PLAYIN' POSSUM

MY MEMORIES OF GEORGE JONES

NANCY JONES
WITH KEN ABRAHAM

PLAYIN' POSSUM: My Memories of George Jones

Published by Forefront Books.
Distributed by Simon & Schuster.
Library of Congress Control Number: 2023911067

Print ISBN: 978-1-63763-222-2
E-book ISBN: 978-1-63763-223-9

Cover Design by Bruce Gore, Gore Studio, Inc.
Interior Design by Mary Susan Oleson, BLU Design Concepts

AUTHOR'S NOTE

GEORGE ALWAYS SAID that I would tell you anything and everything. . . . so I have tried. But I want you to know that I have relied on other individuals to help me describe certain details that I didn't know. I've also drawn upon the recollections of doctors, lawyers, music executives, musicians, and other friends of George Jones to present this story as accurately as possible.

I hope these stories help you to better know the Possum!

—NANCY JONES

"THEY SAY LOVE can change the world. I'm here to testify that it changed one man. Friends, family, doctors, therapists, and ministers had tried to save me, but to no avail. Finally, the power of love from one woman, Nancy Jones, made the difference in my life."

—GEORGE JONES

CONTENTS

1

The White Light

I am not a philosopher and I am not a preacher. I am best known as a feisty, successful businesswoman and the wife of George Jones, the greatest country music singer of all time. For more than thirty years, George and I shared life together—including sensational times and hard times, side-splitting laughs and fun, as well as wall-splitting outbursts of anger. And oh, yes, music—lots of music.

Many people have told me that I saved George's life when he was spiraling toward an early grave, addicted to cocaine and alcohol. That's probably true, but until now, the half has never been told.

A recent spiritual experience of my own, however, has compelled me to share the rest of our story so other people living with addictions or enduring spousal abuse can find hope. If God can change George Jones and me, He can change anyone.

It's easy to take life for granted. We get up each day and go through our routines, never expecting that this day could be our last or that something catastrophic or life-changing may take place. I certainly never dreamed that what I was about to experience would so dramatically change my life. But it did.

On August 31, 2021, in the midst of the COVID-19 pandemic, I moved across town into a new home with a panoramic view, high atop a hill in Tennessee. As I had done previously with most of the moves in my lifetime, I was right in the middle of it all, packing boxes, cleaning rooms, taking items to the trash, and working long hours. It was exhausting and I was ready for some rest.

On a balmy, late-summer evening, a few days after moving in, I was relaxing in the hot tub at the new house with Kirk West, my business manager who had helped me with the purchase and the move, and Dr. Aaron Milstone. Dr. Milstone was a long-time friend and had been my late husband George's personal physician. It was a delightful evening except that I kept coughing frequently. At one point, Dr. Milstone said, "I think you might have Covid, Nancy. You need to go get checked; in fact, both of you should go tomorrow and be tested."

Kirk had been coughing, too. He had already had COVID-19 once before, so even though both of us were coughing, we weren't greatly concerned. Some workers at the house had painted that day, and Kirk had spray-painted the interior of the fireplaces in the house. "Maybe it's just the fumes from the paint," Kirk suggested.

Dr. Milstone raised his eyebrows slightly and slowly shook his head from side to side. "I don't think so," he said. "I think you might have Covid."

"No, I don't," Kirk said. "We're good."

We waited a few more days, hoping to feel better, but neither Kirk's condition nor mine improved. Instead, Kirk, especially, felt even worse. We were tested the next morning and, sure enough, within two minutes, the test came back showing that both Kirk and I had tested positive. My oxygen level was at 96 but Kirk's was only 81.

As the day went on, I felt fine, but Kirk was not doing so well. That was odd, since he had antibodies from his previous bout with Covid. Worse yet, we discovered that he was suffering from double pneumonia, so we drove to our local hospital, Williamson Medical Center, where Kirk could get a CAT scan. Because of Covid protocols, I was not permitted to enter the hospital when Kirk went in for the scan, so I sat out in the car, talking on the phone, texting Kirk's daughter, Lauren. I felt as though I had a cold, but other than that, I wasn't experiencing any serious problems.

Kirk's scan revealed some problems with his lungs, including evidence of double pneumonia, so he contacted a doctor who was a friend, and the doctor gave Kirk a prescription for Ivermectin. Both of us took the medicine and within twenty-four hours, Kirk was completely well! But for some reason, the Ivermectin did not have the same effect on me; I continued to feel weaker and sicker.

My oxygen level dropped down into the seventies so my dear friend and former neighbor, Jessica Robertson, did some quick research and recommended that I see a doctor on the west side of Nashville. We went for an appointment, and the nurse administered intravenous treatments so I could receive some fluids to help boost my immune system and to keep my body hydrated. On September 15, I still felt no better, so I consented to let Kirk drive me back again for another treatment.

I sat in the back seat of the car so the nurse could have more room to administer the IV treatments without me going into their office due to Covid restrictions. They could simply work with me in the parked car.

It was a cool, rainy day as we headed across town, the highway clogged with traffic, threatening to make us late for my appointment. I was hungry so along the way, I said, "Kirk, please stop at McDonald's." Kirk didn't say anything, but he looked at me quizzically. He knew that I'm not a connoisseur of fast foods, but for some reason, I had a craving for a McDonald's cheeseburger. We stopped in the Green Hills section of Nashville, about ten minutes from the doctor's office. I ordered a cheeseburger and a Sprite and ate in the car.

After lunch, we started out again, driving toward West Nashville, weaving through traffic, and pulling into the parking lot at the doctor's office. Kirk texted the nurse, letting her know that we had arrived. The nurse came out to the car with an IV and Kirk held an umbrella over her while she worked on me in the back seat of the car.

The doctor's office was on the second floor, so after inserting the IV in the left side of my neck (she couldn't find a vein in my arm or hand), the nurse went back inside. About thirty minutes into the IV treatment, suddenly, something hit me like a heavy, soaking wet blanket suffocating my entire body. Almost immediately, I could barely breathe. "Kirk, I'm really sick," I called out from the back seat.

"What?" he whirled around and looked at me. Apparently, he realized instantly that I was not kidding. Kirk texted the nurse again to let her know that I was getting worse rather than better, that I was having trouble breathing and needed oxygen.

"Hang on, Nancy!" he shouted.

"Okay," I gasped, "but no matter what happens, do not take me to the hospital." Memories of my good friend, Joe Diffie, the first country music artist who had died due to Covid in March 2020, flashed through my mind. "I'm not doing too well," I told Kirk, as I began coughing up blood. "It's not going to work," I said. "I'm dying. I promise . . . I'm dying."

I could feel myself fading in and out of consciousness and then I was gone. My bowels let loose and suddenly I was sitting in my own excrement in the back seat of the car.

Kirk helped me out of the car and, with the assistance of the nurse, we tried to walk arm in arm toward the doctor's office elevator, but I was too weak. Finally, Kirk picked up my limp body and carried me like a sack of potatoes toward the elevator. I felt awful that I had made such a mess in the car and all over Kirk and me, but I had no strength to walk or to even help him lift my body in some easier way. He carried me from the car to the elevator and just as the elevator doors closed, my bladder let loose and I peed all over Kirk, me, and the elevator floor.

I believed I was dying. When my mother had died, right before she had passed, she had lost control of her bodily functions and made similar messes. I understood what was happening, and I knew I didn't have much longer to live.

When we got upstairs, Kirk and a nurse maneuvered me onto an examination table. Kirk later told me that my oxygen level had dropped to 42. When the nurse checked my pulse, she found none. "There's no pulse," she said frantically to the doctor. "There's no pulse!"

Evidently, they thought I was dead.

"There's nothing else we can do," the doctor told Kirk.

"Well, call an ambulance! Call 911, do *something*!" Kirk blurted. "Call somebody!" Another nurse called 911 and ten minutes went by before the ambulance arrived. When the paramedics came in, the lead EMT examined me and concurred with the nurse. "We have no pulse," he said. Apparently, the paramedics also assumed that I was dead, and did not even bother to perform CPR on me.

I'd like to tell you more about the chaotic scene in the doctor's office, but I can't. At that very time, and for those ten or fifteen minutes from the moment Kirk first lifted me into the elevator and my bodily fluids released, I was experiencing a totally different sort of scene—replete with sights I have never before encountered. Words are insufficient to describe it, but I can tell you this: it was a vision that changed me forever.

I heard no sounds but suddenly I was in what seemed to be a white room. I didn't step into it or drift slowly into it; quite the opposite, the white seemed to spring up all around me and overtake me. Not just any white; this was a white that was brighter than anything my eyes had ever seen. It was brighter than the most brilliant white cloud or cotton ball.

The doctor's office was painted a light beige color but I saw none of that. Everything around me, in front of me, behind me, above and below me was white.

Kirk recalls that he was loudly screaming at the doctor, nurses, and then the paramedics right near me, but I heard nothing, not a sound. I experienced nothing but peace, perfect peace. And white. Pure white.

I remember when I was just a little girl, I heard the preacher at our church talking about heaven as a place that our eyes haven't seen and our minds have not even been able to conceive of all that God is preparing for us. I recall hearing about Jesus being transfigured on the mountaintop, when "His garments became radiant and exceedingly white, as no launderer on earth can whiten them."

That was the sort of radiant whiteness in which I was immersed.

I now believe that I was on my way to heaven. No, I didn't see Jesus; I didn't hear God's voice speaking to me; nor did I see angels waiting at heaven's gate or people who have gone on before us. I saw nothing but white, heard no sounds at all, and felt nothing but total peace.

Recently, I jokingly said, "George Jones must have seen me coming and said to the Lord, 'Oh, God, please! I had thirty-two years with that woman! I've only been here for eight years or so myself. Please send her back to earth for a little while longer.'"

But, of course, I didn't see George or anyone else at that time. Yet everything my eyes beheld was so beautiful, and I sensed a perfect peace.

Back on earth, in the doctor's office, a paramedic placed an oximeter on my finger to check my oxygen level and found that it was still at 42.

"Take her to Williamson Medical Center in Franklin," Kirk demanded desperately, knowing that we had good friends on the medical teams at Williamson.

The paramedic looked him square in the eyes. "We have no pulse. She will not make it to Williamson Medical," he said bluntly.

Nevertheless, the paramedics continued priming my lungs with oxygen as they strapped me onto a gurney and wheeled me to the elevator. Kirk followed along with them. In the elevator, I regained consciousness long enough to realize that I was on a gurney and that they were taking me to a hospital. I mustered every bit of my waning strength and yelled, "No!"

Kirk knew what I meant, that I did not want to go to the hospital, but after losing me for more than ten minutes, he was resigned to the fact that we were out of options. One of the leading medical facilities in Nashville was only a quarter mile away, so the ambulance crew quickly transported me there. Covid protocols prohibited Kirk from accompanying me in the ambulance, so he followed us in his car.

The EMTs rushed me inside the emergency room and nurses there began hooking me up to all sorts of machines. Someone put an IV in my arm and oxygen in my nose.

Kirk arrived at the front entrance to the hospital ER a few minutes later and ran to the receptionist. "I'm looking for Nancy Jones," he shouted through the glass window barricade. "She just came in."

The receptionist peered intently at her computer. "I'm sorry, sir," she said. "We do not have a Nancy Jones as a patient."

"Of course, you do!" Kirk said. "I just followed the ambulance here and then went to park my car. She's here! I know she's here. Nancy Jones. Where is she?"

The receptionist was adamant and the situation was tense. The hospital was packed with Covid patients, and each person attempting to enter the building was stopped six feet apart from one another at the front door. "Sir, we do *not* have a Nancy Jones," she said. "Please. Other people need my assistance."

"Oh, wait," Kirk said. "She's a celebrity. You probably have her admitted under a fake name, a pseudonym of some sort. But her real name is Nancy Jones. Please check for recent admissions."

Kirk convinced the receptionist to peruse the most recent admissions. It took more than an hour for him to figure out my pseudonym, and sure enough, he found a fake name that the hospital had tagged me with when they admitted me, since I had been married to George Jones. The receptionist called for a nurse who guided Kirk back to the emergency room, where he found me hooked up to several machines and not doing well.

Kirk grabbed my hand and held onto it. He didn't let go for more than an hour. "You're gonna make it," he said. "You're gonna be okay." Tears streamed down Kirk's face.

We prayed together and talked a bit. I wanted to tell him about the white room but I was still quite weak. Just then an orderly came in and announced that he was taking me up to the intensive care unit.

Kirk stood to accompany me, but the orderly raised his hand. "I'm sorry, sir," he said. "You cannot go."

He began wheeling me out of the ER cubicle, my hand still clutching Kirk's. "Don't leave me," I screamed as loudly as I could. "Please, don't leave me!" Of course, because of Covid, nobody was permitted inside the ICU area. Kirk had little choice but to leave the hospital. He returned home, and that night the doctor called him.

"I'm putting Nancy on a ventilator to help her breathe," the doctor said. "You want her to die peacefully, don't you?"

"Whoa! Whoa, whoa!" Kirk said. "Let's restart this conversation. If you even think of putting Nancy Jones on a ventilator, I'm suing you personally and I will sue the hospital. You do nothing unless you come through me. Don't even give her baby aspirin, nothing. No Remdesivir, and no vents. My best friend is a lung doctor and he told me that only five percent of the Covid patients put on a ventilator ever come off the machine alive. We don't want Nancy on a vent!"

"Okay, if that's what you want, but Ms. Jones is on 55 liters of oxygen flow right now. That's a very high flow of oxygen, 55 liters. You can go a little higher," the doctor said. "But other than that, we're going on the ventilator."

"No!" Kirk said. "You're not going on the vent. We're not doing it."

The doctor finally acquiesced and hung up the phone in a huff.

Because doctors and nurses had to suit up with extra precautionary coverings and masks, almost like a hazardous materials team, before they could enter a Covid patient's room, making the rounds took on a whole new meaning. Medical personnel checked on patients only when necessary. Some patients went nearly all day without seeing a doctor or a nurse.

Kirk realized that in my fragile condition, that sort of sporadic care could be deadly. He brought a cell phone to the hospital and arranged with a nurse to FaceTime with me from the hospital room. He asked the nurse to place the phone in such a way that I could see him on the screen, talk with him if I had the energy, and most importantly, so he could see me and the monitors in my ICU room. No visitors were allowed for the first two days of my hospitalization. Then Kirk was permitted to visit for only two consecutive hours one time per week, during the first and second week. Consequently, Kirk stayed on the phone FaceTime twenty-four hours a day, every day for the first two weeks I was hospitalized. He didn't sleep all night long, as he sat on the couch at home watching me on the monitor.

One night, in the middle of the night, a flashing red light on the screen above me indicated that my oxygen level was low. Kirk saw it on the phone and called the hospital. "The monitor is flashing red, get in the room right now!" Nobody else had noticed the alarm.

One hospitalist did not like the fact that Kirk was monitoring my care from home by cell phone. Every time he came into my room, he'd push the button and hang up the phone.

When Kirk called back, the hospitalist was brusque with him. "You can't tape this," he said. "This is a hospital."

"I'm not taping anything," Kirk told him. "I'm using FaceTime to keep in touch with Nancy." The doctor continued to hang up the phone every time he walked in my room. By then, however, Kirk had learned some of nurses' names and had asked them for their cell phone numbers.

When he saw that the phone near me was off, he texted another nurse, asking, "The phone got disconnected somehow. Can you go back in Nancy's room and FaceTime me from her phone?" That way, he could keep tabs on my condition and care around the clock.

I was glad for Kirk's watchful eyes, because to tell the truth, I was scared. I never cried, not one time, but I was all alone in the hospital where no one was permitted to visit and few medical people even came in to check on me. I knew my condition was dire, but even worse, throughout the day and night, I could hear the awful sounds in the hospital of other patients dying.

One night I was terrified because I could hear the hospital orderlies pulling out the dead people, taking them from ICU to the morgue. Alone in my room, I cried out, "Oh, God, I'm so scared! I'm really so scared in this place. Please, tell me what to do."

Whether it was in my mind or in some other fashion, I heard a voice say, "Don't be afraid, Nancy. I'm here."

I knew that voice. It wasn't George, and it wasn't Kirk, or any of our earthly friends. It was Jesus.

He didn't say that I would be healed or that I'd be leaving the hospital soon. He simply said that He was with me, and that's all I needed to know. Indeed, my body continued to deteriorate but I was never afraid after that night when His voice spoke such assurance to me.

A week went by and I was still in the hospital, then a week and a half, and rather than getting better, my condition continued to worsen. I could talk with Kirk on FaceTime but I was often too sick to say much.

I was on my own for about a week and a half when the doctor came in one day at 5:15 p.m. and I was barely conscious, so she may have thought that I was sleeping. By now Kirk was permitted to visit with me in my room. The doctors ran numerous tests on me that day while Kirk was there. When the infectious disease doctor examined me, she said, "She's not going to make it through the night."

"What? What are you talking about?" Kirk protested. "We've come so far."

"Yes," the doctor answered, "but she's bleeding and we don't know why. Her pulse rate has been 155 all day long and that, too, is concerning."

The doctors kept checking my heart but they couldn't figure out what was causing the unusual, exorbitant bleeding. They continued to say, "She's not going to make it through tonight."

I heard the doctors say that I was dying, but I did not respond to their words.

Meanwhile, Kirk contacted one of our friends who is a doctor and attempted to explain the situation. Our friend said, "Here's the problem. She's on blood thinners and other medication that has probably caused an ulcer type sore in her stomach and the blood thinners are making her bleed out." He texted Kirk, "Have them do a scope down her throat."

Kirk immediately contacted my doctor in the hospital and read the text. They inserted a scope and found the internal bleeding. As they were inserting the scope, one of the doctors sarcastically said, "I don't know why we're doing this. She's going to die anyway."

Whether the doctors thought I was unconscious or incoherent, I don't know. All I know is that I heard their negative words, but I refused to accept them. I said to myself, *I'm not going to die! I ain't going nowhere. What's wrong with y'all?*

Truth is, had Kirk not contacted our own doctor and taken control of the situation, I may have died that day. Because I was bleeding so much, I was likely less than twenty-four hours from joining George in Nashville's Woodlawn Cemetery.

The ordeal dragged on with little change, other than my weight dropping fast. After two days, Kirk was permitted short visits; later he would be able to stay in my room. He had to suit up in something like a hazmat outfit, completely covering his body and head. He was not allowed to go in and out of the room, only to sit with me, and once outside the door, he had to exit the hospital. It was a strange protocol, but so many people were afraid of Covid, and the government and the Centers for Disease Control were not allaying anyone's concerns. If anything, they were exacerbating the fears.

Once inside the room, Kirk removed his surgical mask and I was glad to see his face. "We need to talk," I said. "I'm dying. I'm not going to make it."

Kirk was not willing to accept that at all. "No, no, you are not dying," he said. "We're not talking like that. We're having faith and speaking only positive statements."

I appreciated Kirk's strong belief in God, especially at a time when mine was weakest.

I remained in the intensive care unit for nearly three months in

2021—September, October, and most of November—before I went to rehab at another facility. My weight dropped from a comfortable 134 pounds down to a frail 92 pounds. My thick dark hair fell out in chunks until I was completely bald. My skin drooped on my body and then flaked off in sheets. I knew I was dying. And that is as close to hell as I ever want to get.

As I lay in the hospital bed, hour after hour, day after day, I thought back to my childhood—which I have never before talked about in public—and how horribly my mother treated me. I recalled how I often wondered, *Mama, why are you being so mean to me*?

I never really got an answer to that question. But lying in that hospital bed, I realized that many of the issues I faced early in life prepared me for life with George Jones, who had major issues with alcohol, cocaine addiction, abusive behavior, and dangerous troubles with the Mafia. Some people said that I was crazy for marrying George. I never saw it that way.

In fact, the more I thought about it, the more I realized that God was preparing me to be tough. He had allowed me to go through those things to help get George ready for heaven. And as Kirk often reminded me during the long days in the hospital, "Nancy, you spent thirty-two years with George Jones, fighting against his alcohol and cocaine, the Mafia, and all the rest. Covid can't take you out. Covid has no power against you. If you can live through George Jones, you can darn sure whip this Covid thing!"

I knew he was right. I determined that I needed to live to tell the story. After all, there were plenty of incidents in my life with George—and even before—when it seemed as though both of us were going to die long before our time.

2
Prep Time

God used much of my early life to get me ready for life with George Jones.

Born February 5, 1949, I was the next to last in the birth order of seven children, with one sister older than me, one younger, and three big brothers. Another sibling passed away early in life. We lived in Mansfield, Louisiana, a suburb on the northwest side of Shreveport.

Clyde Ford, my daddy, was not a tall man, but my brother was six-foot-two and I grew to five-feet, six-inches tall; apparently we inherited our height from our grandpa. Daddy was a good man who read his Bible every day and slept with it at night. A kind, patient man, he taught me many practical skills. For instance, he taught me how to cook, rather than my mom. Daddy called himself Oscar Pancake. He'd putter around in the kitchen and say, "Come on in here, baby. Oscar Pancake is gonna teach you how to cook." And he did!

Apparently, Daddy hadn't been an angel in his earlier years. Before he and our mom got together, he fathered two children—Henry Edward and Lois—that we did not learn about until my siblings and I were adults. Our mother concealed the truth from us all those years. I never knew Henry well, but Lois and I met and grew quite close over the years until she passed away in 2018. Prior to that, she wanted to know everything about our family. She loved country music and often came to George's shows when he performed in Branson, Missouri. She was a good, godly woman and her greatest concern was whether our daddy had come to know Jesus. I was glad to inform her, "Yes, he did! He even slept with his Bible."

Evie Ford, my mama, was a tiny lady—about five feet, two inches tall, she wore a size four shoe—but she was feisty and strong and could pack a powerful punch. She was tough, and my brothers, sisters, and I knew not to mess with her.

One evening my older brother, Bobby, was reading a book while doing his homework and he couldn't comprehend the assignment. Mama tried to explain it to him, "This is how it is, or that is how it is." But Bobby still couldn't grasp it and he started crying. If he thought he could get out of doing his homework by shedding some tears and appealing to Mama's compassionate side, he was wrong. I'm not sure she even had a compassionate side!

Instead, she just wound up and *WHAP!* She slapped Bobby across the head so hard the blow sent him reeling. He tumbled to the floor but on his way down, he hit his head on the fireplace and the impact knocked him out cold. That didn't faze Mama one bit. Bobby wasn't getting any sympathy from her. She ran some cold water over a washcloth and covered Bobby's face and head with it until he awakened. Then she propped him right back in the chair and ordered him to read the book.

I think Mama considered herself a good mother because she was such a strict disciplinarian. Unfortunately, she never learned the difference between discipline and punishment; to her, they were the same thing.

I suppose psychologists nowadays might say that Mama

preconditioned me to accept abusive behavior early in my childhood. Maybe that's one of the reasons why I didn't run, later on, when George Jones did mean things to me. Mama had already gotten me accustomed to mistreatment.

If one of my siblings or I did something wrong, Mama punished us by putting hard, uncooked pinto beans down on the floor and making us kneel on them for hours. If we tried to rest a little, or get up, or lean in some ways so the beans didn't hurt as much, she'd beat us with a switch. Sometimes, we remained kneeling on the beans all day long.

When Daddy came home, he often had to use his pocketknife to dig the beans out of our knees.

Sometimes Mama "disciplined" us by locking us in a large wooden armoire, a big old wooden closet with a little stick that slid across the doors to latch it tightly closed. Once those doors were shut, it was pitch-black dark in there. If my oldest sister did something wrong, even if I was innocent, Mama punished me right along with her. I guess she figured I was probably thinking about doing what my sister did, anyhow, so she might as well get both of us into the closet. She put us in there for hours at a time, "until we'd learned our lesson," whatever that was.

One time, Mama locked my sister in the armoire, and she started screaming, "There's a snake in here!"

Mama said, "There ain't no snake in there, so just shut up!"

Turned out, there really was a chicken snake in there with my sister. Fortunately, the snake's venom was not poisonous.

If Mama got mad at me about something, she'd throw me out of the house, outside in the dark, with all the creepy crawlers and other animals. I think that's probably why I'm scared of the dark to this day.

Mama was tough with all of us but especially to me. I never could figure out why. Looking back now, it is easy to see how God was preparing me, with all of Mama's irrational acts and attitudes and some of her meanness. God was getting me ready for George Jones long before George and I ever met. But at the time, I simply thought Mama was mean.

* * * * * *

I married Manuel Sepulvado on March 3, 1966. Manuel was a good man and treated me well but, truth is, I married him for one main reason—to get away from my mother. I was only sixteen years of age on our wedding day.

Ironically, neither Daddy nor Mama consumed any alcoholic beverages. Mama hated the smell of liquor. My husband, Manuel, on the other hand, hailed from a laid-back, Louisiana Catholic background, so drinking played a part in almost every social activity, public or private. Of course, it didn't take me long to discover the effects of alcohol. By the time I was twenty-two years old, I could drink with the best of the good ole boys, and often did.

One night I was out drinking with a friend and I was imbibing far too much. So much that the bartender refused to serve me any more alcohol and cut me off. "That's all for tonight, Nancy," he said from behind the bar. "You've had too much. Get out."

His attitude made me mad. I walked to my car, got behind the wheel, revved the engine, and floored it! I drove the car right through the front window of the building, sending customers scurrying in every direction. I kept my foot on the gas pedal until the car hit the bar, where the bartender was still standing, with a flabbergasted expression on his face. I turned off the engine and parked the car right there. I leaned out the window and yelled, "Now, serve me!"

He still wouldn't serve me any more booze, but a few days later

I was served with a garnishment of my wages from the factory where I worked at Western Electric, assembling pay telephones. It took me months to pay for the damages I'd done to the bar.

Maybe that's why I wasn't put off by George's drinking when I first met him. I understood what the stuff could do to a person when he or she had consumed too much. I thought, *So he drinks, so what? I can deal with that.* Was I ever naïve!

I still visited Mama after Manuel and I married. I saw her every payday because she was always looking for money. I stopped by her house and gave her two or three hundred dollars, which was a large percentage of my paycheck. But I didn't stay long. I'd just give her some money and leave after I had checked on my daddy, whose health was failing rapidly due to lung cancer.

Manuel never griped about me giving money to Mama. He just said, "Do whatever you feel in your heart."

Eventually, Manuel and I separated, but he still hoped that we could revive our marriage. I had no such hope. We had two beautiful daughters together, but little else in common. It wasn't his fault; he was a good man who had married me when I had desperately wanted to escape my mama's controlling influence.

"Here, just sign the papers," I urged him every time we were together. Although we had been separated for nearly two years by that time, Manuel still didn't want to get divorced, but I did.

Manuel finally gave in and signed the papers. We divorced August 27, 1980. I was ready for a new start in life.

3

THE MAN WITH THE GOLDEN VOICE

I WASN'T IN ANY HURRY to find another fellow. I was content to work at Western Electric, a company in Shreveport, Louisiana, that manufactured telephones when AT&T still held a monopoly on US telephone business—not mobile phones like we all carry nowadays, but stationary office phones, wall phones, payphones, and others that sat or were mounted in one location. At its peak, the Shreveport location employed more than seven thousand people. I didn't work in an office; I worked on the factory assembly line. When I wasn't on the job, as a single mom I stayed busy taking care of my two daughters, Adina—"Dina," as we nicknamed her—and Sherry.

Maybe that's why I was reluctant when, in November 1981, my friend and hair stylist Linda Morris asked me to travel with her from Shreveport to Rochester, New York, to hear country singer George Jones. She was dating one of George's road crew, and she begged me to come along.

I really wasn't interested.

"George *who*?" I asked. I didn't know George's music, knew nothing about him, and was not even a fan of country music. But my friend was insistent.

"George Jones!" she said excitedly. "You know: 'He Stopped Loving Her Today.' *That* George Jones."

"Never heard of him," I said. "Now, if you want me to go see Creedence Clearwater [Revival], I'll be glad to go!" I enjoyed pop music and Creedence Clearwater was one of my favorite groups.

"Oh, come on," Linda urged me. "You don't have to sleep with him. Just meet him. Who knows? You might even like him." She smiled and I finally consented to make the trip with her. I purchased a plane ticket from Shreveport to Rochester. Of course, the least expensive flight I could find also had the most stops along the way. I think I flew over half the country getting to my first George Jones concert.

I wore dark jeans, a white blouse, and a black vest to the show that night. My long black hair had been lightened by the sun and swirled gently around my neck and shoulders. Linda introduced me to George backstage before his show and we quickly hit it off. George seemed real nervous but genuinely friendly and a bit shy, especially for an entertainer. George's friend Merle Kilgore helped break the ice a bit, nodding toward me and saying to George, "Ain't she pretty, George?"

"Yeah, yeah," George replied awkwardly. "She sure is." He then went on stage and put on a spectacular show and the audience loved it. So did I.

I was blown away by his golden voice. I'd never heard anybody that could bend the notes and phrase the words to a lyric the way George Jones did. He was truly amazing.

After the show, Linda and I and George's entourage of musicians and stage personnel returned to the nearby hotel where we were all staying. George and I started talking and didn't stop for more than thirty years!

* * * * * *

We stayed up talking all night long and George confided numerous stories from his childhood with me. For some reason, he seemed to feel safe with me. I knew that he was, but for a big-time entertainer to be that open and vulnerable surprised me. George told me that he had been born on September 12, 1931, in a log house in the small town of Saratoga, in East Texas.

The attending doctor dropped him, resulting in George's arm being broken. Apparently, George was a big baby boy, weighing in at more than ten pounds! "And I haven't grown much since that time," George told me with a whimsical smile.

His parents, George Washington Jones and Clara Patterson, daughter of a preacher, had two sets of twins: Joyce and Loyce, and Doris and Ruth; as well as another daughter Helen who was ten years older than George; a son Herman; and a daughter Ethel, who died at only seven years of age. George was the last born of the eight Jones kids. His parents named him George Glenn Jones, and his mama often called him Glenn to avoid confusion with her husband's name.

George was raised in the even smaller town of Vidor, and often claimed Kountze, Texas, as his hometown. Later, in 1942, the Jones family moved to the port town of Beaumont, Texas, where they lived in a government-subsidized housing project and George's dad worked as a pipefitter at the shipyard for most of World War II.

One incident from George's childhood made a profound impression on him. When he was a little boy of seven, while at the neighbor's house, George spied a beautiful pocketknife on the dresser.

"It was the prettiest thing I'd ever seen in my life," George told me. "I wanted that knife so bad. So I picked it up and I slipped it in my pocket."

He said, "By the time I got home, Mrs. Hodge was already at our house. She told my mom, 'Your son, Glenn, stole my knife.'

"Mama said, 'George Glenn!'"

George knew he was in trouble by the tone of her voice.

"You got that knife?" she asked.

"Yes, Mama, I do," George said.

"I pulled it outta my pocket, gave it back to Mrs. Hodge, and apologized for taking it," he told me. "Then Mama took me outside where she cut a switch off a tree, and Mama whipped me so hard. She wouldn't stop. She said, 'You don't ever steal. You don't *ever* steal!'"

I grimaced as George continued, "I was running through the house and she was still at me, whipping me, whipping me, and whipping me." He said, "I was only seven years old, and it was the only whipping Mama ever gave me. One was all it took!"

He added, "And I never stole another thing in my life after that."

George's mama and the kids attended Trinity Gospel Tabernacle, a Pentecostal, conservative, Bible-believing congregation that took their relationships with God seriously. His mother played the organ at the church and his sisters all sang in the choir. George's dad wasn't so serious about God, but both of George's parents taught him strong values and respect. George and his siblings were forbidden from using profanity, for instance. George said, "If my Pentecostal mother had ever heard us cussing, a whipping was coming for sure."

George Washington Jones had a reputation in Saratoga as a drunk who didn't deserve his godly wife, Clara, who rounded up the kids every Sunday morning and herded them off to church. It was in church that George learned to sing with power and to use his voice to influence people.

George's dad refused to attend church services with the rest of the family. Usually on Sunday morning he was sobering up from being drunk the previous night. He worked five days a week and as soon as he got paid on Friday, he'd make sure the groceries were bought and the bills were paid. The next thing he did was buy whiskey, and he'd stay drunk all weekend until time to go back to work on Monday morning.

Some of George's most emotionally disturbing memories of his childhood included times when his dad came home drunk in the middle of the night. He'd awaken the whole family, especially George and his oldest sister Doris, force them to get out of bed, and make them sing along with him in his drunken stupor.

It's amazing that George ever wanted to be a singer when he grew up. Of course, it's equally as astounding that George developed a penchant for drinking, since he so virulently hated when his dad got drunk.

But at an early age, George developed a taste for both music and booze.

George's father gave him his first "little Gene Autry guitar" that had a picture of a cowboy on a horse with a lariat and Gene Autry's "signature" on the face of the instrument.

"I got my first guitar when I was nine years old," George told me. "I never had a formal music lesson. I learned to sing in church. We lived out in the sticks in Saratoga and the Reverend's wife, Sister Annie, played guitar and sang. She taught me some basic chords on the guitar." His first "big break" in music came when a Pentecostal preacher and his wife, Brother Burl and Sister Annie, invited George to play guitar and sing with them as they sang gospel music during their "revival" services.

"On Saturdays, a bunch of us would stand around the popular hangouts in town or where the people cashed their checks and bought groceries," George said. "We'd sing over a microphone attached to a big speaker on top of the preacher's car, then the reverend would preach a Holy Roller type of message."

George quit school in the seventh grade, after failing that grade twice. He had little interest in book learning, and played hooky sometimes for several weeks at a time before anyone noticed he was missing school.

George recalled, "All I did was play that guitar. I'd stay out in the woods and play that guitar all day long. When I was done, I'd hide it in the woods and cover it with leaves."

He'd sneak into Beaumont barefooted and play his little guitar with a missing string for anyone willing to listen. Some of the people were kind enough to give him some pocket change in appreciation for his playing. On Saturday nights, he listened on an old battery-operated radio to the Grand Ole Opry radio show, broadcasting on WSM Radio from Nashville, Tennessee. He especially loved the music of Hank Williams, Lefty Frizzell, and Roy Acuff.

By his late teens, George picked up jobs playing music in some of the local bars around Beaumont. He told me, "I met Eddie and Pearl Stevens, a husband-and-wife team that had a local radio show on KRIC in Beaumont and played weekends at joints and taverns. They gave me a job playing lead guitar with them."

George got his start on radio, not as a singer, but as a disc jockey on KTRM, in Beaumont.

To George, the greatest voice he ever heard belonged to Hank Williams. Many of Hank Williams's songs resonated with young George Jones. George picked up on the melancholy spirit in Hank's songs and the way he delivered them. He identified with the battle between good and evil that Hank sang about, wanting to be good, but being drawn toward the bad—bad people and bad behavior.

George met his idol when the slim singer with the haunting voice visited KRIC radio station in Beaumont, where George worked the afternoon show with Eddie and Pearl. Williams stopped by the station to help promote his local show appearance. As part of the on-air interview, the hosts asked Hank to sing "Wedding Bells," his latest single. Williams accompanied himself on acoustic guitar, and he invited George to play electric guitar behind him. George picked up his instrument, but he was so intimidated, he froze; he simply stood there and gawked as Hank sang. George didn't play a note while Williams was in the studio.

Hank stayed around a while and talked with Eddie, Pearl, and George. "He was one of the nicest guys I ever met," George recalled later. During most of the conversation, George remained tongue-tied, so Eddie and Pearl told Hank that George sang his songs all the time and sounded a lot like him.

Williams was amused. "Yeah, when I first started out," he said, "I admired Roy Acuff, and I could sing pretty much like him, too. But when I went in to record, I found out that they already had a Roy Acuff, so I had to sing like myself."

Hank Williams turned to George and gave him some of the best advice he'd ever receive: "Always be yourself when you sing."

Over the years, George took Hank's words to heart.

4

The Race Is On

By seventeen years of age, George stood five feet, six inches tall—as tall as he'd ever get. Although music was his first love, when he met Dorothy Bonvillion, the daughter of a local house painter, the couple clicked. Maybe they clicked too much, because not long after they started dating, they discovered that Dorothy was pregnant. The young couple rushed into marriage and George took almost any odd job he could, trying to support himself and his wife. He worked with Dorothy's dad as a housepainter for a while, but he cringed at the thought of painting houses as a profession. "I couldn't stand getting paint all over me," he said. He took almost any job that didn't involve paint. He drove a Coca-Cola delivery truck and even worked for a while as a funeral home attendant, driving the hearse. One night, George's co-workers told him, "Bring that corpse in the casket inside, and we'll hold the door open for you."

George didn't know it, but there was no dead body inside. Instead, one of his buddies had crawled inside the casket and just as George wheeled it through the door, his friend threw open the lid and leaped out. "I was scared to death and ran away as fast as I could," George said. "I never went back to that funeral home job!"

George and Dorothy's marriage lasted less than one year before

Dorothy filed for divorce. She was six months pregnant at the time. His wife claimed that George drank too much. Imagine that.

George was jailed at least twice for nonpayment of support. In the fall of 1951, after George had already moved out, Dorothy gave birth to a daughter, Susan, the first of four children George fathered with three separate wives. A few weeks later, George was in trouble again, but rather than returning to jail, he joined the US Marines. He served in California from November 1951 to November 1953.

Following his stint in the military, George returned home in 1953 and worked at various jobs, but music was his passion. He bounced around with his guitar at local honky-tonks before he was "discovered" by Harold "Pappy" Daily and his partner, Jack Starnes, co-owners of Starday Records, who offered George a chance to record. In February that year, George cut his first recording, "No Money in This Deal," and the song was prophetic. The single sold less than ten thousand copies and George didn't make a dime. But he didn't care. He was twenty-two years old and just wanted to sing. For a while, George even recorded some rockabilly songs for Starday under the pseudonym "Thumper Jones." But George wasn't interested in being a rock and roll star; he wanted to sing traditional country music like his heroes, Lefty, Hank, and Roy.

Years later, George tried to buy back some of those early master recordings, but some shysters found them first. "They knew that someday they could sell that junk and take advantage of the fans, which they did," George said, "and it's the worst-sounding crap that could ever be put on a record." It wasn't simply that he was embarrassed because the music was bad, but he felt his fans may buy it and be disappointed.

Although George never considered himself a great songwriter, he wrote many of his early hits all by himself, including "Why Baby Why" a song that peaked on the *Billboard* singles charts at number four in 1955. He also wrote "Seasons of My Heart," a top-ten single for Johnny Cash.

But it wasn't until George moved to Mercury that he had his first number one hit song, "White Lightning," in 1959. Suddenly, people everywhere wanted to hear more of George Jones's music. He and four other musicians hit the road, traveling in a car and pulling an equipment trailer behind them.

He had married Shirley Ann Corley in 1954, but Shirley was less than supportive of having an entertainer as a husband. She wanted a husband who would stay home and stay sober. She got neither with George. Together, the couple had two boys, Brian and Jeffrey. George achieved an added measure of fame and financial success with hit songs such as "Tender Years" and "She Thinks I Still Care" (a song later covered by James Taylor), keeping George on the road. He and Shirley were living in Vidor, Texas, about eight miles out of Beaumont, and he continued to drink heavily.

Shirley did her best to curb George's wayward ways, but she was having little success. As George later admitted, Shirley "suspected there were other women, and there were. One-night stands were a way of life for my friends and me in those days. Shirley once caught me in the backseat with a gal outside a Texas honky-tonk. On more than one occasion, a member of my band took me home after an extended tour because I was too drunk to get from the airport to my home. I was a bad husband and an absentee father to two boys."

During one drinking binge, George ran out of liquor so he wanted to drive to the liquor store to purchase more alcohol. Shirley was afraid, so she called George's Uncle Dub, who lived nearby. She said, "George came home drunk again, and he's been drinking all day."

W. T. "Dub" Scroggins was married to George's sister Helen. He wasn't really George's uncle, but since he was older than George that's what he called him. Uncle Dub possessed good common sense and an even better heart. He loved George, and George respected him immensely—George would do almost anything Uncle Dub told him to do—so Shirley hoped that Uncle Dub might be able to talk some sense into her husband.

Uncle Dub hurried over to George and Shirley's house. He found George upstairs in a bedroom, so Uncle Dub locked him in the room, and called out, "Don't come downstairs until you sober up." He then went throughout the house and hid all of the car keys to George and Shirley's vehicles. That way, he felt sure George couldn't get to Beaumont to buy more booze.

Uncle Dub went downstairs and fixed a large pot of coffee for George. He sat down with Shirley at the kitchen table and waited for George to sober up.

But Uncle Dub and Shirley underestimated George's tenacious desire to drink.

George looked out the upstairs window and spied his Cub Cadet riding lawn mower parked near a security light. He climbed out the window and made his way to the ground somehow. George later said, "I was dying for a drink." According to George's version of the story (written nearly thirty years later), he recalled, "There, gleaming in the glow, was that ten-horsepower rotary engine under a seat. A key glistened in the ignition. I imagine the top speed for that old mower was five miles per hour. It might have taken an hour and a half or more for me to get to the liquor store, but get there I did. A lot of cars whipped around me on the two-lane highway leading from our house to the store. I wonder if the old-timers around East Texas still wonder about a guy who they swear they saw mowing the concrete."

Truth is, George kept trying to hitch a ride as he made his way from Vidor toward Beaumont on the lawn mower. Eventually, someone picked him up along the way and took George into town, where he promptly purchased another car, a red Oldsmobile that George claimed was a Buick. Maybe Shirley kept the keys to his other car when they divorced in 1968.

Years later, George memorialized the lawnmower drive in a 1998 music video for "Honky Tonk Song," in which he facetiously explained to a police officer and his backups that his wife had taken his keys and wouldn't drive him to drink anymore. By the end of the video, George was surrounded by an army of law officers, some of whom joined him in his cell, as Little Jimmy Dickens tried to bail out George, eventually offering an entire Brink's truck full of cash. It was a hilarious video with George whimsically poking fun at himself. Of course, George wasn't the only one to see the humor in the infamous lawn mower liquor store run.

Hank Williams Jr.'s well-known song, "All My Rowdy Friends are Coming Over Tonight," which served as the opening video to the NFL's Monday Night Football games until Hank said or did something deemed politically incorrect, also featured George riding a lawn mower.

Then in 1993, Vince Gill's "One More Last Chance," included the line, "She might have took my car keys, but she forgot about my old John Deere." The playful video ended with Vince driving a John Deere tractor and passing George on his lawn mower. "Hey, Possum!" Vince called out to George. "Hey, Sweet Pea!" George greeted Vince with his favorite nickname for him.

Vince had done a number of shows with George years earlier, and during one stretch the ticket sales were surprisingly low. "Don't worry," George told Vince. "I won't let you starve." George went to the grocery store and purchased a bagful of comfort foods. He told Vince, "Now, come on over to the bus and get something to eat, Sweet Pea. I've got enough food for all of us." Forever after, George referred to

Vince as Sweet Pea, so, of course, Vince wanted to include the nickname in the video.

John Rich's raucous video "Country Done Come to Town," filmed at John's house, also had George showing up at the party riding on a red lawn mower. Many people who saw the various renditions of George riding on the mower may have thought it was just his country-boy way of having fun. But to those of us who knew the original story, it was bittersweet, even though it usually brought a smile to our faces when someone told it or referred to it again.

Tammy Wynette claimed that George did something similar while married to her, as well. Maybe so. Tammy supposedly hid George's keys, only to awaken around one o'clock in the morning to find George missing.

Tammy said that she got into the car and drove to the nearest bar, which was ten miles away. When she pulled in the parking lot, she claimed she saw George's riding lawn mower by the entrance and found George inside.

Whether that second incident, surprisingly similar to the one at Vidor, ever took place or not, I don't know. George never admitted to it, which causes me to wonder, since George was never bashful about admitting to his mistakes, faults, and failures when he actually did them—but Tammy retold it for years to anyone who would listen.

5

If Drinkin' Don't Kill Me

SIMILAR TO HIS MUSICAL hero, Hank Williams, George possessed an uncanny knack for enjoying success and sadness simultaneously. Along with missing shows, George was wasting away, weighing in at a mere 105 pounds at one point. He regularly consumed large amounts of cocaine and alcohol, and his appetite for nutritious food disappeared. It took an intervention by Waylon Jennings to get George back on track.

Waylon later said, "I was afraid he was going to die. . . . So I called him to come out to the house, and he came out there and I said, 'George, this is going to sound awful funny coming from me, but you've got to do something. You've got to straighten up.'"

Around that time, George said, "The best thing that ever happened to me is when some friends talked me into going to the hospital in Birmingham." Spending time in rehab probably saved George's life, but unfortunately, it didn't save him from his addictions.

Most of George's closest friends knew that he drank too much too often. But they loved him and tolerated his drinking. On one occasion, he and Little Jimmy Dickens—"Tater," as most of his friends called him—were traveling together by car. They did a show and then afterward, George started drinking and didn't stop until he stumbled into their hotel room.

The next morning, George had a colossal headache from a hangover. They started driving up the road toward their next show date, but George was miserable. He said, "Oh, man, I'm dying, Tater. I've gotta get an Alka-Seltzer."

Little Jimmy said, "Well, I have some right here, George." He gave him an Alka-Seltzer tablet, but George didn't take it with water. Instead, he put it in some whiskey and gulped it down!

In a matter of seconds, George started foaming at the mouth like a mad dog. Tater wasn't sure whether George was having a seizure or if it was the Alka-Seltzer and whiskey reappearing. He stopped the car, opened the door, and George tumbled out on the side of the road.

Once Tater realized that George was okay, he laughed and laughed. He thought that was the funniest thing he'd ever seen.

George knew that Tater hadn't intentionally tried to make him sick, and it was his own bad decision to mix the Alka-Seltzer and whiskey. He didn't forget, though, and he looked for an opportunity to pull a prank on Tater. One night after a show with Little Jimmy Dickens and Charley Pride, they had hotel rooms on the same floor. Once they had settled into their rooms, Tater knocked on George's door.

George opened the door to find Tater standing in the hotel hallway, wearing his little red pajamas with feet in them. George said, "Tater, you look like Mickey Mouse!"

Before long Charley joined them and George and Charley cajoled Tater into getting into a rollaway bed. Once they had Tater in the bed, they folded it up, and along with a couple other guys, they rolled Little Jimmy Dickens all the way down the hallway.

They rolled him into the elevator, out through the hotel lobby, and were rolling him down the street, with Tater screaming and hollering all the way. George and Charley were laughing uproariously at the little man in his red pajamas who was yelling so ferociously.

"I'll kill every one of y'all when I get out of here!" Tater screamed. "I'll kill every one of y'all."

Tater never gave George another Alka-Seltzer after that!

* * * * * *

George had planned to fly home with Patsy Cline after a benefit concert date in Kansas City, but some fried chicken kept him from getting on the plane. Similar to many entertainers, Patsy didn't like to eat a heavy meal before her shows, preferring instead to eat after her performance. She loved fried chicken so there was always fried chicken in her dressing room, ready for her to enjoy when she came offstage.

As usual, there was chicken in Patsy's dressing room in Kansas City on March 5, 1963. George knew that Patsy would probably be hungry after her show, but he was drunk and he was hungry too, so while Patsy was on stage, George gobbled down her fried chicken.

When Patsy came offstage and found that her chicken had disappeared, she was furious. It didn't take her long to find a smiling "Possum."

"George Jones! You ate my chicken!" she railed. Patsy knew every cuss word ever created, and she spewed a litany of them at George, calling him every dirty, despicable name she could think of. George didn't care. When he told me the story, he said, "I just stood there grinnin' at her. I'd eaten her chicken. My belly was full and I was ready to sing."

Patsy was still singin' a different tune. She was so mad that she refused to allow George to travel back to Nashville with her on her plane the following day.

That fried chicken saved George's life, because as the entire world soon came to find out, Patsy's plane never made it back to Nashville that night. Instead, it crashed in bad weather near Camden, Tennessee, after refueling in Dyersburg, killing everyone on board, including Hawkshaw Hawkins, Cowboy Copas, Patsy, and the pilot.

George sometimes chuckled about stealing Patsy's fried chicken, but more often, he acknowledged somberly, "I could have been on that plane. God saved my life that night. I've often wondered why?"

George had an aversion to attending funeral services. He preferred to recall people as they were in life, rather than remembering them lying in a casket. But while he didn't even attend his own sisters' funerals, he did go to Patsy's. And years later, at my insistence, he attended Tammy Wynette's funeral as well.

* * * * * *

In 1980, Epic Records producer Billy Sherrill recommended a song to George, not an upbeat, drinking song, but a slow, sad ballad. George was drinking heavily around that time and dipping deeply into the pits of depression, so he didn't respond positively to the song at first. But he trusted Billy and finally acquiesced. He worked on the song off and on, whenever he was in good voice.

Even when George was singing well, he and Billy sometimes heard the song differently. "The melody sounds better like this," George said. He sang the first verse to a tune that sounded similar to the song "Help Me Make It Through the Night."

"I'm sure Kris Kristofferson would say the same thing," Billy responded.

It took nearly a year for George to record the song, along with an emotional reading of the last verse. As he left Billy's office after listening to the rough mix, George told Billy, "That song will never catch on. Nobody will buy that morbid S.O.B. It is just too sad."

Billy said, "Oh, yeah, I'll bet you a hundred bucks that it will."

"You're on," said George, assuming he'd just made an easy one hundred dollars.

Actually, he had just made a lot more than that. The song Billy recorded George singing was "He Stopped Loving Her Today," a colossal hit for George. The only complaint came from the executives of the record label. They lamented to Billy, "Did you have to put all those violins on there?"

Billy responded with one word: "Yeah."

The song was written by Bobby Braddock, who, ironically, had also written one of Tammy Wynette's biggest hits: "D-I-V-O-R-C-E." The single of "He Stopped Loving Her Today" reached number one on the charts on July 5, 1980. The album *I Am What I Am*, which also included "If Drinkin' Don't Kill Me (Her Memory Will)," was George's first to go gold, signifying sales of more than five-hundred thousand units. Before long, the album was certified as "platinum" with sales of more than one million units, and it kept on selling.

Beyond that, the song supercharged George's personal appearance fees. George recalled, "I went from being a $2,500 act who promoters feared wouldn't show up to an act who earned $25,000 per show, plus a percentage of the gate receipts." In 1980, that was a lot of money.

Unfortunately, George never saw most of it.

6

I Don't Even Know You!

George had been married three times by the time I met him, his last marriage a turbulent tumble with Tammy Wynette. They had first gotten together in 1966 when Tammy was an upstart country artist and George was a well-established star. They married in 1969 and divorced in 1975. They produced one daughter together, Tamala Georgette, who was barely five years old when George and Tammy divorced. Despite the smashed televisions in their home, the wrecked cars, their highly publicized, contentious divorce, and their other personal conflicts, they charted some fantastic country music together, duets such as "We're Gonna Hold On" and "Golden Ring." *The Bradley Barn Sessions,* on which "Golden Ring" was recorded, was the first time that George and Tammy had gotten together since their stormy personal and professional breakup. The song—about a relationship that came together and then fell apart—remains one of the most familiar songs George and Tammy ever recorded.

George later said, "During the time that Tammy and I met, we were so enthused with each other for our work. I think we were infatuated more than we were really in love. Even though we both tried to make it work, it wasn't destined to happen."

George won the CMA award for Male Vocalist of the Year in 1980 and 1981, and he took top honors for the Single of the Year award with that song he didn't think anyone would like, "He Stopped Loving Her Today." To this day, the song is widely acclaimed as one of the greatest ever recorded in the history of country music.

* * * * * *

After the show in New York where George and I first met, the man talked my ear off all night long. We had adjoining rooms in the hotel and George came over to mine. We ordered some hamburgers sent in from room service, and we scooted down and sat on the floor next to the bed and just talked and talked as we ate. And then kept on talking. I felt bad for him. He told me about some of the mean things that had been done to him, and I could hardly believe what I heard. Even that first night, I could see that there were things in George—pain, frustration, and other emotional issues—that he wanted to get out, but he didn't know how to release them.

When the sun came up and it was time for me to go home, I asked George, "Are you going with me to the airport?"

"No," he said. "You're not going anywhere."

I said, "Oh, yes, I am."

George asked, "Where are you going? I want you to stay with me."

"I'm going home to Shreveport," I said. "I have two kids and a job waiting there for me."

George's demeanor dropped. He seemed crushed that I would leave him. "Please don't go," he said.

"I don't even know you that well," I told him.

George said, "I don't want you to leave."

I said, "Well, I'm sorry, but I gotta go. Are you going with me to the airport?"

George shook his head. "Nope."

I said goodbye to George Jones. His road manager took Linda and me to the airport. I had flown on a commercial flight from Shreveport to Rochester, and not a direct flight, so it took me all day to get back home.

When I arrived at my house, there was a surprise waiting for me—George Jones! He had chartered a plane and rented a car and was parked, sitting in my driveway, waiting for me to get home. He had a big smile on his face, sort of chuckling at the surprised expression on my face.

Not wanting to be rude, I said, "Well, come on in."

George Jones stepped inside my house and walked into my heart. He looked around my home as I put my suitcase in the bedroom. "Well, this is a nice house," he said. And then to my surprise, he added, "I have that bedspread at my house . . . and the exact same dishes. See, this is meant to be."

I just shook my head and smiled at him.

Over the next few days, George stayed with my daughters, Adina and Sherry, and me. I went to work each morning at Western Electric, working on the factory assembly line, putting together pay phones. The girls went on to school. While the girls and I were out of the house, George prepared and cooked the meals—and that man could cook! In the evenings, he told the kids all sorts of stories. They loved him and thought he was funny. He seemed to really enjoy being with us, and I had no clue about some of the evil demons that were chasing him. Nor did I know that he was missing his own shows to be with my daughters and me. He later figured out that he'd blown off more than fifty thousand dollars in income simply to be with me. Years later, I told him that was a bargain and a good investment!

During his stay in Shreveport, he and I walked and talked . . . and talked and walked. Without the interruptions of backstage fuss and clamor, George had more opportunity to ask about me. I opened up and told him a bit about my childhood, and my running to Manuel to get away from my mother, then divorcing Manuel to make a life of my own—although it seemed simple and mundane when compared to George's life in the fast lane. But I was happy and content working my job in Shreveport and raising the girls.

George seemed surprised that I worked at a manual labor job. I was an hourly employee who worked forty hours every week and usually fifteen hours of overtime just to support Adina, Sherry, and me. I wore work gloves and a heavy apron to work, and by the time I met George, I had worked for the same employer for years—ever since Adina, my first daughter, had been about three weeks old. George seemed especially impressed that I could assemble an entire telephone with all of its components in about a minute or less. Maybe he appreciated that skill because his own family members had worked in blue-collar, manual labor types of jobs.

Regardless, before George left town, he encouraged me to take a leave of absence from my job at Western Electric. "I'll take good care of you," he promised. "And the kids, too."

"I'll think about it," I told him, "but for now, you need to get back to work."

7

Alcohol, Cocaine, and Attempted Murder

George came back to visit once or twice and then went back on the road, but it wasn't long before he called again and asked me to join him. Ironically, it was snowing in Shreveport when he called. It was snowing wherever George was at that time, too, but it was an entirely different kind of snow, which I was soon to discover.

When I told my boss that I needed some time off to spend with George, he adamantly tried to dissuade me. He reminded me that most musicians lived rowdy lifestyles and from what he had heard, George Jones was worse than most. "He's gonna leave you stranded somewhere, just wait and see," my boss warned me. "I can't believe you are going to give up a good job to run off with some singer, like a silly, starstruck little girl," he chided.

I shot right back at him. "I don't want to hear that," I said. "I know what I'm doing." Or, at least, I thought I did.

He said, "Now, listen, I will give you a two-week leave, and I will save your job because you will be back, because that man is dangerous and he's nothing but a drunk."

I said, "Well, I guess I have to prove you wrong."

I told my boss goodbye and packed up some clothes for my fourteen-year-old daughter, Adina, and me. My twelve-year-old daughter, Sherry, remained with her father in Shreveport, as she usually would during the years that followed. My daddy had already passed away due to lung cancer, and I didn't inform my mom of my plans to spend some time with George. Nor did I try to sell my home before we left. After all, I didn't know how long I might be gone. I could be back in Shreveport within two weeks, or even less. I had no idea.

George had been living with a woman in Alabama prior to meeting me, and when someone threatened her life, she had taken off, leaving George alone. Since then, he'd been sleeping in his car. He was ready to hit the road with his band members, whom he affectionately referred to as "The Jones Boys." Most of the musicians had worked with George for a number of years and were no longer boys; they were grown men. But even if the faces changed, they were always the Jones Boys to George. I met them and liked them all immediately. The Jones Boys traveled in George's leased tour bus, but George didn't like the idea of Adina and me riding on the same bus as the boys, so he secured a motor home for us. Adina, George, and I followed behind George's bus in the large recreational vehicle. It soon became our second home.

* * * * * *

I still didn't know much about George's rowdy side. I didn't read the fan magazines or tabloids, and even though George had made some headlines for his run-ins with the law, I knew little about them. I was aware that George drank heavily—far too much in my estimation—and he could be mean when he drank too much, but he also had a softer side that I fell in love with. I didn't know that he had spent time trying to detox in drug and alcohol rehabilitation facilities.

George told me, "When I go in to a bar and get to drinkin', I think I'm supposed to drink every bottle up there. Yeah. I want to drink it all." I didn't understand that, but I sympathized with him.

To me, he was just George—and I liked him. He was fun, he was funny, he enjoyed having Adina around, and he sure seemed to love me.

I soon learned that long before I had met him, George had already earned the reputation and nickname of "No Show Jones" for his proclivity in blowing off a concert date at the last minute. Many concert promoters sued George for breach of contract. Other less-than-scrupulous promoters advertised that George was on the show, when they hadn't even booked him, because they assumed the fans would come but George would not.

I must admit, for a woman of thirty-two-years of age, who had been married with two children, I was still quite naïve about much of the seedy side of life. I had rarely traveled far from Shreveport, and I had no idea of all the bad stuff that George was into when we first met. After being with him for a few months, I realized that besides alcohol, he was addicted to cocaine.

Cocaine was an entirely new world for me. I had never even seen the stuff before meeting George. I didn't know what it was or how it affected a person, so one day while Adina was in school, I asked him, "George, what is that stuff? And why would you want to stick it up your nose?"

If George's drinking was a problem, the cocaine addiction was even worse. Cocaine altered George's mind, but even more importantly, it changed his entire personality and demeanor. It transformed him from fun, jovial George to mean and nasty George.

When I asked George about the cocaine, the mean and nasty George responded as though I was making fun of him. I wasn't. I honestly knew nothing about cocaine, other than what we might have seen in the movies in 1981. But George thought that I was looking down on him and speaking in some condescending manner because he needed the drug and I didn't.

He responded violently and he hit me. In fact, he slapped the fire out of me, hitting me hard with the back of his hand, squarely on my cheek. Pain seared across my face, but I didn't cry.

Maybe it was because I had heard George say, "I can't stand a woman who cries." Or possibly, it was because God had made me tough. But I shed no tears, even if George hurt me. Nor did I attempt to fight him off, which I probably could have done since George was not a big man.

"I don't know why you did that, because I wasn't making fun of you. I don't know what cocaine is!" I said loudly.

"Quit hollering," George said, and for a moment, I thought he was going to belt me again.

"I'm not hollering," I said. "I'm telling you the truth. I don't know what it is. I've never seen cocaine before in my life."

When George sobered up and realized the horrible thing he had done, he was devastated. He apologized over and over to me. "I'm so sorry, Nancy. I know you just want to help. It will never happen again."

He seemed so sincere, so I readily forgave him, and I believed him when he said his violent behavior was an aberration.

Silly me.

I knew there was a good person inside George Jones. But I also knew there was a devil in him, both figuratively and literally. I knew enough about demons to know that they could inhabit a human being if that person opened the door and invited them inside. Apparently, they had taken up residence in Mr. Jones, and it was my job to help get them out of him.

Occasionally, I'd see George pick up a Bible, sit down in his chair, and read a bit of it. He wouldn't say much, but he often sat there for a while, thinking about what he'd read. He never seemed to read an entire book of the Bible or even a chapter, but he'd read a bit, then put down the Bible and think. He seemed to sense that he had some evil spirits within him, and perhaps he thought, *If I read a little bit, they'll go away.*

They didn't.

Shortly after we got together, we moved to Muscle Shoals, Alabama, a town near Florence with a reputation for great musicians and a lot of dope. George frequented a bowling alley in the area, so I went with him. I noticed, however, that while some people enjoyed bowling, a number of folks, including George, engaged in other kinds of activities in the facility. Usually, he said, "Wait here," pointing to a bench. I sat down and watched George step inside a back room. When he came out, his entire personality had changed and Mean George was back. I was naïve, but it didn't take a genius to figure out what was going on behind that closed door. Over time, I saw other famous Nashville music figures slipping behind that office door, as well.

One night I met George's supplier face-to-face. I yelled and screamed at him to stay away from George, but he simply laughed at me. Another fellow heard me . . . or heard about me. His friends called him "Big Daddy," and for some reason, he took a liking to me. Big Daddy knew the drug dealer and his cohorts who were feeding George's habit, and he became an ally in helping me to keep George away from them.

Sometimes when George was in town and a deal was going down, Big Daddy might call me and "accidentally" let me know where George was located. "Don't ever let anyone know that I told you," he warned. I didn't, but when I went to the place where Big Daddy had indicated, I found George high on so much cocaine he looked and moved almost like a zombie. It was all I could do to get him into the car and back home.

Someone told me through the grapevine that the drug dealers

in the area had taken out a high-dollar insurance policy on George. To this day, I think some of those henchmen wanted to murder George. I guess they figured that they'd milk as much money out of George as they could get. Then if George died of an overdose, with his reputation for abusing his own body with alcohol and drugs, nobody would suspect foul play.

During his sober days, I begged George to go to the authorities and ask for help. George wouldn't hear of it. Not only did he want to continue his coke habit, he feared that going to the local authorities would only bring more trouble to us. I didn't know whether he was right or if that argument was all a ruse, but George was adamant that we keep the law out of it.

The boldness and the audacity of the drug dealers continued to frighten me. One night they walked right into George's house, trying to get him to take more cocaine. I knew they were dangerous thugs, but I didn't care. I was furious and I began yelling, screaming, and cursing at them at the top of my lungs. "Get out of here before I call the cops!" I screamed. It is a wonder that one of them didn't put a bullet in my head.

Instead, they simply laughed, and shrugged their shoulders, as though saying, "Another time, lady. And you'll get yours," as they left. But I knew those creeps were not to be messed with. They hated me, and they saw me as a flimsy line of defense, keeping them from destroying George. Even Big Daddy warned me that the suppliers had put out the word that they wanted me out of the way—permanently.

Was I afraid?

You bet I was afraid. I lived in fear for George, and for Adina, as well as for myself. My fears did not prove unfounded.

One night, while George was away, I was driving back to the house where I lived with him in Muscle Shoals with Adina in the car. As we started across a bridge over the Tennessee River that runs through

Florence and Muscle Shoals, suddenly I felt a jolt in the back of our car. I thought I may have blown a tire, but then I felt another jolt, this one stronger than the first. I looked in the rearview mirror and saw headlights and the shadow of a car that was coming right at us again! The car slammed into my bumper, causing me to nearly lose control of the steering wheel and sending our vehicle veering toward the bridge railing.

I struggled to get the car under control and about the time I did, the car behind us rammed us again! And again. I realized that the car was trying to shove us off the side of the bridge into the river below.

Adina was shrieking hysterically in the passenger seat next to me and I could feel my heart pounding like a jackhammer. But there was nothing else to do but keep driving. I tried to swerve into the other lane but there was oncoming traffic. Within feet of a head-on collision, I yanked hard on the steering wheel, pulling the car to the right and out of the way as the cars and trucks zoomed by us. The car behind me slammed into our trunk again, forcing me toward the side edge of the bridge. I could see the lights from our car reflecting on the water below and I fully expected to plunge into the river at any moment.

I wasn't scared.

I was terrified.

But just about the time I nearly lost it, we reached the other side of the bridge—about a sixty-second drive from one side to the other under normal circumstances. As our wheels hit dry pavement, I looked into my mirror but the battering ram swerved abruptly and was gone. It disappeared into the night, but it had left a definite impression. Many of them, in fact. I realized afresh that these boys were not playing cops and robbers. They were serious about wanting me dead. And if it meant taking out Adina, they were okay with that, too, as long as our deaths opened the way to George.

When Adina and I first went to Alabama with George, his house was like a revolving door of shady characters, coming and going at all hours of the day or night. I recall one person walking in and taking the new television George had bought to watch his football games and cowboy movies out of the house. "He's not going to watch it, anyway," the man said. He was involved with some bad people.

George sometimes did well in choosing the good for a while, and then suddenly he turned erratic in his behavior. I knew what that meant, so I tried to keep him happy and well fed. But food was not always enough to distract him. On one occasion, I bought an entire bushel of purple hull peas. He loved them, especially when I cooked the peas and laced some okra on top of them just before the peas were done. The preparation is hard work, though, and requires that each pea be shelled individually.

I shelled those peas for hours until my fingers were purple. I washed the peas and boiled them and put smaller portions in freezer bags, so we could enjoy some later in the season. Then I put them on the counter and put ice in them to cool.

About that time, George came in and abruptly said, "I'm going to Nashville."

I said, "If you wait, these peas will be done in another hour, and I'll be ready to go."

George looked at me and scowled. "You're not going," he said.

"Why not?" I asked. "Why are you going to Nashville?"

"I'm going to Billy's to listen to some songs."

I knew he was lying. I guessed that he was either going to get drugs or possibly go off on another drinking binge. Either way, I knew it was not good to let him go by himself.

I said, "Okay." I shrugged my shoulders and shook my head sideways. George knew that I was not pleased.

He said, "Oh, you're mad, aren't you?"

"Yes, I'm mad because I don't think it's right that you leave me here," I said. "Especially after I went to all this trouble to make one of your favorite dishes." I nodded toward the deep-dish pan filled with the shucked and boiled purple peas.

George walked over to the counter, grabbed the dish pan full of peas, took them outside, and threw them as hard as he could into the driveway, peas, pan, and all. The peas spilled in every direction and the pan clanked down the driveway. He turned and glowered at me as if to say, "There! That's what I think of all your hard work to prepare those peas." He got in his car and sped away, leaving me standing there.

I cleaned up the mess on the driveway. Several hours later, enough time for George to have driven from Alabama to Nashville, Billy Sherrill called me. "Have you heard from George?" he asked.

"No, I haven't," I said. "I thought he was coming to see you, to listen to some new songs?"

"I heard that he is here in town, but I haven't seen hide nor hair of him," Billy said. "I'm afraid he's on another drunken binge."

"Well, I hope he gets it out of his system before he comes back," I said.

George stayed gone for several days. When he came back, he seemed sad and contrite about what he had done.

I told him, "We gotta get outta here, George. If you don't come with me, I'm going by myself. I can't take it anymore."

He looked at me pensively and I think he recognized that I was serious, that I was ready to walk away and not come back. "Okay," he said quietly. "We'll sneak out late at night, so the drug dealers here won't know it till after we're gone."

That's what we did. We didn't take any of our belongings other than the clothes we were wearing, and we left Alabama, headed for Carencro, Louisiana, outside Lafayette. But before we even got out of town, the drug dealers found out somehow and tracked us down. Two large, surly-looking men confronted us. "You need to get back to Muscle Shoals," one of the men said with a snarl. "Or else." We reluctantly returned to our home.

At one point, the drug dealers had planned to kidnap my nearly-sixteen-year-old daughter, Adina, to lure me away from George, but Big Daddy intercepted their moves, found Adina, and hid her for me till I could safely get her and return her to our home. It was crazy. "Let's just leave," I implored George. "Let's move away from this place and these people." George and I planned to pack up and leave our home in Alabama. We loaded our car and Adina's car full of our belongings and started driving out of town. That's when we noticed that Adina was not following us. I was driving, so I turned the car back toward our house, where I thought Adina might go if she were lost. We prayed that she would be there waiting for us.

I eased down the street toward our home when suddenly the night air was ablaze with flashing red lights and the sound of sirens. A police car peeled around me and stopped, forcing my vehicle to the curb, while another police cruiser sandwiched our car from behind. I knew that I had not committed any traffic violations, but two police officers walked up to my window and one of them gruffly yelled at me, "Get out of the car."

Not, "Good evening, Ma'am." Not, "We're doing a random license check." None of that. Just, "Get out of the car!"

That didn't sit well with me, so I retorted, "What for?"

"Just get out of the vehicle."

I took my good old time opening the door and stepping out, while George stayed seated on the passenger's side.

"You ran that red light," one of the officers said, pointing back toward a light that I knew I had crossed under while it was still green.

"You're a liar!" I railed. "How much are you being paid to stop us?"

The cop must not have appreciated my accusations. He spun me around and slammed me face-first against the car. I wasn't going to put up with that, so I kicked him in the shins and cussed him out, as he pulled my arms behind my back and slapped the handcuffs on my wrists.

The officers loaded George and me into one of their cruisers and took us to jail. There, they separated us, me in a cell by myself while the cops led George off to one side. But they didn't put him into a cell. I started fussin' and cussin' again, yelling loudly so everyone could hear me claiming that the cops were being paid to stop us. "I didn't run any red light, and you boys know it!"

"Just calm down, Nancy," George tried to pacify me.

"George, don't you realize what's going on here?" I asked. "They are going to leave me right here in this cell while they take you off somewhere and get you loaded with cocaine."

And that's exactly what they did. They brought George back to the police station in a cocaine-induced stupor about thirty minutes later. They unlocked my cell and nodded toward George. "Take him home," one of the cops said. They didn't even charge me for assaulting a police officer. I don't think they ever intended to charge me; they just wanted me out of the way so they could pour more coke into George. More than that, their actions were a threat to us, a warning, "Don't try to run away. We'll find you." And I was pretty sure they would.

When we got home late that night, Adina was there, frightened but safe.

I called Big Daddy the next day and we talked about what it might take to get away from the thugs who had their claws deep into George. "Get out of town," he told me. "At any cost."

"But where can we go?" I asked.

"Anywhere but here," he replied with a sigh.

I've often wondered if someone had been listening in to Big Daddy's and my telephone conversation. George and Adina and I took his advice and moved away from that area to Lafayette, Louisiana. We were there only a short time when we heard that Big Daddy had been murdered.

8

Why Didn't I Leave? How Did I Survive?

Living together with George outside the bonds of matrimony, as they say in sophisticated circles, or "shacking up," as George coarsely described our relationship, I could have walked away at any time. Over the years, many people have told me that I should have left the first time I saw the cocaine or the first time he raised a hand to hit me. Maybe I should have—that would have been the right response for most victims of abuse—but I didn't believe that was the best course of action for me.

George didn't force me to stay, and unlike some victims of spousal or partner abuse, I wasn't afraid that he would attack my children or me if we tried to escape. I stayed because I loved him, and I was determined to help George get free, not only from the drugs and alcohol, but from the demons within him. Not that I felt I was a spiritual giant. Far from it. But I said it then, and I've said it hundreds of times since, to this very day, "When George was sober, he was the best man I ever knew." I knew there was a good man inside him, and I believed that God could set him free. I just had to help him get permanently clean and sober by starving the bad man to death and feeding the good man.

The one thing I did *not* do was nag George about his addictions.

Oh, I gave him my opinions; I told him straightforwardly what I thought about his booze and drugs. But I refused to nag him. Nor did I preach at him. I knew instinctively those things wouldn't do any good anyhow. More importantly, I believed there had to be a better way to reach George's heart. I noticed that he responded positively when I reminded him that the Lord was watching him, or that he was disappointing his dear Pentecostal mama in heaven. Sometimes George would be talking crazy, and I'd say, "That's fine with me because God hears everything you're saying."

He'd look around and say, "Oh, yeah? Where is He?"

I said, "God is all around you, man, all around you. God hears what you're saying. He knows what you're doing."

George would get suddenly contrite. "I'm sorry, God," he'd say. "I won't do it again." I'm not sure George was serious when he'd say such things, but he always had a reverential respect for God. He also calmed down sometimes when Adina appealed to his better side.

On the other hand, when he was out of his mind on drugs or alcohol, he could be dangerous. Once, he nearly destroyed Waylon Jennings' den, smashing everything in sight. Waylon had to tackle him and sit on George to hold him down and keep him from tearing up the whole house.

On more than one occasion, George smashed up furniture or mirrors or windows in our home, as well. Usually he would not even remember being violent when he sobered up and often, I wouldn't tell him. I simply cleaned up his messes. I knew that George would not have done those awful things had he been sober, so once he was back in his right mind, it made no sense to rebuke him for his actions during his drunken stupor.

It wasn't easy. And there were plenty of times when I feared for my life. For instance, while we were living in Lafayette, George went out to do a show and didn't come home for two weeks. I had no idea where he was, whether he was dead or alive. I hadn't seen his name in the newspapers, so I guessed he was still living—if you can call stumbling around in a drug- or alcohol-induced mess living.

After two weeks, he called and said that he was coming home and that he planned to get professional help to beat his addictions. But when he came home, he was soused again. I was sorely disappointed, and Adina was crushed. We had both hoped that George was sincere when he said he was ready for a new start.

He wasn't.

But I believed that George's time would come. Until then, I had to be wise, protect myself and my daughter, and pray that God would get ahold of George's heart. Whether that would be enough rationale for other women to stay, I can't say. Most counselors nowadays advise a victim of abuse to get out and get away immediately. "Pray for the abusive person from a distance," they may say. But hope motivated me to stay, to love, and to forgive George. I felt that God had given me the mission to help George and that He would protect me.

Some people might say, "Oh, Nancy stayed for the money, or she stayed because it was George Jones, country music star."

That's nonsense.

There *was* no money for the first few years that George and I were together. George wasn't performing many shows. And even some of those he committed to doing, when the dates came around, No Show Jones often blew them off. A few years earlier, he had failed to show up for more than seventy shows!

* * * * * *

For some reason, when George returned to Louisiana, he wanted to stay in a motel, so we booked two adjoining rooms, one for Adina and an adult friend of ours, and one for George and me. Once I saw him, I understood better why George might not want to go directly home. He was a filthy mess after a two-week drunk. We checked in at a motel and Adina went to her room and George and I went to ours. I could tell he was high, but I could not imagine how plastered he was.

Not until he started hitting me, that is. George began lashing out at me verbally, but he wasn't talking to me. His voice had transformed into a horrible, gravel-toned, demonic roar. He loudly yelled out the names of the men who had loaded him up with cocaine, cussing at them and swinging madly at them. I ran to the door between Adina's room and ours and pounded on it, but it was locked. George grabbed me and I whirled away from him, trying to reach the front door, but he caught me again. I slipped out of his drunken grasp and ran into the bathroom where I attempted to barricade myself inside, but George broke through again, swinging his fists madly at me. Blood spattered all over the shower and shower curtain. I fell back into the shower and George continued pounding me in the tub, screaming out the names of the men who had fed him the drugs.

I recognized the names of several of the men George called out. "I am not those men!" I yelled back at him.

"Yes, you are!" he bellowed and then spoke with his fists. "You're trying to kill me!" He dragged me out of the shower and threw me on the bed.

"George! Listen to yourself. You're talkin' craziness," I said. "Those guys aren't here. It's me, Nancy!"

"Oh, I know who you are," he roared. He ripped off my clothes and beat the daylights out of me, fiercely pummeling my face with his fists. He didn't stop until he couldn't function any longer.

I'm not sure which of us passed out first. I know I was the first to awaken. My face was bruised and battered, and I was a bloody mess.

With George passed out, I hobbled to the door and opened it for Adina. Our friend who lived in the area and was staying with Adina came into my motel room and was shocked to see me beaten and battered as a result of George's rampage. George was still passed out.

"Nancy, are you okay?" she whispered fearfully, not wanting to awaken George.

"Yeah, I'll live," I said, although I wasn't quite so sure.

My friend helped me to a chair, then hurriedly tried to clean up the motel room and the bloody bathroom. "We've gotta get you to a hospital," she said.

"I can't," I said. "If I go to the hospital, they're going to want to know how this happened and they'll come back and arrest George."

My friend looked back at me as though to say, "And, so what?"

"I can't let that happen," I told her.

She nodded. "Okay, just tell them that you fell down the stairs."

I reluctantly agreed and my friend rushed me to the hospital. When the emergency room doctor and nurse asked me what had happened, I replied quietly, "I fell down the stairs."

It was a ridiculous ruse and almost anyone could tell that I was lying. The ER doctor and nurse looked at each other then back at me skeptically. I doubt they believed me for a moment, but they were more concerned with my swollen face, my blackened eyes, the cuts on my ear, and the multiple bruises all over my chest and back and other areas of my body.

The hospital kept me for a while, then released me, and my friend took me back to the motel room where she replaced all the bloody towels with clean ones. She went out to a store and purchased a new shower curtain and hung it.

George never moved all day long.

When he woke up the next day, he was horrified at the sight of my black and blue, mangled torso. "Nancy! Are you okay? Nancy, who did this?"

"You did, George," I told him through my tears. "You were drunk or high or both . . . and you did this."

"No, I couldn't have," he whispered. "I wouldn't have."

"You did."

"Tell me who did this to you, Nancy," George begged. "I'll get even with him."

"Look in the mirror, George," I said. "That's the man who did this."

I told him that he had been calling me by the names of the men who had been feeding his drug habit, punching me as though I were them. "At one point, you even came to your senses for a few moments and apologized to me," I said, "asking me to forgive you. And Adina too. She was pounding on the door. You even got down on your knees and begged for our forgiveness," I told him. "Your whole body changed; your face looked evil; your voice changed."

"What did it sound like?" George asked.

"You sounded like the devil," I said.

"How could I do that?" he asked.

"I don't know. But you had a different voice, a scary, ugly, awful-sounding voice. You were not George."

"I don't remember a thing," George told me.

"I'm sure you don't," I told him. "But Adina and I will never forget it."

In a few incidents, George beat me up to the point that my face was nearly unrecognizable. When something like that happened, he always had an excuse. He was either drunk or high on cocaine, or both. When he drank too much, he could be obnoxious or verbally abusive, but when he combined the alcohol with cocaine, the demons took over within him and he became violent. His demeanor changed, his voice changed, and I knew the George I loved was not in control. Yes, it was his body, but it was not *George*—the demons were surging through him. I prayed; I prayed for George's deliverance, and I prayed for Adina's and my safety.

Cocaine increased George's desire to have sex but it also impeded his body's ability to ejaculate, so that made him even angrier. It was always my fault, so he would beat me up, because after all, it couldn't be *his* fault. It was an awful, vicious circle of abuse. I knew the more cocaine George did, the more sex he wanted, but it wasn't going to turn out well.

Where was I gonna run to? I had nowhere to go. Women's shelters were not prevalent back then, and few churches even talked about spousal abuse. Moreover, I deeply believed that if I left George, the devil would destroy him, not merely physically, but eternally. I didn't know much about spiritual battles, but I recognized that the enemy was trying to take George out, and me too.

But I also believed that God's hand was upon me, that He protected me, and no matter what George did, God's purposes would be fulfilled. I didn't go to church during that time, nor did I read the Bible regularly. But I sure did pray a lot!

On only one occasion did I ever fight back against George and after that, I never had to again. We were in Oklahoma staying at a hotel, and George was drunk and cussing and raising Cain.

"I'm not going to do the show tonight," he groused.

"I don't care," I said. I sat down on the side of the bed and crossed my arms over my chest.

George lurched over to the bedside, grabbed my arms, and jerked me to my feet. For a small man, he was incredibly strong. He was country tough. Waylon Jennings once told me, "He's the strongest man I've ever seen to be so little."

And when he was drunk or doing cocaine, he seemed almost superhuman.

George glared at me and said, "What do you mean you don't care? What do you think you're gonna eat and how are you going to pay the bills?"

Usually, when Mean George showed up, I tried to soothe him and placate his irresponsible actions and words, but not this time. I retorted, "I don't care! If you don't want to do the show, don't do it. You don't have to."

George lunged at me, and this time, I pushed back on his chest. He was already wobbly because he was drunk, but apparently, my actions took him by surprise, because when I shoved him, he fell backwards against the heater mounted on the wall of the hotel room. The fins on the heater cut into George's back, and he yelped in pain. "What are you doing?" he yelled.

I didn't know it, but the guests next door had called the police, and the next thing I heard was a banging on the hotel room door. I opened the door, and there stood two officers.

"What's going on in there?" the policeman asked.

I opened the door wider so they could see George. I said, "Well, it's plain and simple. He was going to slap me and I shoved him against that heater and it cut his back."

"Mm-hmm," the officers nodded, looking at the marks on George's back that matched the size and shape of the heater fins on the wall. "Well, George?" the officer seemed to ask for George's side of the story.

George responded, "Boy, it hurt, too!" He didn't try to deny that he had intended to slap me or to downplay my response.

"I'm sure it did, Mr. Jones," the officer said. "Well, if you don't mind, please keep the noise down. We've received some complaints." The officers wished us well and left.

George calmed down, sobered up, asked me to forgive him, and went out and did a great show that night.

I knew that George and I loved each other, and I'm sure George was not afraid of me, but after I confronted his bully-spirit, he never again raised a hand toward me. Not even when he was drunk.

Even when I wanted to leave, something (or maybe it was Somebody) kept saying to me, "No, don't go. If you do, he's gonna die."

At the time, I didn't have sense enough to know that we were engaged in a spiritual battle. Now, when I look back at it, I realize that God and His angels were with me the whole time.

9

Left Behind!

Although I never left George, there were a number of times when he left me. I thought it might help matters if I traveled with George to his shows. In the early days, we traveled to shows in cars and vans. Later, we graduated to motorhomes, then to tour buses. On a sweltering hot Sunday morning, we were traveling in a motorhome and the air conditioning was malfunctioning.

George spied a little old lady walking alongside the road. Already drunk early in the day, George was sitting in the hot motorhome with an open fifth of Jack Daniel's on the table. He called out to the driver, "Pull over!"

"What? Why? Where?"

"Pull over, and pick up that old woman there," George said, pointing at the feeble-looking woman walking along the road. Maybe George thought she was on her way to church and needed a ride. He seemed to feel compassion for her. "Pull over," he said, "and get that old woman. We don't want her walking on the road by herself."

The driver pulled the motorhome off to the side of the road and opened the door in front of the woman. "Hop in," he said. "We'll give you a ride to wherever you are going."

The woman looked inside the motorhome, took one look at

George, and then glanced at the whiskey bottle on the table. She backed away from the door.

"Come on, get in," the driver implored.

"No, thank you," she said. "I'd rather walk."

No doubt, she probably felt safer walking along the highway than riding in the boozemobile.

I got along well with the guys in the band, as well as Bobby Birkhead, George's road manager, and George seemed happy to have me with him, traveling together. That is, until George started drinking whiskey or snorting cocaine. Then I never knew what to expect from George, nor did anyone else; all bets were off.

One night, when George was on a cocaine high, he fell asleep and later woke up angry at about 2:00 a.m. He was mad at me for some reason and was ranting and raving. Bobby was driving the tour bus somewhere in Texas, and he could hear the commotion coming from the back of the bus. George pushed me up the aisle and toward the front door.

"George! What's wrong?" I tried to settle him down with no success.

"Go on, get out of here," he roared. "If you don't like it, there's the door." He shoved me down the steps of the entryway and out the door. The bus pulled away, leaving me stranded. I wasn't even wearing any shoes!

Bobby Birkhead dropped a hundred-dollar bill out the bus window. He knew I'd need some money to get back home. But just as I went to retrieve the bill, a truck came along and blew it away. I never did find it, scrambling around along the side of the highway in the dark.

I wasn't certain where I was—I knew we had been driving through Texas before George and I had gone to bed—so I didn't even know which direction to walk. Fear overtook me when I began to think that maybe one of George's cocaine buddies might try to kidnap me or even kill me so they could have easier access to him. Rather than risk walking the dark road alone, I crawled down into ditch alongside the highway and stayed there all night long. The next morning, I walked to a service station and called George's brother-in-law, "Uncle Dub," and he came and found me.

On several occasions, George threw both Adina and me off the bus, leaving us alone along some highway. Bobby usually was able to slip me some money when he saw what was happening.

On one occasion, George wasn't even mad when he "accidentally" left me behind. We were on our way to do a show in Kentucky, traveling along the Bluegrass Parkway, when we pulled in at a service station to purchase some fuel. I was all "dolled up," and looking good, dressed in a beautiful leather skirt and wearing a pair of fancy boots. I looked out the window and noticed that there was a shop that had a little wagon in the window. I thought the wagon would be a great gift for a child of some friends of ours, so I got off the bus and walked inside to check out the wagon. It wasn't exactly what I wanted, so I browsed around the shop a while.

Meanwhile, George was watching an NFL football game and reading the *USA Today* newspaper. George loved football and often bet on games, so he hadn't even noticed when I'd gotten off the bus.

When I went back outside, the bus was gone!

"Where'd that bus go, that one that was sitting over there, getting fuel?" I asked an old codger standing nearby.

"Oh, hun," he said with a slow drawl, "they've been gone for about ten minutes."

"Are you kidding me?"

"No, ma'am, they pulled out a while ago."

"Well, can you call the state police or something?" I asked.

"For what?"

I said, "I'm Nancy Jones and I'm married to the man in that bus that just took off and left me here!"

The old guy grinned. He said, "Well, ma'am, undoubtedly he didn't want you to go."

"That's not funny," I said.

I went back inside and called the police. Within ten or fifteen minutes, a Kentucky state trooper showed up and found me. I explained to him what had happened and asked him, "Can you just go and catch that bus?"

He said, "I don't understand this. Is he drunk? Did your husband get mad and throw a fit?"

"I don't know," I said. "All I know is that I was in the store looking at a wagon."

The officer looked at me as though I was wacky. He tried to radio the bus driver but couldn't make contact, so he said, "Come along with me, Ms. Jones." I got in the state trooper's car with him and he said, "Where are they going?"

I said, "They're scheduled to play at a civic center somewhere tonight with Conway Twitty."

"Oh, I know where they're headed," the trooper said. He punched down on the gas pedal and the cruiser roared away from the service station and up the highway. We sped along the Bluegrass Parkway until the officer spied George's bus and pulled alongside it, flashing his lights. The bus pulled over to the side of the road and the officer and I stepped on board.

When George saw me, he said, "Honey, *where* have you been?"

I said, "You left me at that service station!"

"I thought you were in the back of the bus," he said. "And then Bandit [our dog] wanted to go out and pee. So I went back there and I couldn't find you."

Sad, isn't it? He really didn't know I was gone till the dog had to pee.

The state trooper came on the bus and George autographed some pictures for him. I said, "See, I told you he wasn't mad at me."

The trooper smiled, tipped his hat, and was gone, carrying with him George's pictures and my sincere thanks.

When we arrived at the venue, Conway Twitty was fixin' to go on stage. When he saw me by the bus, he cracked up laughing. "Ha! I heard that you got left at a truck stop."

"You shut up, Conway!" I said, "I don't want to hear a word from none of y'all."

I tried to go inside the building, but I was so mad, and I had changed out of my fancy clothes into my blue jeans by then, and I didn't have my backstage pass. So the security guy raised his palms in front of his chest said, "Oh, whoa! Whoa, you can't get in back here."

I glared at him and said, "Honey, you don't want to mess with me tonight."

"Let her in," Conway said with a chuckle. "She's had a bad day and she's in a bad mood."

Throughout his set on stage that night, George quipped to the audience, "I left Nancy at a truck stop." He paused for a moment, and with a twinkle in his eye, said, "But she found me."

Occasionally, George flew on a private jet to some of his shows. That was a wonderful way to travel, but I didn't always make the round trip. Somewhere along the way, George would get worked up into an alcohol or cocaine fit and would order the pilot to take off while I was still in the restroom, leaving me in some strange city with no luggage or money.

I always made it home, and I always went back to him, but I kept two credit cards packed inside my bra for nearly two years.

Even on bad days, George always verbally expressed his love for me. "Well, you know I love ya," he'd say.

"Yeah, but you sure have a strange way of showin' it," I'd often respond. I loved George, and I knew that George loved me—we never went through a day without telling one another, "I love you"—but sometimes he'd get mad about the silliest things. On one occasion, I made a meatloaf for dinner, using tomato sauce and seasonings. I thought it was pretty tasty, but George didn't like it.

I was a Louisiana girl, and our style of Cajun cooking was not what George was accustomed to eating. He was a Texas boy, and although he had left there years before I met him, his tastes in food still drifted back to the Lone Star State. When he tasted the meatloaf I had made for dinner, he turned up his nose.

Before long, he was arguing about how to make a better meatloaf, but I wasn't backing down. George finally got so mad, he picked up the whole pan of meatloaf and threw it at me from across the room. The meatloaf sailed right over my head, barely missing me. It splattered against the wall, making an awful mess all over the floor, as well.

But at least he didn't shoot up the house, as he was prone to doing. I considered George's throwing the meatloaf as progress, rather than him beating me physically.

Let me tell you, if George had wanted to kill me, he could have done so easily. Hurling the meatloaf at me was just George's way of saying, "I'm still in control here." Yes, it was a warning shot, but it was more of his way of blowing off steam.

He was drinking heavily again but he was not using cocaine at the time. He didn't do cocaine the entire time we were living in Texas. It was just alcohol that he sought constantly. He was a great man when he wasn't drinking. Give George one drink and he was funny; two drinks and he was hilarious; three or more drinks and he started to get mean. Those evil spirits were in him, and Jesus and I had to get them out.

10

Love, Luck, or Lunacy?

It didn't take me long to figure out that although George could earn good money, he was blowing more money than he had in the bank account. For the longest time, it seemed that George Jones—country music superstar—possessed no money at all.

Maybe even more astonishing was George's ability to go out and perform concerts during that time. He had several hits playing on the radio during the early 1980s, so concert promoters were still seeking him out, despite the risks that he might not show or that he might leave the stage early so he could go watch the television show *Matlock*, which he often did.

As George said later, "I had been drunk for nearly thirty-five years before I met Nancy. But because of her, I quit drinking and doing drugs."

Unfortunately, when George said that he quit drinking, he meant that he had quit drinking Jack Daniel's whiskey and other hard liquors. He still freely enjoyed beer and other alcoholic drinks. "That's not liquor," he claimed. George pooh-poohed the power of any alcoholic beverage except whiskey. And that continued to be a problem for him and for me, as I was soon to discover.

Sometime in 1982, George said that he wanted to get off cocaine and whiskey. He suggested that if we could get to Texas, his sister Helen and her husband, W. T. "Dub" Scroggins, would help get him committed to a rehabilitation center to treat his drug and alcohol abuse. That sounded like a good idea to me, and I was hopeful that he could get some kind of treatment that might help him.

I should have known better.

George and my then sixteen-year-old daughter, Adina, and my dog and I started out traveling toward Texas in George's huge Lincoln. During the first part of the trip, George sat in the back seat and was really messed up on cocaine and whiskey. He'd been snorting cocaine right in front of Adina, but I knew there was little use in pleading with him to stop, so I pulled out my "ace."

I looked in the rearview mirror and said, "George, it's a good thing your mama's not alive to see you doing that. It would break her heart."

I knew that George loved his mama, and she was a good, godly woman who no doubt spent many a night praying for her boy, George Glenn, as she called him. At times when George was totally out of control, I'd invoke the memory of his sweet mama, and it always calmed him down.

"You can whip that stuff," I encouraged George. "Just throw it out the window. Go ahead!"

"Please, throw it out!" Adina agreed with me. We continued to encourage George, and in a burst of Mama's determination, he tossed a large, costly bag of cocaine out the window.

Adina and I clapped our hands and cheered for George. But a short while later, George began having second thoughts. He wanted more cocaine.

I was driving the car somewhere near Corinth, Mississippi, when George climbed over from the backseat and plopped down in the front passenger's seat. "You're not going fast enough," he complained. "I want to go see Uncle Dub and Helen, and you're not going fast enough."

I knew that earlier George had been doing drugs in the back seat of the car, so I attempted to ignore his belligerence. Meanwhile, Dina was hollering, "Mama, please don't go any faster! Please!"

George stretched his leg across the floorboard and stomped his foot down hard on top of mine on the accelerator. Our car sped up, roaring like a dragster. "George! What are you doin'?" I yelled. "Get your foot off me!" I tried to keep the vehicle under control, but as I looked up, right ahead of us was an eighteen-wheeler. I yanked hard on the wheel, swerving out into the oncoming traffic lane and around the tractor trailer, then back into my lane and in between the semi and another eighteen-wheeler in front of him.

If anyone would have seen me driving so erratically, they'd have probably thought that I was the person who had been drinking or doing cocaine.

That's probably what the state trooper who pulled us over must have been thinking, after clocking me on his radar as going more than ninety miles per hour!

I saw the flashing lights behind us and pulled the car to a stop on the side of the road. A state trooper loomed behind my window. Another walked over to George's side of the car.

When he pulled us over, I had a verbal blow-out. I was so mad. Still, insulting the state trooper wasn't a smart thing to do. The police officer pulled me out of the car and handcuffed me. He charged me with speeding and reckless driving.

The officers instructed Dina to get out of the car, along with our little dog, and stand next to the vehicle, but they didn't handcuff Dina. Then one of the officers must have recognized George. He ordered George to get out of the car, although he didn't handcuff him. Only me.

"Is this your car?" one of the troopers asked me.

"No," I said. "It's his." I nodded toward George.

The police officer said, "Okay, Mr. Jones, we gotta call the dogs because we saw you throw something out of the window."

I said, "Yeah, he did."

We continued to stand on the side of the road until the drug-sniffing police dog arrived and began sniffing all around the car. Sure enough, some of the cocaine that George had thrown out had flown back inside the car window when George had attempted to toss it. The dog put up a fuss and the officers found the cocaine residue in the car.

The officers took all of us to a jail in Mississippi. Once inside the building, I told the police officers, "I'm not gonna take the blame. He was pushing down on my foot on the accelerator." I looked across the room at George and said, "Tell them the truth, George."

George hung his head and looked at the floor. "Well, I might have done it," George said sheepishly, "but I really don't remember."

I knew that he remembered all too well!

They put us all in jail—Adina and me in one cell, along with our little dog—and they took George to another room to question him. I put up an awful fuss, yelling and screaming the whole time.

When the sheriff—a huge George Jones fan—came in, he took one look and said, "What is that kid and that woman and that *dog* doing in that cell?"

I said, "Umm . . . because George was doing coke and I was driving and he was pushing the accelerator, and I guess I'm guilty."

The sheriff glared at his officers and said, "Get them out of there right now!"

They not only released us, they didn't charge George with possession of an illegal substance and they didn't give me a ticket for reckless driving. I struck a deal with the local authorities for George to return and do a free benefit show. We got back in the car and drove away, leaving behind several smiling George Jones fans.

Unfortunately, George reneged on his promise to go to rehab again if we got to Texas. In fact, we turned around and headed back toward Muscle Shoals, Alabama, where George knew he could easily score more cocaine.

Along the way, we stopped at a motel and George got plastered again. The next day, he insisted on driving, accusing me of setting up the arrests. He got crazy, slammed on the brakes, and pushed Adina and me out of the car, along with the dog. George roared off, leaving us in the dust along the side of the road.

Adina and I walked to a nearby farmhouse, and I knocked on the door. A kind woman answered and I told her that we had been stranded along the highway.

A perceptive woman as well, she looked at me kindly and asked, "Were you riding in a car with George Jones?"

"Yes, ma'am, we were," I said.

"Well, my police scanner in the house here said he was just in an accident about two or three miles down the road."

She took us to the scene and sure enough, George had wrecked the car. An ambulance took George to the hospital emergency room, and after patching him up, sent him on to Hill Crest Hospital in Birmingham, a detoxification center. As awful as our day had been, I was hopeful that the detox center might help George accomplish the mission he had aborted in Texas.

But once again, my hopes were dashed.

George spent thirty days in rehab, but somehow managed to find someone who was willing to supply him with cocaine while inside the hospital. After all, he was George Jones, the "King of Country Music."

When the hospital personnel discovered that George was still using while he was supposed to be detoxing, they asked him to leave—which George was only too happy to do.

* * * * * *

On another occasion, when we were living in Lakeland, Florida, we went to the dog races in Orlando and George got drunk. On the way home, George insisted on driving our old, white Mercedes. Coming back from Orlando toward Lakeland, he ran off the road and the Mercedes flipped in the air and landed on its roof. Neither of us was hurt, but somebody called the cops. When the Florida state trooper arrived on the scene, George whispered to me and said, "Tell 'em you did it. Tell 'em."

I said, "Why do I have to tell them that, when you were driving?"

"Cause I'm drunk, crazy!" George shouted.

No doubt the officer could hear him, but when he walked up to us, I told him that I had been driving the car. Silly me. I was charged with reckless driving, and they didn't even cite George for public intoxication. As I often did, I took the heat that he should have taken.

I think professionals call that "enabling," making it easier for George to escape the inevitable confrontation between him and his addictions. To me, my actions expressed my love for George. I didn't yet realize that sort of love could kill him.

Somehow, in the midst of his continued cocaine and alcohol abuse, George teamed up with his buddy Merle Haggard to record the album *A Taste of Yesterday's Wine*, a really top-notch recording. But for most of that year, George was a mess.

For a while in 1982, George was so down and so far out of his mind on drugs and alcohol, every day brought new adventures in delusional lunacy. George repeatedly bounced back and forth over the line between sanity and insanity, crossing the line numerous times in almost every conversation. Many of those conversations were between himself and two characters that he created in his mind, figments of his drug-darkened imagination, but all too real to George. One character was an old man; the other was a duck with a voice that sounded like the cartoon character Donald Duck. George carried on loud, virulent, often crude and coarse conversations with the Old Man and the Duck, dialogue laced with the foulest of profanity and insults, with George providing the voices for all three characters. George made the Old Man sound like the surly actor Walter Brennan, and he quacked like a duck—Donald Duck's style of English—when the Duck responded. When "George Jones" spoke, it was George's own Texas drawl. Imagine the cacophony when the three voices started arguing with each other, which they did daily. It was sheer lunacy to listen to those conversations.

It was useless for me to argue with George, trying to convince him that the Old Man and the Duck didn't exist. They *did* exist—at least to George. Sometimes George's conversations with his imaginary characters were funny; sometimes they were pitiful. Most of the time they were exasperating.

I often thought, *This is crazy!* But I was determined to stay and help George. A lot of people in the Nashville music business made fun of George about his imaginary characters. I couldn't blame them because that's how far gone he was. Although I wasn't part of his life in 1978 and 1979, a friend, Maxine Hyder, from Lakeland, Florida, recalled an incident in which George stood in front of thousands of people at a show and began singing some of his hit songs in the Duck's voice. Maxine left the venue in tears, and George's fans treated him to some nasty voices of their own.

The Old Man and the Duck stretched me about as far as I could go with as much as I could take, but just about the time I thought I couldn't take any more, I'd sense God speaking to me, saying, "You can do better. You can do more. Come on. I will help you."

So I stayed and wouldn't leave George. But it was far from easy.

For some reason, the Old Man and the Duck always sat in the back seat of the car as George rode down the highway—and we drove a lot, especially when George was having a mental episode. We traveled by car from Nashville to Birmingham three times in one day, a distance of 190 miles each way. Nashville, Birmingham, Nashville, Birmingham, by car, just driving. Meanwhile the three of them would get into the biggest arguments and to George it was real.

During the third trip to Birmingham, the Old Man and the Duck really got into it; the Old Man was fussing, and the Duck was fussing, and George was fussing—with George doing all three of their voices. It got so bad, I finally yelled out at the top of my voice, "Shut up! Y'all just shut up. I'm tired. I'm hungry. *Shut up!*"

George looked over at me and raised his eyebrows, as though to say, "Wow, that was impressive."

I glared back at him and said, "Pull the car over."

"Well . . . okay . . ."

He pulled the car over to the side of Interstate 65 and I climbed out. I jerked open the back door and I pretended that I was dragging George's two "friends" out of the vehicle. "Both of you, get out!" I screamed at the invisible characters. (I hope there were no farmers out plowing their fields along the highway that day, because they'd have thought that *I* was the nut job.)

George's body stiffened with terror. "They're coming back in!" he cried.

"No, they're not!" I yelled equally as loud.

"Look! They're in the car," he shrieked.

I said, "No, they're not." And then I directly addressed the Old Man and the Duck again. "Get out. Get out!" I screamed at nothing. But

I dragged them out again, slammed the back door, and jumped into the front seat. I yelled at George, "Go! Get going!"

We left the Old Man and the Duck on the side of Interstate 65.

I never heard from either one of them again.

Not until years later, that is, when George and I were at an event in Nashville, and Jamey Johnson's beautiful little daughter, Kayla, saw George and ran over to him. "Do the Duck!" she begged. "Do the Duck!"

Noooooooo!

* * * * * *

I prayed every day and every night. I never asked God to get me out of the relationship or away from George. Instead, I said, "God, please help me. 'Cause I know there's a good man in there. We just gotta get those evil spirits out of him."

Looking back, I now understand that there were probably more than a few evil spirits in George. I think there were hundreds of demonic entities attempting to control him, to rob him, harm him, and eventually hoping to kill George Jones.

Nevertheless, I lived in hope. The Bible tells about a fellow who lived among the graves, running around naked and cutting himself, and he had twelve thousand demons in him. Jesus cast out those demons and set him free. I believed that Jesus could do something similar for George.

11

Mr. and Mrs. Jones, March 4, 1983

I FELT STRONGLY that if I could keep George away from some of his cocaine cronies and his whiskey-guzzling, undesirable "drinking buddies," and keep him physically busy, he could stop abusing his body—and mine. Prior to getting married, we rented a home in Carencro, Louisiana, for a while and then moved to East Texas, ostensibly so George could live nearer to his sister Helen. We worked together building Jones Country Music Park, a one-hundred-fifteen-acre country property near Colmesneil, Texas, about sixty miles from George's birthplace. The park featured live country music and good country food, most of which was cooked by me. George enjoyed hosting live music at his own venue, and over the years he had owned several nightclubs and music theme parks, from Possum Holler, a five-hundred-seat nightclub in downtown Nashville near the famous Ryman Auditorium, to the Old Plantation Music Park in Lakeland, Florida, and several other music parks. George loved making country music accessible to the fans. When he suggested another theme park in Texas, one large enough to accommodate recreational vehicles and campers, I said, "Let's do it."

For more than a year, we worked long hours, day and night.

We cleared the land, built the buildings, grew our own food, and lived on the property. It was hard work but both George and I enjoyed it. He was pulling up stumps and cutting down trees and was the happiest he'd ever been. We planted flowers—well, one of us did, anyhow—in every shade of bright red, school-girl pink, and golf-course green. We laid hundreds of yards of sod. And for a while, George stopped drinking. He had a goal and he was intent on reaching it.

One day I was out working in the garden when George came over to me and said, "If you're going to be the next Mrs. Jones, you'd better get up from there and let's go get a blood test." George had already been married three times previously, so I guessed that he'd wasted all his fancy, flowery proposals on my predecessors.

I stood up from where I was working, brushed the dirt off my clothes, and wiped the sweat off my forehead. "All right, then," I said. "Let's go."

We didn't even change out of our work clothes. We simply washed up a bit and drove to Woodville, Texas, where we took blood tests and purchased a marriage license. We returned to our mobile home at Jones Country, and George called Helen and asked her to round up a preacher and some witnesses for a wedding the next day—at her house!

I didn't wear a beautiful wedding dress and George didn't even own a tux. Instead, George and I got up the following morning and put on our work clothes as we usually did. The only difference, on this day, was that we drove over to Helen's place where she and Uncle Dub were waiting for us, along with a preacher, Brother Patrick, pastor of Katy Baptist Church, and a small cake.

George and I stood before the preacher in front of the fireplace, and the pastor walked us through the ceremony. We both repeated some vows after the preacher and said, "I do" and "I will," while Helen took some photos with her Kodak Instamatic camera. We shared a piece of cake and then headed back to Jones Country to get back to work.

Along the way, we stopped in Jasper, Texas, and ate lunch at Burger King. I guess you might call that our wedding reception dinner.

While working so tenaciously on Jones Country, George and I lived in a double-wide mobile home—a trailer—on the property. We were pinching pennies, but that didn't keep George from going out and buying a new Corvette. George loved cars, although he had no concept of money, so he rarely knew how much his vehicles actually cost him. He just ordered them or signed the paperwork to buy them and then let someone else work out the details of how he was going to pay for them. It didn't matter if the electric bill got paid or not; George was going to have a new car.

George pulled the Corvette in front of the double-wide trailer and blew the horn. A number of guests were visiting that day, including one of George's adult sons, with his wife and three young children. When they heard the horn, everybody ran outside to see the new car. When the excitement faded, most of them drifted back inside the house.

What happened next was possibly the saddest chapter in George's relationship with one of his sons. The battles between George and his sons have been well documented, and I am not going to get into them beyond saying that the boys always seemed convinced that George owed them things. George felt entirely otherwise, to say the least. I was convinced then, and am now, that George's sons had an inappropriate sense of entitlement and that George had been more than generous.

In any event, here's the scene I recall:

After the crowd had dissipated, one of George's sons nodded toward the vehicle and asked his father, "Is that mine?"

"No," George said happily. "No, it's mine."

The son went back in the trailer and yelled to his wife, "Collect the kids, we're leaving." He walked out the door and looked toward

George again. "So, it's not my car?" the son asked.

George was irritated by now. "No, it's not your car."

His son said, "I'm going to ask you one more time. Is that my car? Did you buy that beautiful car for me?"

"No, I certainly didn't," George answered. I wasn't surprised when George responded the way he did, but I was extremely surprised when I heard his son retort, "Well, if you won't give me that car, you will never see me or your grandkids again. Ever."

"What?"

"That's right. If you don't give me that car, you can forget about ever seeing your grandkids," George's son stated brazenly.

I could hardly believe what I heard. Surely he wasn't serious.

But he was.

George shrugged. "Well, I guess I'll never see them," he said. And we didn't. His grandkids grew up without knowing their grandfather. George was not about to be emotionally manipulated by his sons or anyone else. Nobody told George Jones what to do.

George did have a great love for his daughter, Susan, though. She was his first child, and ironically, she was the sibling the rest of George's family seemed to ignore, almost as though she didn't exist. But she was clearly George's favorite, and over the years she became my favorite of George's kids as well. Quiet and unassuming, much like her father, Susan never expected anyone to notice her or serve her just because she was George Jones's daughter. Quite the contrary, Susan possessed a kindness and a humility just like her dad.

In the meantime, we were having a 3,700-square-foot log cabin built for us, located on the edge of Jones Country. The home had high ceilings and pine beams in the living room, where George enjoyed boasting about a large trophy elk head above the fireplace. "I shot him with a BB gun," George often told guests. Of course, anyone who knew

George well recognized the twinkle in his eye and knew that George was no hunter. The home had lots of cedar throughout the house and because it was our first real home together since being married, in the bedroom, we put a big brass bed with an embroidered pillow that read: Nancy and George, March 4, 1983.

I ordered built-in shelves to safely display George's many music awards, some of which had been stored in boxes and others that I had tracked down and retrieved for him. I had gotten some back from Tammy Wynette, and I had traced a few that George had given away or that had been stolen from him when he was so messed up on cocaine. Several would eventually be discovered on display at various yard sales, including George's prestigious Country Music Association Male Vocalist of the Year award. In a few cases, I had to trade the promise of a "George Jones show" with a promoter to get back awards George had squandered while drunk or high on drugs. Over time, many of George's awards found their way back home and onto those shelves.

One source of constant frustration as we tried to move ahead was the Internal Revenue Service's demands that George owed more than $1.5 million in back taxes. It was almost impossible to calculate what George had paid or not paid the government in the years before we were married, and trying to wade through the morass was demoralizing and depressing. Our good friends and devout George Jones fans Paul and Bernice Chaney, from Roanoke, Virginia, attended one of George's shows in their town and afterwards stopped by our bus for a visit. Down-to-earth folks, the Chaneys had earned a fortune in the coal mining business, but they put on no airs, and no one observing their dress and demeanor would have guessed that they were wealthy.

About that time, one of George's former managers, also from Roanoke, had demanded payment for something for which George didn't owe him and for which we did not have the money to pay, anyway.

"That's alright," he said. "I'll take your wedding rings as payment." The police showed up with a seizure warrant and demanded we turn over our wedding rings as collateral. We sadly removed our wedding rings and handed them over to the officer.

Paul heard about it and searched until he found those wedding rings. He bought them back for us and brought them to us on the bus after the show.

We were elated!

Paul was still upset that someone would demand our wedding rings for a business debt. "I can't believe someone would do such a thing," Paul said.

"Oh, we've gotten used to it," George said casually. "Shoot, I stay in trouble all the time. The IRS is suing me now for back taxes. That was poor management because I thought the taxes were being paid."

"Really? When are you meeting with those people?" Paul asked.

"I'm going to see them next week," George said.

"Okay, I'll go along with you," Paul offered. "Let me know when and where and I'll be there."

"Naw, Paul," George said. "You don't want to get involved in that mess."

"Just tell me where," Paul said.

Sure enough, when we went to meet with the IRS about the taxes, Paul came along. He was dressed in jeans, a pullover shirt, and wore Hush Puppy shoes. "How much do you want?" Paul asked the IRS examiner. "Will you settle for a million dollars? I'll write a check for it right now."

"Sure," one of the examiners shot back sarcastically. "If you'll write a check for a million, we'll settle." No doubt the IRS examiners, as well as our accountant, would not have thought that Paul possessed a dime.

Our accountant eased the IRS examiner aside and said, "He

The man with the golden voice.

Evie Ford, my mom; she preconditioned me for George.

My dear daddy; he loved God and slept with his Bible.

I was an adult when I met my half-sister, Lois, for the first time.

I was a single mom with my daughters Sherry and Adina when I first met George Jones (picture here taken before I met George).

LEFT: George always respected his godly, Pentecostal mama, Clara Patterson Jones.

ABOVE: George served two years in the U.S. Marine Corp long before I met him.

George's passion was to sing traditional country music.

I had never heard anyone bend a note and phrase a lyric like George could.

Pure class.

George loved introducing me to his favorite animals.

George was messed up here, but I knew there was a good man inside him.

Our wedding day. We got married on a whim and a prayer.

I cut the ribbon when we opened Jones Country.

Me, Uncle Dub, Helen Scroggins (George's sister), and George relaxing at Jones Country.

George and I share a laugh with Ray Charles in the mid 1980s.

LEFT: Johnny Cash always referred to George as "Little Pal."

BELOW: Waylon Jennings and George. It tore George up when Waylon died.

George riding a lawn mower down the street to get another drink became a classic story (this shot is years later).

George called Vince Gill "Sweet Pea," and the nickname stuck.

George loved recording duets, including one with Keith Richards of the Rolling Stones.

George was rarely without some lemon-flavored chewing gum in his mouth.

George loved artists such as Alan Jackson, who sang traditional country music.

George and Jamey Johnson relaxing on the bus before a show.

George and I said "I love you" to each other every day for more than thirty years.

doesn't *have* a million dollars."

But Paul overheard him. He looked at me and said, "Nancy, will you please step outside the office with me for a moment?"

"Sure, Paul," I said.

Once outside the office with the door closed behind us, Paul looked at me and said, "I'm going to write that check for a million dollars . . . on one condition." He paused for a moment and looked me right in the eyes before continuing. "If you fire that accountant."

I smiled. "What accountant?" I quipped.

We went back inside the office and the IRS officials checked with Paul's bank to make sure he had sufficient funds to cover a million-dollar check. He did. Paul and Bernice paid that debt for George and me, with no questions asked.

Over the next few years, I paid every penny back to them, although they did not expect that or want that. "I don't want the money back," Paul said repeatedly. "We just wanted to help."

"No," I said. "I don't do business that way. I'll get your money back to you. It might just take some time."

Paul and Bernice asked for nothing in return. "We don't want any praise for that," Paul said. Nor did they want any credit. Once, when some reporters somehow caught word that Paul had paid George's debt, they showed up at Paul and Bernice's home wanting to hear more about the story. Paul ran them off the property.

What a great fan he was! And what great friends he and Bernice were too.

* * * * * *

By May 1984, we were ready for the grand opening of Jones Country. Early in the morning, cars loaded with people were already lined up and down the two-lane highway approaching our place. Many others showed up as early as Thursday evening, more than twenty-four hours before the first show. I was afraid some people might get discouraged when they saw the long lines to get in, so I hopped onto a four-wheeler and worked my way down the highway, selling tickets to folks in their cars as they inched toward the entrance. They seemed excited to see me, especially now that many of them knew that George and I were married, and I enjoyed talking with them. I was also happy because I felt sure that once the fans had purchased tickets, they weren't going to leave.

I needn't have worried. Not only were they not going to leave, most of them came for the entire weekend. The seventy-foot staging area was covered with a roof, but there were no bleachers or comfy seats. The audience brought their own lawn chairs and blankets and placed them out on the hillside early in the morning. Most people stayed till the last note was sung at night, then were back first thing the next morning, throughout the weekend. Technically, the shows ran from eight o'clock at night until midnight, and they began at noon again on Saturday and Sunday and ran till six o'clock Sunday evening, but many of the fans rarely left the performance area—even when it poured down rain. They didn't want to miss a thing!

In addition to the natural amphitheater where concerts were presented, we also opened the Possum Holler Restaurant and Country Cookin' Buffet. Of course, we had live music performed in a dancehall as well. Some new upstart artists from Beaumont, such as Mark Chesnutt and Clay Walker, performed in the dancehall long after the shows on the mainstage were over.

We had camper hookups throughout Jones Country. We charged $12.50 per day, or $35.00 per weekend, regardless of the size of the camper or recreational vehicle. Admission to the shows was also $12.00

per person per day. Sunday's show was $15.00 per person.

We opened for business on Memorial Day weekend 1984, featuring musical guests Johnny Cash and his wife, June; George Strait; Johnny Paycheck, best known for his song "Take This Job and Shove It;" Leon Everette; Cajun Jimmy Newman; and George. On later shows, such as on the Fourth of July, Labor Day, or other Memorial Day weekends, we hosted Conway Twitty, Lacy J. Dalton, Steve Wariner, Billy Joe Royal—who was still riding high from his pop hit "Down in the Boondocks"—and of course George, assuming I could keep him sober enough to perform.

More than twenty thousand people showed up for our opening day, and most shows after that drew crowds of at least ten thousand people and usually reached upward of fifteen to twenty thousand people. Fans around that part of the country were starving to hear some major county music acts, and Jones Country was a fun, family-oriented place where they could get their fill. As successful as Jones Country was, by the time we paid all our artists and paid for the supplies, we didn't really come out like we thought we might. We were lucky to break even.

We were busy getting Jones Country up and running, so we stayed right on the property unless George was out working a show. Since we didn't get out much, our good friends came to Texas to visit us. They enjoyed seeing our progress and we enjoyed having company. We often spent the evenings around the kitchen table playing games, which always brought out George's competitive side.

George wanted to win at everything he did—even if it meant cheating to come out on top. On one occasion, an older couple, Cliff and Maxine Hyder, flew from Florida to Houston and then drove an hour or more to visit with us at Jones Country. Cliff and Maxine were longtime friends of George's, dating back to when he had been married to Tammy Wynette.

After dinner, we played Aggravation, a board game similar to Chinese Checkers, played with marbles moved from hole to hole in the board. We were sitting around a round table in our kitchen and having a good time, but George was not winning. That's when he started surreptitiously moving Cliff's marbles.

Before long, Cliff noticed and said, "Now, George, don't move my marbles. I can move my own marbles."

"You don't know how to play," George huffed.

He didn't want to lose, but now that Cliff was on to him, George fixed his gaze on another part of the board, and stealthily attempted to move Maxine's marbles. "No, no, no, George," she said. "Don't go moving my marbles. We move our own marbles. You play yours; we'll play ours."

I sat across the table and could almost see the steam coming out of George's ears, or was it the green slime of jealousy because he was losing? Regardless, as I observed George trying to cheat and getting caught, I thought, *Oh, watch out, it's fixin' to happen.*

Sure enough, the next time Cliff or Maxine chided George for cheating, he got mad. He leaped to his feet and flipped over the entire table. Marbles flew everywhere as the game board soared through the air too.

George stormed out of the kitchen like a little child who didn't get his way. He left our guests stunned in the kitchen as he went in his room and slammed the door.

We waited a few minutes and George didn't come out, so Maxine said, "We wanna go home. We're not gonna put up with this. We've seen too much of George doing this."

"I understand," I said, "and I'm sorry. I don't know what has gotten into him tonight." That wasn't exactly true, but I knew that Maxine and

Cliff could relate.

I asked one of the employees at Jones Country to take the couple back to the airport. "Take them to Houston and stay with them till they get on the plane," I instructed our employee.

Maxine and Cliff flew back to Florida, abbreviating their visit.

George finally came out of the bedroom about two hours later. "Where's Cliff and Maxine?" he asked.

"They went home," I said.

"All the way back to Florida?"

"Yep, I guess they figured there was no use to stay here any longer."

"Well, I guess I messed that up, didn't I?" George said.

I just raised my eyebrows at him and didn't say a word. Nor did I pick up the marbles or the mess in the kitchen. Nothing. I left it just as it was.

George always played at Jones Country on Sunday afternoons—a much-anticipated show for all of the fans. But that sometimes meant George and the band had to travel long distances between show dates on Friday and Saturday nights to get back home in time to perform at Jones Country on Sunday. On one such weekend, I was busy with all the preparations at Jones Country, as well as entertaining our guests, and I couldn't accompany George on a road trip where they finished up with an afternoon show at Ponderosa Park in Salem, Ohio. The group hurriedly packed up after the show and headed for Texas. They were making good time when suddenly a traffic accident shut down both sides of the interstate highway, and our buses were stuck there. Traffic was at a standstill.

When it became clear that they weren't going anywhere soon, George said to Bobby Birkhead, who was driving George's bus, "Hey, Bobby, why don't you fix up some spaghetti back here? Nancy made up some sauce so all we have to do is cook the spaghetti noodles there on the stove." Bobby did as George asked and poured the sauce into a large pot on the stove. "We'll have the boys come over and eat with us," George suggested, talking about the band members who were traveling in a separate bus behind his.

With the buses idling on the interstate highway, Bobby walked to the band bus and invited the Jones Boys over to eat. They gladly took him up on the offer, but they had no sooner gotten in the bus than George said, "Let's wait and eat later. Since we're stuck here in this traffic, let's play some cards."

Four of the musicians and George sat around the table, drinking and playing poker and drinking some more. The game got steep with each hand worth $700 to $1,000 or more, and they were playing for cash! Meanwhile, Bobby Birkhead remained in the driver's seat for more than an hour and a half, waiting for traffic to move, but it wasn't budging. One by one, the musicians folded until it was just George and the guitar player holding their cards. And drinking.

George and the guitarist ran the pot up to more than $1,600 as they sat across the table from each other trying to bluff their way to victory. "I think I got you, George," the guitar player said.

"Naw, I don't think you do," George said. And back and forth they went. Finally, George said, "Well, whatcha got, son?"

The guitar player laid down a flush, and George's face went pale. He was holding two deuces.

Remember what I said earlier? George didn't like to lose—at anything. Now, his guitarist had bested him for $1,600. He laughed out loud at George. "Ha! HA! See, I told you I got you, Chief!"

"Get off my bus!" George roared. The two men slid out from behind the table and as the guitar player scarfed up the cash, George grabbed him, and the two inebriated men stumbled backwards, off balance, and slammed right into the pot of spaghetti sauce on the stove. The pot ricocheted off the floor and literally bounced to the top of the bus, splattering spaghetti sauce all over the white ceiling and the furniture in the bus.

The guitar player grabbed his money and headed for the door. He should have left well enough alone, but he couldn't resist turning around and yelling back, "Better luck next time, George!"

At that, George picked up one of the empty, long-necked beer bottles on the table and hurled it at the guitarist like a World Series pitcher firing a strike. The bottle missed him and zinged right past Bobby Birkhead's right ear, smashing into the lower portion of the bus windshield, right next to the center post between the two large pieces of tempered glass. George had thrown the bottle so hard that it shattered the bottom portion of the windshield, leaving a large indentation.

About that time, the traffic jam on the interstate broke up, so George went back to his bedroom, the Jones Boys boarded the band bus behind George's, and Bobby drove all night with the mess of spaghetti sauce all over the front of the bus. On the way, he called for a new bus windshield to be overnighted to Jones Country because he was afraid the window was going to blow out as they traveled.

The next morning, George got up and poured himself a cup of coffee. Looking around at the mess of spaghetti sauce everywhere and the broken windshield, he said to Bobby, "What happened up here?"

Bobby turned his head and looked up at George, who still had spaghetti sauce in his hair. "Really, George? You don't remember?"

"No, I don't," George said, rubbing his jaw. "What are we going to tell Nancy?"

Bobby raised his eyebrows. George wasn't concerned about how the window was going to be fixed or how they'd explain it to the police if they were to get stopped. "Ahh, George, I'm not certain how it happened," Bobby said. "Hmm . . . Maybe we hit a bird or an owl or something," Bobby suggested. "I don't really know what it was that could smash a windshield like that. It must have been a big bird."

George nodded. "Yeah, I think it was a bird," he said. "Yeah, that's what it was . . . a bird."

When the bus pulled in at Jones Country, George got off, hugged and kissed me, and headed straight to the house to get cleaned up. I stepped inside the bus to greet Bobby, and I could hardly believe my eyes. It looked as though there had been a Hollywood production of a Texas chainsaw massacre, with spaghetti sauce used as fake blood. And then I saw the large dent in the front windshield. "What happened in this bus?" I asked Bobby.

"Well, ma'am," he hedged, "I'm not really sure."

"And what happened to your windshield?" I asked nodding toward the gallon-sized dent in the shattered glass.

Bobby did his best to conceal a smile. "We think a bird hit us," he said with a straight face.

I stepped up inside the bus, past the sitting area to the stove, and looked around. I said, "You know, Bobby, there's one thing bothers me."

"What's that, Miss Nancy?"

I said, "You wouldn't think that a bird could get to flying fast enough inside this bus to make that big of a dent in that windshield."

Bobby looked up sheepishly from the driver's seat and smiled. "No ma'am, you wouldn't think that." We both got off the bus and Bobby told me the whole story.

A few hours later, George went on stage at Jones Country, still convinced that his bus window had been attacked by a bird. It had been—a dirty bird named George!

Maintaining and running the business at Jones Country was hard work. George encouraged me to hire more help, but it was difficult to keep them, probably because I had such a fiery temper back then, too. I enjoyed dealing with the fans and I loved the artists who played Jones Country, although they could be exasperating. I often had to wake up Johnny Paycheck where he was sleeping off a drunk on our couch so he could go sing "Take This Job." I'd yell at him and get after him, and I took out a lot of my anger on Johnny. At the same time, I had to keep George sober enough to get on stage, and I'm happy to say he never once pulled a "no-show" at his own venue. Good thing. I'd have killed him!

Like buying and selling a boat, my best memories about Jones Country were the day we opened and the day we sold it—which we did in 1989. We moved to Brentwood, Tennessee, a short drive south of Nashville. I was ready for a rest.

12

Managing George

We were still struggling financially while we had been living at Jones Country, and there were many nights when I'd sit at the dining room table trying to figure out how we were going to pay the light bill. I stared at the stack of bills and wondered who I should pay first, or last, or at all.

Although George had a string of hit records, he wasn't making good money then because concert promoters didn't trust him enough to book him at their best shows. They could never be sure if he would show up or not. So when George did earn some money, I tried to pay a little bit here, a little bit there.

Often, I'd be sitting at our table, and George would come in and see me discouraged or frustrated in front of the large stack of unpaid bills. "What are you doing?" he asked.

"I'm trying to figure things out," I said. We don't have enough to pay this." I waved a bill in the air.

George stepped over to the table, grabbed the paper bill, and threw it in the trash.

"George, we don't have the money," I protested.

"Oh, don't worry about it, Mama," he said. He sometimes addressed me as Mama rather than Nancy, as a term of endearment.

"I'll have it for you next week." He picked up more of the bills and threw them into the trash.

"George! Are you crazy? We need to pay those," I said.

George smiled. He left the room and came back a few minutes later with a phone number on a piece of paper. "Here," he said, handing me the paper. "Call this guy."

I called the fellow who owned Texas Longhorn, a popular club nearby that featured live music. I spoke to the owner honestly and said, "Man, I need some help. I've got electricity bills due and I have water bills due, and we don't have the money. Do you have a spot on your show schedule where you can use George? Soon?"

"Bring him on," he said. "I'll let him work."

For a couple of nights, George performed at the Texas Longhorn, and he was paid well enough that I could get caught up on our bills again. That was our pattern.

Even before George and I married, I had begun helping him with his business. George never worried about money and always assumed he could simply call up some honkytonk club on a whim, play the venue for a portion of the gate, and walk away with $20,000 or more in a weekend. He did that often, refusing to show up for a large, well-promoted event, and then going to some club with his guitar and playing for hours along with the house band. It made no sense.

Moreover, his previous no-shows had resulted in many lawsuits from promoters suing George for not fulfilling his contracts. Many of George's no-shows were drug or alcohol related, but some were simply due to George's playfulness or his stubbornness. For instance, we drove to Longview, Texas, one night by car so George could do a show along with the Jones Boys in a saloon. We were parked across the street from the venue, sitting in the car, when George said, "I don't wanna do the show tonight."

"Why not?" I asked. "We drove here just so you could do the show."

"Yeah," he said, "I just don't want to; I'm tired of singing in bars."

I continued debating with George, trying to persuade him to go inside, when he spotted the Jones Boys going in to set up and do a sound check.

George continued to sit in the car and even started laughing. "What is so funny?" I asked. "You've got to get over there and do the show."

"I'm not doing the show," George said. "In fact, let's see how long it takes before the Jones Boys come out."

Sure enough, after a while they did. And sure enough, we got sued.

We went to court—or I should say that *I* went to court, since George didn't go—and met with lawyers in Nashville to see what could be done about all of the legal cases against George.

It didn't take long for me to figure out that the lawyers considered the procedure a waste of time. One of them said to another, "George didn't show up. He was probably drunk. That's why he didn't show up at the venue. He probably won't be at the next one, either."

Even the judge seemed resigned to the inevitable conclusion. "George is going to have to pay all these damages," he said, nodding toward the stack of lawsuits.

"No," I said. "No, he is not. He can't earn that kind of money."

The judge looked at me kindly. He said, "Well, what are you going to do, Ms. Jones?"

"I don't know yet, but I will figure out something."

The judge smiled knowingly and adjourned our session.

Once our lawyer and I were out in the lobby, I told him, "Let me have every one of those lawsuits. I'll find a way to settle them."

"No," he said defensively. "I haven't been paid."

"I don't have any money to pay you," I said with a bit of a snarl. "George has hardly been working any shows."

"Well, I'm not letting go of these until I am paid," he replied.

So right there, right outside the courtroom, I kicked George's supposed legal counsel right in the shins. The erudite attorney hollered, "Oww!" as he dropped his briefcase and the whole stack of lawsuits against George spewed onto the floor. While the lawyer was still rubbing his leg, I got down on my knees and grabbed every one of the legal documents.

Just then, Judge Faimon, the presiding judge, came out of his chambers and saw me scrambling on the floor. "Nancy, get in here," he said.

I scooped up the last of the lawsuits and slipped inside the judge's office.

"What have you done?" he asked with a bemused expression on his face.

I put my hands on my hips and said, "I just kicked the fire outta that attorney. I grabbed all the lawsuits and I'm going to find a way to settle each one of them. Those lawyers aren't helping."

The judge chuckled. "Okay," he said. "Stay in here till they leave."

I kept all of the lawsuits against George and took them with me. It was foolish to pay the lawyers to do nothing. I decided that I could do better on my own.

When I first met George, he had more than two hundred outstanding lawsuits, most of which were for breach of contract for not showing up to do a concert or not fulfilling his obligations to do a full show when he did show up. Back in those days, I never knew if George was going to stay on stage for ten minutes, fifty minutes, an hour, or much longer. It all depended on how much he'd had to drink or if he was snorting cocaine. When George didn't perform a full show, more often than not, the promoter sued.

When I took over George's business dealings, I inherited that whole mess. There were some tight times. It was hard. I would pay one person a portion of what George owed him, and then maybe pay a bit to someone else. It was a delicate juggling act, simply to keep George from going bankrupt again, as he had done earlier in his career. But I never asked anybody for money. I did it all on my own.

I knew, though, if I could keep George from blowing the money he made, it wouldn't take long to repay the people he legitimately owed. One of the ways we could do that was by playing casinos. George loved playing casinos, anyhow, so that was an easy ask.

Once I got him back working regularly, I solved most of the "no show" lawsuits by agreeing to have George return and do a free concert for the promoter he had stiffed. I *guaranteed* that he would show up—or else! Along the way, I assumed a new role as George's manager. He trusted me and let me call the shots. If I told him that he needed to do a free show for someone, he went along with my decision. Eventually, every lawsuit against George was settled, and we started to bank some money.

I didn't really have anyone helping me or even advising me. I simply did what I thought was right, what was best for George, and what was in our best interests. Because of George's erratic nature and his unrealistic approach to handling money, it was sometimes hard to track down all the information I needed. George didn't exactly keep good accounting records or even a list of all his performances, who had booked him, or how much they had promised to pay him. For years, he had left that sort of thing up to other people—and they had not always done a good job for him. So I was often just winging it as I tried to bring his business dealings into some sort of manageable form.

I talked with Tony Conway, at the time with Buddy Lee Attractions, one of Nashville's premier talent agencies. Tony had helped with George's bookings for a number of years. More recently, though, because of the question marks surrounding whether or not George might show up, Tony had been booking dates for as low as $7,500 per show. I said, "Tony, golly, you know that George has proven himself. We gotta go up a little in price."

Tony wholeheartedly agreed, and we soon hiked George's basic performance fee back up to $15,000 per show. With some newfound consistency in George's appearances, Tony kept moving the fee higher and higher. Before long, we were making really good money.

George especially loved working the casinos. They paid well, plus he only had to be on stage for forty-five minutes per show, which left plenty of time for George to enjoy gambling—and he enjoyed it immensely!

George's favorite game at the casinos was blackjack; that's where he spent his time and his money; that's all he ever played. He often won big in blackjack, but right at the end, when he might be up $5,000 or $10,000, he'd just push in everything he was holding, all in at one time. "That's stupid," I told him, but George paid little attention. He didn't flinch at risking it all. If I could distract him, I sometimes went to the table and tried to get some of his chips.

"You can't do that!" the dealers protested. "You can't get his chips."

"Watch me," I said. They didn't want me to hold on to any of his chips because they wanted him to lose. Like me, they knew if George stayed there long enough, he'd lose everything he had won. I didn't want George's winnings to play myself; I was trying to get his chips to hide some. After a while, George might say, "Oh, here; take this and go. You can have this much." He'd slide some chips toward me. I put his winnings in my purse because I knew we were going to need the money the next day.

George was stubborn but he never got bitter, not even when a promoter did him dirty. For instance, a promoter who lived in California booked George to play at a casino operated by some Native Americans in Oklahoma. The agreed-upon fee was $100,000.

We arrived at the venue in plenty of time for the show, but then Bobby Birkhead came on the bus and said, "I've got some bad news."

I said, "What?"

Bobby looked down at the floor as he answered. "The guy in California kept the money. The chief here doesn't have it."

"Don't you have a deposit?" I asked. "Wasn't there a deposit sent to you?"

"No."

"What? Why not?" I demanded.

"Well, Nancy, we know the guy. So I figured it was fine, that he was good for the money."

I said, "Bobby, you know our policy: we must have half of the money as a deposit in advance, or we don't work the shows."

"I know, I know," Bobby said. "But I was sure this guy was good for the money."

The casino was sold out, but when George heard that the promoter had stiffed him, he said, "Okay, then; I'm not doing the show. I want my money."

I went to the casino office and talked to the chief. He was somewhere between irate and scared stiff. "George has got to do the show," the chief said. "If he doesn't, I don't know what will happen."

"But, Chief," I said, "we're getting ripped off. He's getting nothing."

The chief shrugged his shoulders and stretched out his empty palms, as if to say, "Tell me about it." We both felt helpless to do anything about the situation.

I went back on the bus and explained our dilemma to George, fully expecting him to say, "Pack it up, boys. Let's go home."

But he surprised me. He said, "You know what, honey? God's been good to me, and I'm gonna do the show for free."

I smiled at him and thought, *Hallelujah!*

That chief was so happy. He just kept hugging me and thanking me.

"I didn't do anything," I said. "It was George's decision; he's a good man."

The chief threw his hands up in the air. "Oh, yeah, he is. George can come back and play here any time. He can come five times a year if he wants to."

George played the show and we had a good time, but we never did get that money.

It was probably no accident that we had been booked at the casino for $100,000. That was George's go-to number for everything. Whenever anyone asked him how much he wanted for something, his favorite answer was, "A hundred thousand dollars." Everything was a hundred thousand dollars to George, even if it was worth exponentially more than that. George didn't care. He would have sold almost anything he owned for a hundred thousand dollars. He simply had no comprehension of money. If you gave him a hundred thousand dollars, you got it. Do you want my $2 million tour bus for a hundred thousand dollars? I'll take it. There was no rhyme or reason to George's answer. But he knew that 100k was a lot of money, so to him, everything was a hundred thousand dollars.

I fought him over this all the time, for his own protection, and sometimes George was his own worst enemy when it came to getting less than he deserved. For instance, one time he got mad at me because I wouldn't sell the rights to our concessions for one hundred thousand dollars.

When I first took over as George's manager, his sons, Brian and Jeffrey, were handling the sales of merchandise such as T-shirts, caps, photos, and other George Jones souvenirs sold at the concert venues. They were terrible at it.

Velton Lang, father of T. G. Sheppard's wife, Kelly, worked for Conway Twitty. Velton asked George if he could handle our merchandise sales at concerts (online sales had not yet become popular). George liked Velton and was going to give him our concessions—all of them: T-shirts, hats, CDs, coffee cups, and all sorts of other "George Jones" products. "Velton's a good man," George told me. "He'll sell all that stuff."

"What are you going to get out of that deal?" I asked.

"Oh, I don't care about that mess," George replied.

"Oh? You don't?" I asked, pursing my lips and nodding my head.

I guessed that George had already considered selling the rights to his concessions to Velton for a hundred thousand dollars. To George, that was the magic number, notwithstanding the fact that on good nights, George's concessions often took in more than $100,000 at one show!

I went to Bobby Birkhead and said, "Bobby, we need to get those concessions, because if we don't, George is going to give them away for next to nuthin'."

Bobby nodded; he understood. "Yes," he agreed, "but what can we do?"

"I have an idea," I said. "Go to SunTrust Bank and talk to Brian Williams. Tell 'em we want to borrow a hundred thousand dollars, and we'll get those concessions."

Bobby got the loan from the bank, and we bought our own concessions. When I flashed that hundred thousand in front of George's eyes, he was done. "Thank you," he said. He did not even know where the money came from, and he didn't ask. He didn't care. He had his one hundred thousand dollars. He went out and bought himself another car.

Bobby and I made a fortune on those concessions. It was a lot of hard work, but it was fun, too. I went out to the lobby every single night and sold concessions before, during, and after George's shows. I put the profits in a bank account that George didn't even know he had.

When George wasn't working in December and January, sitting at home and not doing shows, guess what money he wanted? He wanted a cut from the concession money. More specifically, he wanted *my* concession money. "Nancy, do you have any concession money?" he asked ever so sweetly.

"Oh, no, buddy," I said. "You got paid a hundred thousand dollars for those concessions. Don't you come around here tryin' to get my concession money."

"Now, Nancy, I know y'all are making money," he probed.

I should have said, "Your portion of the concession money is sitting out there in the driveway," but I was nice. For his own good, I told George a "convenient truth," which, of course, was a downright lie. I said, "George, stop and think. We're buying the T-shirts, we're buying the CDs, and all the other products. So when you get through with all of that, at the end of the year, there's not much money left." I conveniently didn't tell George that the profits were in a separate account.

"Well, we went to Canada and y'all were selling stuff left and right," he said. "I heard everybody talking about it."

I said, "Yeah, but we had to replace the products we sold. Do you understand that, George?"

That was another half-truth. The reason we had to purchase more product was because we had sold out of almost everything we'd had.

"Well, I guess so," he said sadly.

George looked so forlorn that I agreed to give him $5,000 a

month out of that concession money. That usually worked well when we were doing shows, but George still wanted his $5,000 per month even during the holiday months when we were sitting at home and not doing shows.

That was his "talkin' money," as he put it. He carried at least $5,000 in cash with him all the time, wherever he went. Whenever he wanted to make a point, he'd pull out that wad of cash and start peeling off one-hundred-dollar bills. People tended to listen better when George pulled out his "talkin' money."

* * * * * *

Not long after I took over George's business dealings, I started recording his concerts. Not because I enjoyed his shows that much—although I did love to hear him sing, and nobody did it better than George when he was in his right mind—but I recorded his shows to avoid lawsuits. Thanks to George's reputation as No Show Jones, promoters were especially diligent about making sure that George fulfilled his contract obligations. Moreover, sometimes George did indeed show up, but he was too drunk to do an entire show. Or, if there was a good NFL football game on television, or if we were close to airtime for *Matlock*, George might try to slip off stage early. So if the agreement was for a sixty minute show, and George did only forty-eight minutes, the promoters sued us for breach of contract.

Granted, there were plenty of times early on when George did not complete the full show for one reason or another, but not nearly as often as some promoters contended. To prove that George fulfilled his contract obligations, I recorded the entire show, from start to finish. I still have many of those recordings to this day.

One day, our lawyer, Joel Katz, called to inform us that we were being sued by another promoter who claimed that George did not do a complete show. Joel said, "George only did forty-eight minutes, and the show was supposed to be an hour long, so this promoter is suing."

I said, "No, that's not right. George did a full hour show and more."

"Let's just go ahead and settle with the promoter," Joel suggested, "and get it over with."

I said, "No, I'm not settling it. George did a full show, and I can prove it. I've got the tape."

About that time, George came in and saw me talking on the telephone. "Who are you talking to?" he mouthed the words quietly.

"Joel Katz," I mouthed back to him.

"Oh, okay." George waved goodbye and went outside riding around on the farm.

I stepped outside on the patio so I could talk to the lawyer without anyone else in the house being able to hear me. I said, "I'm not doing it, Joel." He and I talked further and argued back and forth. We were still talking a while later when here comes George back to the house, driving his car, and pulling up close to the patio.

I waved the phone at him so he could see that I was still talking.

George responded by drawing an imaginary "cut" line across his neck with his finger, signifying that he wanted me to cut off the conversation. I shook my head no. I'm still talking.

He drove around a little longer and then came back again. He pulled in front of the patio and honked the horn. I was still talking with the lawyer.

George pulled around again, and this time he rolled down the window. "Come on!" he growled quietly.

I flipped him off. That made him so mad he gunned the engine and took off in the car by himself.

I saw him go, but I thought, *I don't care. I can't worry about George. Right now, I've got a bigger problem than him being mad.*

George roared out the back gate and drove all the way around our property and back through the front gate. He pulled in front of the house and sat there and pouted. After a few more minutes of sulking, he pulled in the garage, got out of the car, and slammed the door.

By that time, I was through talking with the lawyer, so I hung up and addressed George. I said, "What are you doing?"

He yelled at me from across the room, "Don't you *ever* flip me off again!"

I said, "Well, don't you ever go 'cut' to me again, either."

George sat there a bit, then he went into his room. I called after him, "What did you want, anyhow?"

"Are we ever gonna *eat*?" George asked. He didn't care that I had just saved him a ton of money. All he cared about was his empty belly.

George sat there and continued pouting.

I said, "We're gonna go eat. What do you want?"

"No, I'm not going nowhere, now. Now, you have to fix something for us to eat."

"That don't bother me none," I told him. "I can go in the kitchen and cook whatever you want." I went into the kitchen and started pulling out some pots and pans and dishes, so I could prepare a meal.

A few minutes later, George ambled into the kitchen. "Honey," he said. "Don't be mad at me."

I said, "I'm not mad at you. Whatever gave you that idea?"

"I know you are," George said. "I can tell by the way you are slinging those dishes around."

I looked at him and tried to glare at him, but I cracked up laughing and so did he.

Oh, and I did win that lawsuit, too. I sent the tape to the lawyer and proved that George had done a full show. It's probably a good thing he hadn't been hungry during that show!

No question about it, when George was hungry, he could be impatient—and impertinent.

When George woke up in the morning, he was ready to roll. One morning, he jumped out of bed, threw on his jeans, and covered his messy hair with his favorite baseball cap. "Get up, honey," he said. "Let's go to Cracker Barrel."

"Well, okay," I said. "But I gotta get dressed."

"Honey, hurry up. I'm hungry," George said.

"Okay," I said. "I'll be right with you." I went in the bathroom and started to get ready. I was naked except for my panties. That's when I heard George in the garage honking the car horn, trying to get me to hurry up. The noise echoed through the entire house.

Okay, I thought. *I've had it. I'm gonna teach that man a lesson about patience.* I walked out of the master bedroom without a bra, without any other clothes, either, except my panties. I marched across the house toward the garage.

Our longtime housekeeper saw me walking through the house nearly naked and she must have anticipated what I was about to do. She called out, "Oh, no, Miss Nancy! Oh, no!"

I gave her a playful, dirty look and continued walking out the door and into the garage. I slipped into the front passenger seat without saying a word.

George didn't even look at me. He was grasping the steering wheel with both hands and staring out the window. I could tell he was mad.

He pulled out of the garage and drove all the way down our long driveway toward the front gate of our property. George still hadn't noticed his naked passenger.

Uh-oh! I thought. *If he goes out that gate, I am dead!*

Just as George was about to pull through the gate, I made a slight noise and he glanced over at me. His eyes about popped out of his head. "Well, good God, honey!" he exclaimed. "Go put you some clothes on. That's ridiculous!"

It was a close call for me, but George never honked that horn at me again, trying to rush me in getting ready.

George and I had so much fun together. People who heard us in restaurants must have thought we both were drinking but we weren't. We simply enjoyed being together. George was the funniest man I've ever met. And he didn't even know it.

Cracker Barrel and Carrabba's Italian Grill were his two favorite places to eat close to home. He could go in there and eat without people bugging him. Fans or local folks never bothered us when we went out for a meal in Franklin. If we drove to Nashville, that was a different story because Music City drew far more tourists, and if they noticed George, it was impossible to finish a meal. But in our hometown, folks were always kind. "Hey, George!" someone might call out a greeting if they noticed us at a restaurant. George smiled and waved, and he kept right on eating.

He didn't hang around long enough to attract a crowd. When we'd go out to eat, even if some of the kids and grandkids were with us, it wasn't a social event for George. We'd order our selections, and as soon as he finished his meal, he was ready to go. He wasn't going to sit around and enjoy the dinner conversation.

We'd say, "We're still eating!"

"Well, okay. I'll meet y'all in the car." And he was gone.

George didn't like to go out after dark, which was rather odd since most of his shows took place at night. But George was afraid of the dark. We turned down most invitations to attend dinner parties or other events if they took place after dark. We wouldn't even go to the movies at night.

"I'm going to run to the mall," I might say.

"No, you're not; it's dark outside," he said. He kept lights on at night. He didn't want to go out by himself, and he didn't want me to go out by myself after dark, either. Even when he was working in the studio with producer Billy Sherrill, George would often quit before dark. He'd say, "Hit it again, boys! I gotta go before the five o'clock traffic." Maybe it had something to do with his youthful experience working at the funeral home; I never knew.

Because George was so kind, he sometimes had a hard time saying no to a salesperson, even if he didn't need what they were selling. On one occasion I planned to meet George at a mall near our home. George arrived before I did, so he passed the time by browsing around some shops in the mall.

He passed by a kiosk where they were selling lotions and creams that were supposed to make a woman's facial skin beautiful. I think the salesman must have seen a sucker coming, because he sold George every item on his shelf.

When I arrived at the mall, George was walking out with a large, heavy bag filled with skincare products. It was so heavy he was huffing and puffing from carrying it. He could barely tote it.

I said, "What are you doing?"

He said, "Hun, I spent eleven hundred dollars."

"On what?" I asked.

George nodded toward the bag of skincare items.

"Well," I said, "that is a rip-off!"

"Oh, no," George said. "The guy said it's supposed to do all sorts of good things for your skin."

"Really?" I fumed. "And did you pay cash?"

"Oh, yeah," George said, patting the wad of cash he carried in his pocket. I don't think George even knew how to write a check.

"Give me that bag," I said angrily.

George noticed the look on my face. "Oh, honey, don't go startin' nothing."

I said, "Give me that bag!"

I took the heavy bag from George's arms and walked over to the kiosk where he had made the purchases. "My husband just bought this," I said. "I don't even know what all he bought, but I want the money back."

The man at the kiosk said, "You can't get your money back."

"Why not?" I asked. "It hasn't been opened. Everything he bought is still in the bag. I want my money back."

The man at the kiosk shook his head. "No, can't do it."

"Look," I said. "The money is in that cash register right there." I pointed at his cash register on the kiosk. "I'm gonna hit that register and get the money."

"Money not here," the man said in broken English. "Already transferred to Iraq."

I knew that George had paid with cash rather than a credit card so I said, "You couldn't have done it that fast. Give me the money back."

He said, "Nope. I call cops."

"Fine," I said. "Call them!"

Sure enough, he called the police, but while we waited for the security officers to arrive, I kept calling out to people passing by in the mall, "Don't come over here. This is a rip-off!"

"You can't do that," the man cried out. "You can't do that!"

When the cops arrived, I recognized them, and they recognized me. One of them said, "Nancy, what are you doing?"

I said, "Let me tell you what happened . . ." After I explained the whole matter to the police officer, he turned to the kiosk operator and said, "You have to give her money back. She hasn't opened anything her husband purchased. It's still in the original bag."

The salesman said, "We don't have the money. It's not here."

I yelled out, "It's in that register." I said, "Don't make me come and push that button."

The police officer interjected, "Step back, Nancy. You have to behave. We'll get to the bottom of this." He took George's receipt to the register and demanded that the kiosk operator open it. When he did, there was George's eleven hundred dollars.

The officer gave the money to me. I went to George and gave the money back to him. I said, "Here, don't ever do that again."

George was amazed. "How'd you do that?" he asked. "Did you create a scene?"

"No, I did not," I said.

George never knew the cops were there. I appreciated that he thought he was doing something nice by buying all those skincare products for me. That was sweet of him, but it was rip-off. After that, I tried to keep George from going to the mall by himself anymore.

13

Tammy, Waylon, and Johnny

I FIRST MET TAMMY Wynette after she and George had been divorced for nearly ten years and before George and I were married. Tammy had custody of their daughter, Georgette. George wanted to have visitation rights with Georgette on weekends since he and I were now together, but Tammy balked at that. By then, she had a new husband, George Richey, a keyboard player on several of Tammy's recordings and later a producer at her label. (I simply called him Richey to avoid confusion between the Georges.) No doubt they had their reasons, but they didn't think it was a good idea for Georgette to spend the weekends with us.

So one day I called Tammy and said, "Tammy, you don't know me, but I think you should because I'm really a nice person. I'm not like some of the women George used to date." We talked on the telephone for a while, and Tammy invited me to visit her at the gorgeous Nashville home she and George Jones had purchased together during their marriage.

I went to her house and we talked. We got along well, and after we got past the initial awkwardness of sitting in the same room with someone who had shared intimate life with George, we hit it off. I liked her, and apparently she liked me, because she agreed to allow Georgette to spend some weekends with George and me.

I later heard a rumor in Nashville that, in reference to me, Tammy had told others, "I tried to hate that woman. I just can't. In fact, I really like that woman."

Tammy and I became friends, and her husband, George Richey, and I also got along great. We laughed a lot and had fun together.

My George, of course, was skeptical. His eyes twinkled as he warned me, "You're gonna wish you hadn't gone over there."

"But George, I like that woman," I protested. "Why don't you come along with me when I visit?" I knew that from the time George had first heard Tammy's voice that he admired her as a singer. Even if their marriage had been volatile, I sensed that he wouldn't mind singing with her again someday, if and when the pain of their divorce subsided.

George went with me a couple of times to his former home to visit with Tammy and George (Richey), but he said it felt uncomfortable. Truth is, I didn't really like him going along with me to Tammy and Richey's house, because my George and Tammy would jab and dig at each other the whole time, trading sarcastic remarks.

"Oh, baloney!" I said. "Enough of all this bickering. I'm not having fun now." After that, Tammy and I mostly got together by ourselves without the men. I had no grandiose plans about Tammy and George ever working together again, but I didn't rule out the possibilities either.

George and I had plenty of friends, but there were few with whom I felt comfortable enough to confide about George's addictions. That was a lonely place. But I just didn't trust too many people in the music business. The two country music stars that I trusted the most during the time George was doing all of his stuff were Johnny Cash and Waylon Jennings. They had both fought their own battles with addictions—Waylon with cocaine and Johnny with pills—and had gone through some tough times as a result. They knew all too well the demons that George confronted. Johnny and Waylon were there for George, and they were there for me as well.

Occasionally, Waylon would try to talk with George about his self-destructive behavior and my efforts to save him from it.

"Yeah, I know," George said, as he nodded his head.

"George, you got a good woman there," Waylon said. "She's tryin' to help ya."

"I know it," George replied. "I've gotta straighten up."

Johnny stayed on George's case quite a bit too. And June Carter Cash, Johnny's wife, tried to encourage George as well. By that time, June and Johnny had established a strong relationship with the Lord, and they were not bashful about sharing spiritual truth with George.

George always listened appreciatively, and he usually agreed with what our friends were saying. But he simply couldn't find the power within himself to choose the right things rather than the things that were killing him.

Johnny always took time to pray with George before leaving our house. He'd even pray on the phone before he'd hang up a telephone conversation with George. George later said, "Johnny Cash was one of the nicest, most beautiful people I've ever known—and one of my very best friends."

Waylon didn't pray with George, but his wife, Jessi Colter, was strong spiritually, and I knew she prayed for George—and for me. "Hang in there, Nancy," Jessi encouraged me. "It's going to get better."

I appreciated her trying to lift me up, because I knew she had survived plenty of rough times with Waylon. And of course, June had lived through some difficult times with Johnny and she had hung in there. They were strong women and dear friends to me.

All three of us women knew our men were good people underneath their rough exteriors.

When George and I moved to Franklin, Waylon visited our home quite often, and I'd let him know what I thought about the whole drug and alcohol thing. Sometimes I'd get after both of them, Waylon and George. "Y'all gotta stop it," I said. "You've got to stop the drugs. You gotta stop drinking." He'd tolerate me for a while before loudly saying, "Put a muzzle on her mouth, George!"

But I'd give it right back to him. "Just shut up, Waylon," I'd say.

But even if Waylon did get tired of my tirades, give me the fake evil eye, and put his big old hand on my head and turn my mouth away from them when I got on a roll, I still loved him.

I knew Waylon and Johnny loved me, and I knew they loved George. So I didn't hold back in trying to enlist their support in helping to get George away from the cocaine and alcohol.

Johnny rarely called George by his name. Nor did June. Instead, Johnny referred to George as "Little Pal." It was always Little Pal.

The first time Johnny called for George, we were living in Louisiana and I didn't really know Johnny.

"This is Johnny Cash," he said. "I want to talk to Little Pal."

When I heard that deep voice on the phone, I worried that it might be one of George's drug dealers trying to get past me to him. "You're not Johnny Cash."

He said, "Look, I wanna talk to Little Pal."

I said, "If you are really Johnny Cash, then sing me a song."

"Really?"

"Yeah," I said. "Sing something."

Johnny sang "I Walk the Line" over the phone.

That was the first and last time I ever questioned Johnny's voice.

From then on, whenever Johnny Cash called our home, he'd say, "Nancy, let me talk to Little Pal." I guess the nickname made sense: Johnny Cash was six feet two, and George Jones was five feet six. "I'm five-feet-six *and a half* inches tall," George would protest.

I'd simply smile.

To me, Johnny and George were both giants.

Most other country artists with whom George shared the stage felt the same way about him. His peers respected him immensely. Some of the younger artists were downright intimidated by him. For instance, George loved Randy Travis and Randy loved George. They were kindred spirits when it came to music, and they became good friends. George felt that Randy was performing true, traditional country music and had a fantastic future in the business, so George was always glad when Randy was booked on a show with him.

After they had toured together for a while, George felt confident that Randy could close the show. At a venue in Virginia, George suggested that Randy be the closing act. That was a compliment to Randy, but it also gave George the opportunity to do his hour-long set and be back to the bus in time to watch his favorite shows on television.

Besides being enormously talented, Randy was one of the nicest, most humble fellows in the music business. Although he had enjoyed phenomenal success with his first two albums, he was still reluctant to sing after George.

He came over to the bus before the show and said, "George, I know you want me to close the show, but please don't do this to me. The people won't stay after you do your show. I'll be singing to an empty room."

George smiled at Randy. "No, son, they ain't gonna leave," he said. "You're as hot as a pistol right now. You'll do fine."

And he did. Randy performed several of his hits, including "I Told You So," "1982," "Diggin' Up Bones," "On the Other Hand," and a new song that audiences loved, "Forever and Ever, Amen." Randy brought the house down and did an encore, and George missed it all. He was already watching *The Andy Griffith Show* reruns on the bus TV.

George did something similar when Faith Hill first came on the country music scene. Faith had scored a couple of big hit songs on the radio and was the opening act with George at a number of shows. At one venue, there was a football game on in the afternoon and another on in the evening, closer to show time. Of course, George wanted to watch all the games because he had placed bets on every one of them!

"Honey, you or Bobby go over and talk to Faith about closing the show tonight," he said. Bobby and I exchanged glances, and I was glad to delegate that responsibility to him.

Bobby reluctantly walked over to Faith Hill's bus and asked to speak to Faith. She welcomed him, and Bobby got right down to business even though he was nervous. "Ahh, Faith, uh, George asked if, uh, if you wouldn't mind . . . uh, if you would close the show and let him open tonight."

Faith stared back at Bobby as though he had dropped in from Planet Zulu or someplace. "Bobby, have you lost your mind?" she asked.

"Well, yeah, maybe," Bobby said, "but that's what he sent me over here to ask you."

Similar to Randy Travis, Faith Hill had tremendous respect for George, and to even consider going on stage after George, much less closing a show after George, was daunting. She spent the next twenty minutes or so telling Bobby all the reasons why she couldn't close the show after George performed, with Bobby doing his best to convince her that she could handle it.

She finally consented and did a fantastic job closing the show while George was flipping channels between one NFL football game and another, checking on his bets.

In October 1986, George's song "Who's Gonna Fill Their Shoes" was a top-five hit and won a CMA Video of the Year Award. George loved that song, especially because the lyrics included the names and images of many of George's musical heroes, although it asked a poignant question that many people still wonder about even today.

George had another top-ten duet in 1990, this time with Randy Travis on "A Few Ole Country Boys." He appeared with Alan Jackson in a 1991 video for "Don't Rock the Jukebox," in which Alan sang the iconic lines, "Don't rock the juke box; I wanna to hear some Jones." Then in the final chorus of the song, Alan got even more specific, singing, "I want to hear *George* Jones."

In 1991, after twenty years with Epic Records, George left the company and signed with MCA Records in Nashville. That was a bittersweet move for George, since he had worked at Epic with producer Billy Sherrill, and he loved him both as a music producer and as a personal friend. Billy, of course, was already well established in the music business long before George walked into his studio with Tammy Wynette to record some duets. Billy had recorded artists including Marty Robbins, Charlie Rich, Barbara Mandrell, and some pop artists such as Bobby Vinton and even Andy Williams. Later, he also produced Tammy Wynette's "Stand By Your Man" and George's "He Stopped Loving Her Today."

Billy had a low-key personality, almost dour, and George had warned me before I met him, "Now, let me tell you, Billy has a dry sense of humor, he probably ain't gonna like you, but don't worry about it. He doesn't like anybody at first."

"Oh, Billy will like me," I said.

"I don't know," George replied, raising his eyebrows and looking toward the ceiling.

But Billy and I hit it off almost instantly. Billy had first played music as a boy in his Alabama church. He appeared stern, but he had a quick smile when he wasn't sucking on a stogie. He loved it when I accompanied George to the studio because he knew that George wouldn't be drunk if I came along. We became each other's strongest advocate when it came to helping George, and we remained good friends.

Later that year, George recorded *Friends in High Places*, an album of duets, along with Ricky Skaggs, Emmylou Harris, Randy Travis, Buck Owens, Vern Gosdin, Shelby Lynn, Sweethearts of the Rodeo, Ricky Van Shelton, and Charlie Daniels. The album stalled at number seventy-two on *Billboard's* Top Country Album charts, but "A Few Ole Country Boys," George's duet with Randy Travis, turned out to be a hit.

* * * * * *

Around that same time, Debbie, a woman who worked for George in our office, called and said there was a large piece of property for sale at Nestledown Farms, a neighborhood in Franklin, about a thirty-minute drive from downtown Nashville. The land had previously been owned by Jimmy Velvet, a 1960s pop singer and former friend of Elvis Presley.

"The gates are already up," Debbie said, knowing that we wanted a gated property.

George and I were living in Brentwood, Tennessee, at the time, in a house right along a main road, so our home was extremely accessible to fans, curiosity seekers, and snoopers. George sometimes grew tired of people peeking in our windows. He said, "You can't even go to the mailbox without the tour buses being out there."

We went and looked at the property in Franklin, and George

fell in love with it, so we bought it from Jimmy Velvet. Then George kept adding on. He bought more acreage first in one direction and then another, and he kept stretching our boundaries farther. Eventually, we acquired more than one hundred acres at Nestledown. We hired the contractors to build our dreamhouse on the property according to our specifications, just the way we wanted it.

The home was such a blessing to us. When George and I first got together in 1981 and then married in 1983, he was already a country music superstar. He earned enormous amounts of money, but he squandered most of it on cocaine or alcohol. What he didn't blow, people stole from him, everyone from his managers on the road to people in the office. It was a sad joke that after a concert, the musicians' first act after packing up their instruments was to go find the promoter to make sure they got paid their percentage of the show's receipts for that night's show. If they didn't, the money would be gone.

George taught me about the music industry, and I slowly but surely began taking over most of his business dealings. George didn't care a whit about money, as long as he had $5,000 in cash in his pocket at all times. He just assumed the money would be there. He'd order a brand-new car, and never even ask "How much?" Nor would he write a check to pay for it. He figured someone else in his inner circle was responsible for that; he was responsible to bring in the money.

But when I took more control of the business, I also began saving and investing George's money, which was now my money as well. We paid off past debts and started from scratch, putting money to work for us. George finally had a beautiful estate with his finances on solid ground.

14

The Funniest Man I Knew

Shortly after George and I married, I also started handling the many requests for interviews he received. Members of the media knew that George was always good for a colorful quote on almost any subjects except politics or religion ("Those are personal," he'd say), but he didn't really care to do in-depth, formal interviews. To tell the truth, he *hated* doing those kinds of interviews and avoided them as long as he could. "They always want to know about the same old things," George said.

On the other hand, George enjoyed talking with reporters as friends, but he would often tell too many details about certain aspects of his career or even our lives together. We really had nothing to hide, but sometimes George could be his own worst enemy by giving out too much information. Slowly but surely, I began to assume more managerial control over matters, tending to his career, and carefully guarding what he said in interviews. That wasn't always easy with George being such a loose cannon.

He was doing an interview at our home one day with a reporter from *The Tennessean,* our local newspaper that also had national ties to *USA Today*. George liked to sit in his recliner as he did interviews, so when the reporter arrived, I ushered him in to George's "sitting room," made sure he was comfortable, and then left the two men alone. I purposely didn't close the door as I walked out, and I went into George's and my bedroom on the first floor nearby. I sat down on the bed where I could hear George and the reporter talking, but I really wanted George to do his own interview. I didn't want to interfere, but I didn't want to miss anything, either.

Their conversation moved along just fine, and George was doing a good job in the interview when the reporter asked, "George, do you have any grandkids?"

"Yeah," George said with a smile. "I do." He paused as he thought through the list of names. Then he said, "I got two by Susan." He didn't mention the names of Susan's two children. "Yep, two by Susan and one by Adina." George rubbed his chin as though thinking through the family tree. "And Sherry, Nancy's daughter, which is my daughter too, she can't have any kids. But she ended up getting them by having incest."

Sitting on the bed in the room next door, I nearly choked. I went running into George's sitting room and said, "Stop!"

George looked up at me with shock on his face.

I glared back at him and said, "Do you know what *incest* means?"

"Well, yeah," George said. "I know what it means. That's what Sherry did. Her and her husband, Kirk."

I said, "Oh, George! She had artificial *insemination!*"

George wrinkled his nose. "Artificial *what?*" he asked. "What does that mean?"

"That's a big difference from having a baby as the result of incest," I told him.

"Well, what is incest anyhow?"

"George, incest means you have a baby by your brother or your father, or someone else you are related to."

"Oh, no," George said, looking at the reporter. "She didn't do that."

The reporter was rolling with laughter. I knew the reporter fairly well, so I looked at him sternly and said, "Don't you dare print a word of that. I mean it."

"I promise you, Nancy." He chuckled. "I won't."

And he didn't.

Some of George's funniest interviews were not with reporters at all. They were with police officers. On one occasion, George drove the car as we left our house and pulled out onto Highway 96, the busy two-lane road fronting our subdivision. We hadn't gone far when we passed a Tennessee state trooper who had pulled over another driver on Highway 96.

According to the law, and to help protect the lives of police officers and highway-department workers, cars passing by were supposed to move over, away from the vehicles alongside the road. George was supposed to move over into the other lane to avoid an accident, but he didn't. When I saw the trooper's car, I said, "George, you gotta get over."

"No, I'm not," he said.

"Okay," I said, shrugging my shoulders.

A few seconds later, the state trooper pulled up behind us, blue and red lights flashing.

George pulled off the road and parked on the berm.

The state trooper came right up behind the driver's side window. He recognized George immediately. He said, "George, when I'm pulling somebody over, you're supposed to move over."

George wasn't giving an inch. He said, "Son, let me tell you something. This road is known as Murder Highway. So when you're pullin' somebody over, why don't you go onto the other side and you won't get hit?"

The state trooper rolled his eyes, shook his head, and said, "Nancy, take him home."

George never considered himself a lawbreaker. He simply didn't pay attention to the laws, especially when it came to driving. For instance, he never quite grasped the concept of a High Occupancy Vehicle (HOV) lane on the interstate highways. Or maybe he just didn't want to.

In Tennessee, HOV lanes, intended for vehicles carrying at least two passengers during certain hours of heavy traffic, were clearly marked with large signs and diamond shapes painted on the pavement in the restricted lane. George rarely paid any attention to the HOV lanes.

He had just purchased a new vehicle and he wanted to add chrome to it. George loved shiny bright chrome on all his cars. Anything we got had to have chrome, or George would have it specially chromed. I think he would have chromed *me* if he'd have figured out how to do it. The man loved chrome.

He woke me up early one morning and said, "I gotta be down at the chrome shop by eight o'clock."

I said, "It's too early, George. I'm not getting up."

He pouted a while and then said, "Okay. I'll go myself."

"Okay," I said. "Have a good time." I rolled over and went back to sleep.

Meanwhile, George headed toward Nashville on Interstate 65 during the HOV lane restricted hours. Not surprisingly, he was driving too fast in that HOV lane when he got pulled over by the state police. The trooper recognized him and said, "George Jones, you can't be in this lane unless there are two people in your vehicle."

George looked back at him and presented his defense. He said,

"Well, I couldn't get Nancy up!"

No wonder George was on a first-name basis with most of the law officers in our town.

At Nestledown, George busied himself by acquiring a number of full-sized horses, several miniature horses, and cows. At first, he loved his cows, but then the animals began getting hoof marks in George's grass and leaving other telltale evidence. After that, George didn't care so much for the cattle because they messed up his lawn. Our property looked more like a golf course than a ranch.

On one occasion, as a joke on George, Carl Smith and Douglas Green, better known as "Ranger Doug" from the group Riders in the Sky, made off with some of George's Black Angus cattle and took them to Carl's house.

Carl called George and said, "George, come on over. I know you've got some Black Angus cattle. I want you to see the ones I've got."

George said, "Okay." So we went over to Carl's farm. I knew something was up because Carl and his buddies had a video camera filming the whole time. Nevertheless, George started looking at the cows and he was duly impressed. He nodded his head and told Carl, "Yes sir, those are some nice-looking cows there."

Carl played it like a pro. He said, "Yeah, George, they are." Carl rubbed his chin, and then said, "But I have to tell you . . ." Carl lowered his voice as though telling a secret. "They're stolen."

George was aghast. "You stole them cows?" he asked.

"Yeah," Carl deadpanned. "Ain't nobody out here gonna turn us in." Then he drew closer to George and spoke quietly, "You wanna go in with me on them? You want half of them?"

George looked around a little bit, looked at the cows, then back at Carl, and said, "Well, I guess so . . ." as though he wasn't quite sure.

About that time, Carl Junior, who worked for the Sheriff's department, cracked up laughing so hard he nearly fell over. He said, "George, it's a joke. They're *your* cows!"

George still didn't get it. "What? What y'all doing with my cows?" he asked.

Carl and his buddies stood there grinning from ear to ear, and finally George realized that they had indeed pulled a prank on him. He had been close to buying back his own cows!

"Carl Smith," he railed facetiously. "I'll get you for that one!"

* * * * * *

Long before George ever got sick, he decided where he wanted to be buried when he died—in Nashville's Woodlawn Cemetery. We went out to the cemetery to look over what grave sites were available in the popular burial spot. We walked all over the cemetery, it seemed, before George finally pointed at some open grass and said, "I want that plot right there."

"Okay, fine. Let's tell the funeral director," I suggested.

But George wasn't done yet.

"And I want that one," he said. "And that one . . . and that one . . ."

Before he was satisfied, he had picked out sixty-eight separate plots!

I said, "George, we don't need sixty-eight plots in the cemetery. There's only you and me, and we might need a few more, if any of the kids want to be buried in the same area."

I looked at him quizzically. "Why in the world do we need to buy sixty-eight separate grave sites?"

George looked back at me and without missing a beat, said, "I'm not going to be crowded out here!"

I cracked up laughing, but sure enough, we purchased sixty-eight cemetery plots, including the two for George and me, and sixty-six others around us.

Still, I never anticipated using them.

Later, after he quit drinking, George used to say, "I hope it rains when I die. Because I'll be the only one dry at the funeral."

* * * * * *

George and I were visiting in California when I saw a sign at a hotel for an auction of custom-made bronze lawn statues. I told George, "I'm going to look inside here and see what they have."

"Alright," George said. "Don't be gone long."

"Okay," I said. "I'll meet you back here."

When I stepped inside the hotel ballroom, I was amazed at the sight. The exquisite statues were huge! They were beautiful, life-sized renditions of everything from a flamingo; to a deer with large antlers; to a little girl reaching up on her tippy-toes to get the mail, with a little bird perched atop the mailbox; to a tall football player throwing a pass. I knew that we had plenty of space to put several of the statues on the lawn next to the entryway to our home at Nestledown, so I grabbed a bidding paddle, slipped up to the front of the room, and took a seat. Before long I began bidding up a storm on the various bronze statues.

These were not inexpensive pieces of art. The auctioneer began most bidding at $1,000 and moved up quickly from there. I bid on several pieces, but the moment I raised my bidding paddle, somebody behind me bid the price up higher. I'd bid again, and the person in the back of the room bid more. After getting outbid on several pieces, I was getting mad.

During the bidding on the next piece, I stood up and turned around to see who it was who was bidding against me. Sure enough, there was a man holding up a bidding paddle in the back of the room—and it was George! Apparently he had come in off the street looking for me, and he had started bidding on the pieces without realizing that he was bidding against me.

I called out to the auctioneer. "Stop the bidding! This is not fair!"

The surprised auctioneer's face looked as though he might choke. I continued as I whirled around and pointed at George. "That man back there is my husband, and we have been bidding against each other. That's not right. We gotta start this auction over again!"

Everyone in the ballroom was laughing hilariously at George's and my bidding against one another. The auctioneer graciously started the bidding all over again, but before he did, he said, "Mr. Jones, why don't you bring your paddle and come sit up front here with your wife."

The audience howled in laughter again as George made his way to the front of the room. George sat down and raised his paddle before the auctioneer even finished his description of most pieces. "We gotta hurry up," George said to me. "I'm ready to eat."

I might have been better off letting him remain in the back of the room, bidding against me, because together, the two of us purchased fifteen of those large bronze lawn statues! We loved them. We didn't love the expensive shipping bill to transport them from California to Tennessee—we had to hire an eighteen-wheeler to move them—but those beautiful statues, including a bronze pony, a woman pouring water from a pot, and a large bronze fountain, graced the front of our property along the driveway from then on.

George was a prolific gum chewer. He never chewed tobacco, but if he wasn't eating, he was rarely without some lemon-flavored chewing gum in his mouth. He special-ordered that stuff by the case and had it sent directly to our home. He chewed gum out in the fields when he rode around the property in his golf cart, he chewed gum in the recording studio, and he chewed gum right up to the moment before he went on stage. He probably would have kept it in his mouth all through the show, but I usually caught him before he stepped out on stage. "Spit it out," I'd say, and George would reluctantly unload his wad of gum right in my hand.

He even chewed his gum when he went to the dentist. George would try to hide the gum from our dentist, Dr. Spalding Green, while he was in the dentist's chair. Dr. Green knew the gum was usually tucked under George's tongue or stuck to the roof of his mouth. It was almost like a game to George, to see how long before the dentist discovered that George had a fresh batch of lemon gum lodged in his cheek somewhere.

For nearly fifteen years, George regularly relied on Dr. Green for his dental work, but he never showed up in the office without his favorite chewing gum. Other than hiding his gum from the dentist, George was a good patient. He had such confidence in Dr. Green, he once fell asleep in the dentist chair while Dr. Green was still working on him! Dr. Green later told me, "George always said his lemon gum was sugar free." The dentist smiled. "But I really don't think it was."

George wasn't real good at keeping secrets. People closest to him knew they didn't dare tell him anything confidential that they did not want shared with the world. It wasn't that he was not trustworthy; he simply had no filters for private information. He'd tell you just about anything, and if he wouldn't, I would. George always said, "I don't have any secrets. Nancy will tell you anything you want to know!" And I usually would.

But even I knew enough to have some discretion when Elvis Costello and his wife, Diana Krall, shared a secret with us when they came out to George's show at Carnegie Hall and visited with us backstage before the event. Elvis had grown up listening to George and had recorded "A Good Year for the Roses," one of George's hit songs he'd recorded years earlier. George and Elvis were buddies and we were delighted to see them. Diana was pregnant and the couple was so excited because they were going to have, not just one baby, but twins! "We haven't even told our parents yet," Diana said. "They're going to be so excited!"

The couple's mistake, of course, was telling their secret to George. That night, right in the middle of his show while on stage, he mentioned that he had enjoyed working on a duet with Elvis Costello in the studio, and that some of Elvis's family members were in the audience. And then, without even a pause, George told the entire crowd, "And Diana and Elvis are soon going to be the parents of twins!"

Oops!

The couple was shocked that George had slipped up about their pregnancy secret. I wasn't.

They took it in good humor, although that's how the Costello and Krall families first heard the news. Early in December, Diana gave birth to two healthy boys, Dexter Henry and Frank Harlan.

George made me laugh so much. He was such a funny man, even though he never saw himself that way. Sometimes, he'd say something hilarious and everyone in the room would burst out in laughter except George. "What are you guys laughing about?" he'd ask sincerely.

Maybe it was better that he didn't know.

15

Dynamic Duos

George enjoyed recording duets with other artists, and he was especially excited about putting together the 1991 album *Friends in High Places,* on which he was joined by Waylon Jennings, Randy Travis, and other top country traditionalists.

Then in 1992, George recorded a new album, *Walls Can Fall,* produced by Emory Gordy Jr. for MCA Nashville. The first single epitomized George's attitude about growing older, the music business's tendency to kick older artists to the curb, and his desire to keep performing music. The song, written by Billy Yates, Frank Dycus, and Kerry Kurt Phillips, was "I Don't Need Your Rockin' Chair," and as George described it, "It's my attitude set to music."

For George, the song was a bit bittersweet. He had previously recorded a duet with Dolly Parton titled "Rockin' Years." George really liked the song and felt the recording had great potential to be a hit. Unfortunately, the record label executives didn't see it that way. In fact, not only did they deny George the opportunity, they took his vocal *off* Dolly's album track and substituted it with that of newcomer, Ricky Van Shelton. George took that as an insult, and although that may not have been the only reason for his departure, he felt that the record company had done him wrong and George soon parted ways with the

Epic record label.

At the time, one of Nashville's premier songwriters was also one of our finest hairstylists. I regularly got my hair done by Billy Yates. I was sitting in Billy's salon chair, with him working on my hair as I told him how George had been treated regarding his duet with Dolly. The more I talked, the hotter I was getting. "Who would do such a thing, Billy?" I asked. "What kind of record company operates like that?"

"Shhh!" Billy tried to calm me down. "There's an executive from the record company sitting just on the other side of that partition over there."

"I don't care!" I said loudly enough for the whole salon to hear. "To treat George Jones that way just isn't right!"

"Well, why don't I just write another song for George?" Billy asked. "Something about 'I don't need this sort of thing.' Do you think he might want to do that?"

"I think he might," I told Billy.

When songwriters Billy Yates, Frank Dycus, and Kerry Kurt pitched their song "I Don't Need Your Rockin' Chair" to George, he liked the tune, and the lyrics immediately resonated with him.

But he wasn't going to record it for Epic. I met with Bruce Hinton and Tony Brown at MCA Nashville and they were interested in having George on their record label. When I told George, he said, "Oh, Nancy, they don't really want me over there. Nobody cares anymore. I'm not even going to record any more music."

"Oh yes you are," I told him. "They really want you at MCA."

"Well, I like Tony and Bruce," George said.

George was sixty-one years old when he recorded "I Don't Need Your Rockin' Chair" for MCA Nashville, and it became something of an anthem for him and other "older" artists. Helping George on the chorus of the song were Garth Brooks, Alan Jackson, and a bevy of major country music stars, all of whom had credited George with paving the way for their careers.

The video for the song was a statement in itself. Appearing in the opening scene along with George was the former World Heavyweight Boxing Champion George Foreman. The two Georges sat together in rocking chairs in the center of a boxing ring.

George looked over at the gregarious boxer and asked, "Hey, George, ole pal?"

"Yes, George?" Foreman responded.

"George, do you think we're getting a little old for this kind of business?"

At that, the video featured a full-screen shot of George Foreman bellowing, "Old?" Foreman felt that this was a sort of heavyweight punch at the record executives who said Dolly's song "Rockin' Years" was not a hit with George Jones on it. The boxer bounded to the middle of the ring, now wearing bright-red boxing gloves. "Here I am knocking all the young kids down, and there you are packing all the young kids in night after night! We're the best rockers in the business!"

Both Georges now wielded red boxing gloves, and they looked directly into the camera as they stood and emphatically stated, "We're not ready for the rockin' chair yet!"

George and the Jones Boys took it from there, performing the song inside the boxing ring. At the close of the video, George kicked the rocking chair as though booting it out of the boxing ring. George Foreman and George Jones then returned together, standing defiantly and triumphantly over a pile of rocking chairs splintered into a bonfire stack of kindling on the canvas. It was a humorous but powerful statement.

The fans loved the song, but many of the country music radio stations were reluctant to play it regularly and it peaked at number thirty- four on the *Billboard* charts.

Nevertheless, for the 1992 Country Music Association award show, held at the (Grand Ole) Opry House in Nashville, the producers asked George to perform the song along with many of the stars who had appeared on the record with him. George agreed, and when Reba McEntire introduced him, he ambled onto the stage wearing a black tuxedo and a black bowtie with two long strands to the cheers of the entire audience.

From the first line of "I Don't Need Your Rockin' Chair," the crowd clapped and sang along. George sang the first chorus and verse by himself, then side panels raised and the lights came on in the corners of the stage revealing many of the stars who worked with George on the recording. They took turns answering George in a "call and response" manner during the second verse, with George singing the line and Alan Jackson, for example, repeating the line in the third person, "He don't need your rockin' chair," then other artists joining in, including T. Graham Brown, Patty Loveless, Vince Gill, Joe Diffie, Mark Chesnutt, Clint Black, Travis Tritt, Pam Tillis, and Marty Stuart. At the close of the song, the entire audience leaped to its feet in a standing ovation that went on and on.

George loved it and was still saying thank you when Randy Travis slipped up behind George and surprised him. While the crowd continued to applaud, George looked at Randy and said, "What are we doing?"

Randy put a hand on George's shoulder to help steady him in place on the stage until the audience's applause subsided and they were seated. Randy spoke to the crowd, "I have the best job in the house tonight." He looked at George and grinned. "Nobody here or watching at home wants to see you retire to your rocking chair"—the crowd interrupted Randy with loud cheers and more applause—"but, . . . but we do want you to enjoy being the next member of the Country Music

Hall of Fame!" Randy handed George a plaque signifying his induction into the Hall.

The audience erupted in another standing ovation.

George was honored but he was also shocked and said so. "I'd like to thank the Good Lord above first of all . . . He made it all possible . . . and I have to thank the fans. I want to thank one more person . . . between her and God, she saved my life . . ." George then thanked me in a heartwarming word of love and appreciation. I stood and mouthed the words "I love you!" to George, then waved at the cheering fans as the ovation continued to fill the Opry House.

George concluded, "I've won a lot of awards—I'm not braggin' . . . but this has got to be the greatest one in the world."

A month or so later, George was officially inducted into the Country Music Hall of Fame, which was, to him, one of the greatest honors he could ever receive in his life.

At the October 1993 Country Music Association's award show, held at the Grand Ole Opry House and again broadcast live on television, "I Don't Need Your Rockin' Chair" was one of the nominations for the Vocal Event of the Year award. Other nominees included Clint Black and Wynonna Judd singing "A Bad Goodbye," Reba McIntire and Vince Gill's "The Heart Won't Lie," Tanya Tucker and Delbert McClinton's performance of "Tell Me About It," and Trisha Yearwood and Don Henley's song "Walkaway Joe." All of these were strong nominees and George knew it.

We sat through the show, enjoying the wide variety of country music and awaiting the announcement of the Vocal Event award. George grew more fidgety as the night wore on, and I could tell that it wasn't simply because he was nervous. He wanted to get out to get a drink, even though he had supposedly stopped drinking . . . again.

Just about the time the Vocal Event award was coming up on

the program, George leaned over to me and said, "I'm going to the bathroom."

"George!" I said. "Do you have to go right now? It's almost time for the vocal event award."

"Oh, don't worry," he said. "We're not going to win anything anyhow. There are a lot of great performances in the category this year. They won't even miss me."

"George, you're going to win this award," I said.

"No, I'm not," he said, as he gave me a smirk. "Look who we're up against. Honey, I'm goin' to the bathroom."

"Well, you better hurry!"

"I'll be right back," he promised, easing out of his chair and heading toward the aisle. The CMA ushers noticed and quickly moved a handsome young substitute into George's seat while he was gone, so when the television cameras panned the audience, they didn't come across an empty space—especially in the front rows of the artists' sections.

Just then, Vince Gill, one of the show's hosts, introduced Shelby Lynne and Steve Wariner to present the Vocal Event of the Year Award. Clips from all five of the nominated performances were shown on a large screen in the Opry House, as well as on national television. Shelby then did the honors, opening the envelope and announcing, "And the winner is . . . George Jones, 'I Don't Need Your Rockin' Chair'!" She tried to announce the other stars who had sung on the song with George: "Garth Brooks, Vince Gill, Patty Loveless, Alan Jackson, Joe Diffie, Mark Chesnutt, Clint Black, Pam Tillis, and Travis Tritt," Shelby called out—as the song filled the room behind Shelby and Steve. There was such a roar from the crowd, it was hard to hear the names of the other artists.

But then an awkward hush fell over the room as Shelby and Steve waited on stage for George to step to the platform to accept the award. But George was nowhere to be seen.

Steve quipped, "Did he show?"

The audience chuckled nervously, perhaps wondering if No Show Jones had struck again. Vince Gill and Clint Black eased onto the stage, soon joined by Pam Tillis . . . but no George Jones.

Sitting in the audience, I knew I had to do something—and fast! A few seconds of dead air time on television seems like an eternity and can be a death knell for a production. I got out of my seat and hurried toward the stage as fast as I could move in my long black evening dress. By the time I got up the stairs and onto the side stage, about a dozen of the other performers who had recorded the hit song with George had arrived as well. Garth Brooks playfully nudged me out onto the stage.

I rushed toward center stage, calling out into the microphone, "I promise that he showed up!"

The audience burst into laughter and cheers.

"He's in the bathroom!" I added, evoking more laughter, cheers, and applause, along with mine.

Knowing my aversion to speaking in public, Clint Black stepped up to the microphone, put an arm around my shoulder, and said to the audience, "I think we need to make her say something, don't you?"

The audience roared its approval.

"I'll have him here in a minute," I promised lightheartedly, looking furtively toward my left off stage. "Somebody find him!"

Once again, the crowd crowed in laughter. I tried to express George's gratitude and mine. "He's gonna kill me," I said. "But if George was standing here, I think he'd say 'thank you,' and . . . what am I doing?"

It was another one of those classic George Jones moments on television, making a scene when he wasn't even in the room!

When George returned to his seat, I told him, "You won. I told you that you were going to win." He was upset that he had missed the award. "I wasn't gone that long," he fumed.

At the celebrations after the show, everyone was congratulating George on winning the award. "You did good, man! We're so proud of you."

"Well . . . ah . . . I didn't get to see that part of the show," he said.

A talented young fellow named Brad Paisley opened a few shows for George in Parkersburg, West Virginia, around that time, then moved to Nashville to chase his dreams. We invited him out to the house at Nestledown to hang around with us, and he often came out to the farm to fish in the ponds on his days off. Afterward, I'd invite him to stay for dinner, and he usually would. We sort of adopted Brad as our own. Later, he bought a horse and had nowhere to stable the animal, so George said, "Son, bring him out here to the farm." Brad did and it was not unusual to see the future star out riding through the fields while the Possum kept up with him in a golf cart.

After dinner, we'd sit around watching something on television together or simply talking about matters important or mundane. George enjoyed talking about the future of country music with Brad, and Brad seemed to appreciate George's perspectives and insights. George especially emphasized the importance of taking care of the fans to Brad. "Treat those people right, son, and they will always be there for you."

George enjoyed imparting wisdom to the younger artists, but mostly he enjoyed their friendship, especially those who continued to perform traditional country music rather than the more "pop" forms of country. But he never put on airs around them. One night, Denise and Alan Jackson came over for dinner, and after a time of conversation, while our guests were still sitting on the couch, George simply got up, went in the bedroom, and changed into his pajamas.

When he came back out, Alan looked at Denise, and in his low-key drawl, said, "Well, darlin', I guess it's time for us to go home."

I said hasty goodbyes to the Jacksons, knowing that by the time I returned from the front door, George would already be in bed, watching a movie.

George was funny, but he could also be stubborn. Sometimes that worked in his favor, but at other times, it was nearly deadly.

For instance, we made plans to celebrate George's sixty-third birthday on September 12, 1994, with a big party in the barn at Nestledown. George didn't like to make a big deal about his birthday, but I did, so I invited a slew of people and arranged to have the party at our property because I knew George would balk and complain about going somewhere else.

As it turned out, George wasn't feeling well that day, and after the party, he began to experience pains in his chest. When I went to check on him, I found him sitting in his chair in his den. "My arm is hurting for some reason," he said. "And I have bad indigestion. Can you get me some Alka-Seltzer?" Since we lived near a hospital, I said, "Come on, George. We're gonna go to Williamson Medical Center and have you checked."

"Oh, no," he said. "I'll be fine. It's just indigestion."

I said, "No, it's not, George. Let's go over to the hospital and let them have a look at you."

"Oh, alright," he groused.

I knew he wasn't happy about it, but at least I got him to the emergency room. At the hospital, they ran some tests but they were inconclusive and did not indicate that anything was wrong. George was elated with that. "See, I told you," he said. "I was just having indigestion."

He was still hooked up to the heart monitors, when suddenly, George burped. Immediately, the monitors went crazy, and all sorts of alarms sounded. I was never a nurse, but I knew this wasn't right.

"Y'all need to do an EKG right now," I called out to the emergency room doctor and nurse who had come running.

They did. And that's when they found severe blockage in George's arteries. They said, "George, we're going to have to admit you in the hospital so the cardiologist can have a look."

George said, "I ain't gonna stay in the hospital; y'all are known to kill people!"

I was embarrassed that he had been so rude, even if he'd been joking—which I guessed that he had not been—so I tried to smooth things over. "Can we transfer him to Baptist Hospital in downtown Nashville?" I asked.

"Sure, we can do that," the ER doc said.

I nodded in the affirmative, letting the doctor know that's what we should do.

George was mad! He didn't want to stay in that hospital or go to any other hospital. All he wanted to do was to go home and eat his chocolate pie that I had made for his birthday celebration.

He looked at me and said, "You and your d*** PKG!"

PKG?

"Oh, do you mean EKG, George?"

"Yeah! You and your PKG! Now look what you've done."

I snapped right back at George, "It's an EKG, George. An electrocardiogram, and if we hadn't done it and they hadn't found the blockage in your heart, you'd likely be dead by tomorrow morning!"

The hospital transferred George by ambulance to the much larger midtown hospital, better known for handling heart disease. I followed the ambulance in a car, and when I arrived and went inside, I found

George already on a gurney, ready to be examined. In an effort to maintain some semblance of privacy and as much anonymity as possible for George, the staff had placed a white sheet over him and pulled it up high on his head so nobody would recognize him.

George was still angry that he was there, so he pulled the sheet down and started singing at the top of his lungs, "He stopped loving her today!" As loudly as he could sing. People could hear him all over the corridor, and their heads snapped around, as though to say, "That sounds like George Jones!"

"George! Be quiet," I said. "I know you're mad but don't be stupid."

The doctors admitted George in the intensive care unit, and housekeeping brought in a bed for me to stay right there with him, since the doctors planned for him to have surgery first thing the next morning.

Dr. Taylor Wray came to see George in the ICU, to talk with him about his test results and the planned surgery for the following morning. George already had tuned in a football game on the hospital room television. He was not one bit interested in listening to what Dr. Wray had to say.

The doctor prattled on and then finally realized that George was paying no attention to him. He nodded toward the action on the screen. "George, did you bet on this game?" the doctor asked.

"I bet on every one on there," George said, nodding toward the television.

The doctor shook his head. "Well, thanks a lot," he said, facetiously. "Thanks to you, now I've got to spend the night up here."

"Why do you have to spend the night here?" George asked.

"George, you don't realize, but you have serious blockage around your heart. If you don't win these games you're betting on, you might have a heart attack."

"Oh, don't worry, doc," George assured him. "I don't win half the time anyway."

Dr. Wray stayed at the hospital that night to be certain George was okay, and the following morning he and his team performed open-heart surgery on George, with a triple bypass of his heart arteries. They kept George at the hospital for more than a week, and when the doctor released him, he strongly encouraged George to follow an eight-week cardiac rehabilitation program. "George, you can't drink or smoke. We cleared out those blocked arteries and you have a new clean system. So take care of it."

He didn't.

Nor did he do well at rehab. At one of the first rehab sessions, George walked into the hospital gym and there was Waylon Jennings, who suffered from diabetes. The two men sat down and talked . . . and talked . . . and laughed . . . and talked. The nurse kept calling out to Waylon, "Mr. Jennings, it is time for your session."

"Wait a minute," Waylon responded. "My buddy is here." He nodded toward George. Neither one of them did much rehab that day, and I know George did very few rehabilitation sessions after that.

Nevertheless, I was glad that I had gotten him to the hospital in time for the doctors to save his life. Apparently, my PKG was more important than George realized. Maybe that PKG was a *Possum* Cardiogram.

And apparently, Jesus wasn't done with George Jones just yet.

16

Tammy and George— Not Again!

When love is lost, it's not always easy taking the high road. Throw in a messy divorce and new spouses and it gets even harder. And when your names are Tammy Wynette and George Jones, well . . . it's nearly impossible. Maybe that's why some people thought it was odd that I was instrumental in bringing George and Tammy back together to record an album entitled *One.*

George and I were talking casually one evening when I suggested, "Now that you and Tammy are happily remarried and everyone gets along fairly well, it might be a good time for the two of you to do a new album."

George looked back at me as though I had lost my mind. "Heck, no, I ain't doin' an album with that woman," he said. "You better just leave that idea alone."

I didn't. In fact, I made a similar suggestion to George Richey, Tammy's husband. He, too, thought it was a grand idea. I stopped in at MCA and talked to Tony Brown to gauge his thoughts on a potential George and Tammy reunion album. "I think it will do well," Tony said. To me it simply made sense. Holding on to bitterness and rancor never helped anyone. But it made sense from a musical perspective, and also from a financial standpoint. George and Tammy simply put on a great show.

I went back and suggested the idea to George again.

"I'll do it," he said, "but I'm telling you right now. I ain't puttin' up with no crap from that woman. Nothing. So you better be there at every recording session."

"I'll be there, George," I promised. "And Richey will be there too. We'll keep it all together."

That was much easier said than done.

Norro Wilson did a superb job producing the album for MCA Nashville under the direction of the company president, Tony Brown. Renee Bell, MCA's artist and repertoire director, sifted through hundreds of songs before helping everyone settle on enough for an album. Renee was also instrumental in coming up with the album title: *One*. It had been seventeen years since George and Tammy had last toured together, fifteen since they'd last recorded together. In the interim, they had barely spoken to each other. They didn't get along in the studio and often fired searing remarks at each other during the sessions. But they did the album together—it took forever to get that album done—and I thought it came out rather well. So did Tammy and Richey, and so did the label. Everyone loved it, it seemed, except George.

Undeterred, I suggested to George Richey, "Wouldn't it be great if George and Tammy did a show together?"

"Oh, I don't know about that," Richey hedged. "But I guess it wouldn't hurt to ask them."

Tammy responded positively to the idea of a reunion concert; George responded . . . let's say, poorly.

"No!" he bellowed when I broached the idea of him doing a show with Tammy.

I knew it would be useless to attempt convincing him by myself, so I said to Richey, "Why don't you and Tammy come over to the house for dinner and we'll talk about it."

Richey gladly accepted my offer.

George reluctantly acquiesced.

When Richey and Tammy arrived at our house, even I was surprised at Tammy's appearance. She looked excessively old, her face looked sunken, her skin seemed to sag, and she had a disoriented and unkempt look about her. I had seen Tammy "doped up" at various times over the years, but now she didn't look high; she looked low, skinny, and haggard.

Ever tactful, George opened the evening conversation when he saw her by asking, "What's wrong with you? You got AIDS?"

Tammy was not amused. Nor was I. I was embarrassed for her. "Oh, George, stop being so ugly," I said. I turned toward Tammy and George Richey. "Welcome. We're glad you came."

We had a pleasant dinner and talked through the possibilities of touring together. George finally saw the sense of it all, but he still had the final word. "I'll do it," he said, "but I'll tell you right now, there are going to be some rules."

Tammy agreed, then they prepared to tour. Before the album tour, I joked to the media, "Some promoters are asking, 'Do we need to put up a stage or a boxing ring?'"

Still, all over Nashville, music lovers raved, "George and Tammy, together again!" The trade magazines proclaimed the message too, even though they knew that both of the stars had remarried. Tammy and George had been married to each other from February 16, 1969, to March 21, 1975. "Six of the worst years of my life," George often quipped. "It was six years of hell!"

A former Birmingham beautician, Tammy sang at local clubs

in the evenings after working at her day job. Eventually she moved to Nashville and signed a recording deal with Epic Records, where she was produced by Billy Sherrill.

George fell in love with Tammy's singing when he first heard her on the car radio as he was driving. He told the person riding with him, "My lord! What a singer! Listen to that. That girl is going to be hotter than a firecracker."

They later did some shows together, and while visiting in Tammy's home, George heard her husband, Don Chapel, "talking ugly" to her and he went crazy. "I started breaking up the furniture and telling him he'd better shut up," George recalled years later. "I told him that he was talking about the woman I loved! I don't know who was more surprised to hear me say it—me, him, or her—it just came out. We had never even been alone together, much less dated." Before long, George and Tammy were a couple.

During their contentious marriage, George drank heavily and Tammy was often high on something, creating even more tension in their relationship. Tammy claimed that, in a drunken rage, George had once aimed a loaded gun in her direction; on another occasion, she accused him of shooting up their home. George adamantly denied both accusations. At one point, Tammy had George constrained in a straitjacket and committed to a mental asylum in a padded cell. They divorced ostensibly because of George's drinking, but not before they recorded the ironically titled *We're Gonna Hold On* in 1973, an album that soared to the number one spot on the charts.

George and Tammy had produced some great music together, as well as a daughter, Georgette. In the divorce, George willingly gave Tammy everything she wanted—and she wanted almost everything associated with their seven-figure portfolio.

No wonder the music world was shocked in the mid-1990s when, at a key intersection on West End Avenue in downtown Nashville, a huge billboard touted an enormous photo of George and Tammy with the message: "They're back together!"

In some ways, when I'd hear people say that, it turned my stomach, because I knew the truth. Tammy and George could be together in the studio as long as we had referees, and maybe even on stage, assuming we had long hooks on the side-stage to pull one or both of them off so the other could sing.

But "together again?" Uh-uh. No way.

Naturally, the record company wanted to promote that image, even if it was false, because it appealed to country music fans—both Tammy's and George's. The buzz created by the romantics *oohing* and *awwing* all over about George and Tammy's reunion was good for album sales.

Of course, none of those people mushing and gushing over George and Tammy being back together saw them up close, on the road, or at concert venues backstage or behind closed doors the way I did. It was like World War III every night!

When the album released in June 1995, George and Tammy toured together all across the United States. We also did shows in England, Ireland, and Switzerland. George was still drinking and Tammy—I'm not sure what she was doing but she seemed higher than a kite almost every night. Each show was a battle. It's a wonder they didn't kill each other.

But they'd get on the stage together and the people thought they were back in love. They were quintessential performers. Both of them. And they were good—*really* good.

Tammy opened the show and performed her forty-five-minute set alone, followed by George's set. They planned to close the show together performing their popular duets and songs from their new album. But if Tammy prolonged her set and stayed on stage too long, George would gripe at *me*. "Get her off that stage!" he'd say. "Unplug her! She has been on there ten minutes over time."

From side-stage I'd look at Tammy and give her a signal to quit, but many times, she'd keep right on singing—especially if she knew she was irritating George, who was waiting to do his solo portion of the show.

When she finally came off stage, George would cuss her out. She often ran to her dressing room in tears. But they still had a set they were to do together to conclude the show, so I'd go to Tammy's dressing room, wrap my arms around her, and try to console her and calm her down. "Go baby her," George called out after me.

I'd sit with Tammy and say, "Now, Tammy, you know how he is. By the time you two get on the stage together, he'll be over it."

"But I don't like him anymore."

"Well, so what? He don't like you, either," I'd tell her and we'd laugh through the tears. On more than a few nights, I thought, *What have I done? I should never have brought them back together. This is the tour from hell!*

George Richey felt much the same way. "I'll be glad when this tour is over," he told me.

But we pulled it off and the audiences loved it.

There was an emotional cost, though. I got so tired of hearing how much George was in love with Tammy. After all, when he was up on stage, singing with Tammy, they put on a great show, looking at each other all lovey-dovey, singing to each other and smiling real sexy-like. For a few minutes every night, it really did look as though they were back together and madly in love. At times, it was hard for me to watch Tammy eying my husband. After all, one of us divorced him, and one of us didn't.

I told them both, "Y'all are such good actors; you really need to be in a movie."

I think George felt good that he finally had a chance to apologize to Tammy for the tough times they lived through together and apart. At least they didn't seem mad at each other anymore. They ended the tour rather harmoniously.

Through it all, I got along with Tammy just fine, but George kept telling me, "You're gonna be sorry one of these days. She'll turn on you like a rattlesnake."

"It was wonderful getting back and singing again," Tammy told some reporters.

"Yep, we got into it just like old times," George quipped.

By 1995, George was slowing down a bit, and after open-heart surgery, he was a bit more philosophical about his career. In an interview, he said, "I think I've accomplished about everything I set out to do."

He had enjoyed success again with MCA Nashville, including the albums *And Along Came Jones* and *The George Jones Collection*, but his sales numbers were nothing compared to the skyrocketing sales of younger artists such as Garth Brooks. George understood. He called Tony Brown one day and said, "When y'all get through with me, just let me know. You're not going to hurt my feelings."

Tony was kind, but a few weeks later, he called George back and said, "George, I hate to say it, but we're going to have to let you go."

"That's fine," George answered. "Nancy and I think the world of y'all."

George put on a happy face, but I could tell the rejection hurt him. It was the first time in his entire career that he was released from a label because of poor sales.

* * * * * *

Although George and Tammy constantly picked at each other, he was nonetheless saddened by Tammy Wynette's unexpected death in April 1998. George's former wife died at only fifty-five years of age.

When we heard the news that Tammy had died, we were at home at Nestledown. I said to George, "We need to go over to their house."

George didn't want to go. He said, "There will be too many people over there. It's none of our business. We don't need to go."

I said, "George, let's just go over there and pay our respects at the house."

"Oh, alright," George acquiesced. He changed from his jeans and sneakers to his jeans and boots, and we drove across town to Tammy and Richey's house. When we arrived, Georgette and Jackie, Tammy's daughter from a previous marriage, were there crying. We all hugged and Georgette said, "We gotta go to the funeral home to meet with the funeral director."

George said, "Well, okay. We'll just go with you."

I'm not sure who was more shocked, Georgette or me, but she responded first. "You will, Daddy?"

I looked at George and then back at her and said, "Yeah, we'll go with you."

So George and I accompanied the women to the funeral home and helped plan the whole thing—Tammy's private funeral at the church, as well as the public funeral at the Ryman Auditorium in downtown Nashville.

When we got back to the house, Tammy's daughters, Georgette and Jackie, thanked George profusely for accompanying them and lending support. I smiled to myself, knowing that he wouldn't have been there if it hadn't been for me encouraging him.

George didn't want to go to Tammy's funeral, but I felt that it was important that he attend. "Don't you want to go?" I asked him.

"No!" he said. "They don't need me there and I don't want to be there."

"That's not right, George," I chided him. "You need to be there."

He stomped off and huffed and puffed for a while back in his den, but about a half hour later, he came out and said, "Honey, you're right. We'll go to the service at the church."

We did. And we went to the memorial service for Tammy at the Ryman too.

Months later, I went out to the cemetery and saw that Tammy's remains were located in a mausoleum type of wall, with a bunch of tacky-looking pictures and notes taped to it. I said, "That ain't right. Tammy is a country music legend. We need to put up some sort of monument for her."

Since George and I owned sixty-eight cemetery plots, we certainly had the space.

But Tammy's family balked and made it sound as though I was a gravedigger, wanting to do something morbid by relocating Tammy's remains.

That was a lie. I simply wanted to do something to honor her. But it never happened.

Throughout the early to mid-1990s, George and I had fun doing things he wanted to do rather than letting him be bossed around by other people who did not have George's best interests at heart. I knew that good man was in there from that first night we met, but it took me two years to make much headway and then thirteen more years before I felt confident that George was on a good path.

We enjoyed being together and we had fun together. We were

truly best friends, as well as lovers and marriage partners. For a while, we had a place in Cocoa Beach, Florida, where we could get away and George could just be himself, not George Jones, Country Music Star. We enjoyed doing simple things. We'd go out walking or fishing together. George didn't often swim in the ocean, but he loved to walk the beach and get the sand between his toes. We'd almost always hold hands as we walked. Later, we'd go to dinner, George would put on his baseball cap and sneakers, and nobody would recognize him unless they heard his voice, or if they did, they didn't bother us. We drove around in a convertible and acted like teenagers. It was great fun.

People have often asked me, "Why do you think George was so self-destructive for so much of his life?"

I'm not a psychologist, but I think for the longest time, George didn't like himself. His attitude was, *Who cares if I live or die?* It took quite a while, but after ten or fifteen years of marriage, I felt as though George finally liked George.

Of course, he always credited me with saving his life. Maybe I did, I don't know. George often told people, "They say love can change the world. I'm here to testify that it changed one man—me! Friends, family members, doctors, therapists, and ministers all tried to save me, but to no avail. But finally the power of one woman—Nancy Jones—made the difference."

We both knew it wasn't me alone. It was Jesus and Jones.

But the devil doesn't give up his property easily.

17

Love on the Rocks

Wedding anniversaries are supposed to be happy times; times of celebrating the years of marital bliss together, reminding each other of the reasons why you and your spouse married in the first place. George never quite figured that out.

One of the reasons why he never took our anniversary too seriously was probably because he didn't plan a great deal for the wedding itself, back on March 4, 1983. We'd been together by that time for about two years, and I was all too aware of his addiction to cocaine and his alcoholism. He'd sometimes leave to go get a loaf of bread at the grocery store and not come home until a week later. He rarely tried to explain where he'd been, and sometimes, I'm not sure he even knew.

George once told me that he never had expected his previous wives to stay. Maybe that was another reason why George never took celebrating anniversaries too seriously. Despite having been married for sixteen years, on March 4, 1999, I wasn't surprised when we had plans to go out for a simple dinner to commemorate our wedding anniversary. I wasn't sure where George planned to take me, but I figured that any place that wasn't fast food was progress.

But even that didn't happen.

On our anniversary that year, George disappeared. He took off early in the day and he didn't come back. I assumed that he had found some vodka somewhere. I thought, *Okay, we* were *going out to eat, but I guess we're not going anywhere, now.*

Late that afternoon, I heard his car pull in our driveway, but when I looked out the window, I was surprised to see that it wasn't George driving. It was Tanya Tucker. Somebody else had followed them in Tanya's car and she, George, and her dog were in George's vehicle. She didn't come in the house, no doubt, because she guessed that I would be mad. She'd have guessed right.

I went outside and sure enough, George was loaded. He had been at Tanya's house listening to some new songs. He hadn't been using cocaine, she assured me, but he was drunk as a skunk, so Tanya had driven him home.

I took one look at George and said, "Oh, yeah. Happy anniversary!"

"Oh, it's your anniversary?" Tanya asked.

I glared back at her.

"Ah, well, er . . . happy anniversary, Nancy," Tanya said as she quickly dove into the front seat of the car behind George's. "See ya soon!" she called.

Yeah, I thought. I was furious but it was sort of funny, too, seeing Tanya so flustered as she and her driver pulled out of our driveway.

I walked over to George's vehicle and looked inside, wondering, *How much more booze is in here?*

I didn't find any more alcohol, but I found Tanya's dog in the back seat of George's SUV!

But Tanya was already long gone.

George stumbled out of the vehicle toward the house. When he saw me, he threw his jacket up in the air and in a thick, drunken voice, said, "Don't you fuss at me!"

I replied angrily, "I don't care what you did. It was *just* our anniversary, but that's okay."

Once I got George in the house and into bed, I called Tanya Tucker and said, "Tanya, come get your dog."

"Oh, my God!" she said. "Did I leave my dog in your car?"

"Yes, you did," I said icily. I wasn't really mad at her. It wasn't her fault that George was drinking again. It was his.

Tanya drove back across town to Nestledown to retrieve her dog. "I'm so sorry, Nancy," she said in her gravelly voice. Whether she was sorry that George was drunk or that she had left the dog, she didn't say. At that point, I didn't much care.

George went to bed and slept from that afternoon all the way till the next morning.

When he got up, he tried to apologize to me. "I just got over to Tanya's and we started playing music," he said.

I ignored his flimsy excuses. I was still as mad as a hornet at him, not only for blowing off our anniversary dinner, but that he'd gotten drunk again on our special occasion. I didn't know how much more I could take. And I wasn't sure I wanted to find out.

* * * * * *

Over the years, people have frequently asked me, "Nancy, with all of George's drinking, cocaine use, and other faults, why did you stay with him?" It's a good question and deserves an honest answer. I've always responded, "Because I knew that underneath all of that was a really good man." When George wasn't drinking or doing drugs, he was a wonderful gentleman, a kind, fun man, with a fantastic sense of humor. He made me laugh so much. He was one of the funniest people I've ever met, unpretentious, and he didn't even realize that he was funny.

So throughout our marriage, I kept trying to help him get clean and stay clean.

But by 1999, I was ready to call it quits. Although for nearly a decade George had publicly declared that he had stopped drinking—again—I knew better. He was no longer doing cocaine, but alcohol was a different story. A man who had befriended George—and who George had allowed to live on our land rent free—was facilitating his drinking by stashing vodka in various places around our property. We had more than one hundred acres of land beyond our home at Nestledown Farms so the "friend," who wanted to be George's Jones's buddy, filled tiny bottles of vodka and concealed them in places where George could find them as he went out to check on his cows, or simply rode around the farm. George got good at playing an adult version of "hide and go seek."

"Honey, I've quit drinking," George told me repeatedly. And he had. He no longer drank Jack Daniel's whiskey as though it were water, but he had those small bottles of vodka—which, of course, looks like water—stashed everywhere: in the bedroom furniture drawers, in his boots, as well as out on the range. George thought that by drinking the clear vodka he was able to disguise the smell of the alcohol. But anyone who has been around the stuff knows better. I could smell the alcohol and even found and destroyed some of his stash. "You make me so mad!" George had railed when he found out that I had discovered and dumped out several bottles of vodka hidden in our home.

I knew it was happening. I went out there one time and found that George's facilitator had bought a big gallon jug full of vodka. I snatched it up and poured every ounce of it down the sink.

When George came looking for his vodka, his buddy said, "Your wife got it!"

"Oh, Lord," George sighed. "That woman." He reached in his

pocket and pulled out some cash. "Go get another bottle," he told his supplier.

One night early in March 1999, George had gotten really wasted on vodka. When I saw him staggering into the house, I was furious. I yelled at him, "George! If you don't quit tomorrow, I'm out of here." And I meant it. I said, "I have spent so many years with you, listening to your lies, with you telling me you're gonna quit . . . and you don't. No more. I've had it."

For the first time in our long marriage, I seriously considered divorce. In my mind, I was already gone. I couldn't take anymore. I'd lost weight because of the stress, and I didn't want to spend the rest of my life searching in our closets, looking for booze. I'd put up with so much for so long, but now I was done. I finally gave George the ultimatum—either quit or I'm gone—and whether he realized it or not, I was dead serious.

The next morning, George was badly hungover and he looked terrible. His clothing was disheveled, his hair was messed up, and his face sported a scruffy growth of beard. I took one glance at him and I got mad all over again.

George leaned on the kitchen counter and held his head. "Can I just have one shot?" he begged, his voice still thick from the previous night's drunk. "I've got a hangover so bad."

I crossed my arms over my breasts and said, "I don't care. Drink all you want. It don't bother me."

Of course, it *did* bother me, but I wasn't about to tell him that. Not now. Not again. *No más;* no more!

George knew I was fuming. When I told him he could drink whatever he wanted and it wouldn't bother me, I think he recognized that I had given up. I was over him and his drinking.

He said, "Honey, listen to me. I'm gonna ride around and I'll get it right. Just don't leave me. When I come back, I promise you, I'll never touch another drop."

I'd heard that line before.

I said, "I don't believe you. I *don't* believe you, George!" I said, "Every time you say that, you do it more. So this time . . ." I paused to make sure I had George's full attention. I looked straight at him and said flatly, "Whenever you come back, I won't be here."

"Please! Just wait for me," George groaned. "Don't leave me. I promise; I promise. Just let me ride around and think. I'll get it right. Just don't leave me." He went out the door and climbed into our brand-new, black Lexus LX 470 SUV, replete with George's well-known license plate: NOSHOW1, and drove out the back exit from our property.

Later, George told me, "I prayed to God out there in the back field, and said, 'Lord, I can't afford to lose my wife.' I asked Him to hit me in the head with a sledgehammer and wake me up."

Well, God did more than that. He hit him with a bridge down on Highway 96.

18

Hit By a Sledgehammer

I was still stewing, my emotions somewhere between boiling hot mad and feelings of futile frustration. Meanwhile George was out driving and listening to some songs from a rough mix of his upcoming album *Cold Hard Truth*. Before long, he had eased the Lexus west on Highway 96 and had started up Interstate 65, heading toward Nashville. About that time, he spotted a young woman on the side of the road, whose vehicle had a flat tire. George pulled over to offer his assistance.

"Ya got a flat, honey?" he asked, nodding toward her car. He noticed the woman had several earrings, including one in her tongue, as well as a nose ring, and a stud through her lip. George was not fond of body piercings.

"Yes, sir, I do," she said. She recognized him. "You're George Jones, aren't ya?" she said.

"Yes, I am," he said. "I'll tell you what I'll do. If you will take all that metal off your face and throw that stuff away, I will take you down to the service station and buy you four new tires."

She looked back at George in amazement. "Are you kidding?"

"Nope, I'm not kidding," George said. "Throw it away."

She went to work unfastening and undoing all the earrings, the nose ring, and the lip stud. She tossed them into the ditch nearby and looked back at George. "Okay, I'm ready!"

True to his word, George took her to a tire store, bought her four brand-new tires, and paid for a serviceman to put them on for the young woman.

She later noted in an interview with the local CBS affiliate, "He was so nice! There ain't nuthin' bad about George Jones. That was one of the sweetest men I've ever met. He was drinking 7UP out of a can."

(Have you ever noticed that clear 7UP and vodka look a lot alike?)

George waved goodbye to his new friend and said, "My wife wants me, so I gotta get going. I'm on my way home."

George started back toward our house, still listening to the new album. Little more than a mile away, the car's audio system began playing "Choices," one of George's favorite songs on the album and one that the label thought might make a great first single for radio play.

Maybe he thought it might reduce my aggravation with him before he walked in the door, but for some reason, when he was just a short distance away from our home, he called our thirty-three-year-old daughter, Adina (Estes).

Adina and her sister, Sherry, were together in her car on their way to a cooking party, so Adina answered her phone. "Tell momma I'm almost home," George told her. "Hey, don't hang up. I want you to hear this new song."

George began playing "Choices" as he was talking with Adina, but as soon as he spoke, the Lexus automatically reduced the volume of the song. George got angry and started cussing and telling Adina, "I can't get the song to play. I don't know what's wrong with it. I can't get the song to play!" He didn't realize that a feature on the new

Lexus automatically reduced the volume of the audio system when it detected conversation in the vehicle. Adina tried to explain that to George.

She said, "Dad, listen, you're in a Lexus. You're talking on a speakerphone. So the music won't play."

George was unconvinced. "That's nonsense," he said. "That's a bunch of bull!" He banged his fist on the dashboard. "Of course, it will play. Here, listen to this."

The next thing Dina heard was George crying out in a spine-chilling scream, "Oh, God!" And then, with her ear still to the phone, Dina heard a loud, metal-mangling crash. And then silence.

Dina frantically called me at my home where I was working on some details with our housekeeper, Verb. "Mom!" Dina said. "I think Dad just had a wreck!"

"What?"

"Yes, Sherry and I were together and Dad called. He was trying to play us a new song, but the volume kept cutting out because he was in the SUV. He said he was almost home, but then I heard a crash. I think Dad may have wrecked the car."

I hung up, pressed George's number on the phone. No response but his voicemail message. I yelled into it, "George!"

No response.

"George!" I yelled again. "Where are you? Are you okay? George!"

When I stepped outside onto the porch, I could hear the sound of sirens on the highway nearby. Instinctively, I knew that something terrible had happened.

I was dressed casually, wearing a pair of jeans, sneakers, and a sweatshirt, so I grabbed a light jacket and said to Verb, "Let's go!" We jumped in my car—a white Lexus SUV matching George's black one—and headed toward Highway 96, the two-lane road near our neighborhood. But when we got to the highway, a traffic jam caused by the crash had already clogged the road and vehicles were stopped, with a long line of cars and trucks backed up, so Verb and I pulled off, hopped out of our vehicle, and took off running in the direction of the sirens and flashing lights. I didn't know for sure where the accident had occurred, but I knew there was an old concrete bridge nearby and several tree-lined embankments along the road. Whatever had happened and wherever George had crashed, the impact had stopped him and his music dead in his tracks. I frantically ran as hard as I could for more than a half mile along the side of the highway, frightened by thoughts of what I might find. Funny, a few hours earlier, I had been furious with George for drinking again, and now I feared for his life.

When I got to the scene of the accident, my heart leaped into my throat at the sight. Police and fire department vehicles blocked both sides of the bridge, their red lights flashing, and communications speakers blaring. Apparently, George's vehicle had swerved across the highway as he was fumbling with the audio controls, and he had slammed full force into a concrete bridge, demolishing a section of the heavy concrete-and-steel, fence-like bridge railing, and hurling it into the water below. No telling how fast George had been going, but the front of the Lexus looked like a scrunched accordion.

I felt tears coursing down my face as I pushed through a crowd of onlookers and rescue workers that had gathered. One of the police officers grabbed me. "Back up, back up!" he said. "This is really bad."

I lost it emotionally when I peered at George's body trapped inside the vehicle. Apparently, he had not been wearing a seatbelt. George didn't like to be constrained so, as he often did, he had fastened his seatbelt behind his back, simply to silence the warning chimes in the Lexus. "Yeah, that's gonna save your life," I had sometimes chided him. With my eyebrows raised, I cajoled him about the useless belt. "Yeah.

You're saving your life all right." *Right.*

George would look at me and smile . . . but he refused to buckle up. Consequently, when he hit the bridge, upon impact, his body had been flung forward, under the steering wheel and dashboard; his rear end was pushed up, off the seat; his knees were pinned behind him; and his body was trapped there. No doubt, had it not been for the airbag deploying, he would have been thrown through the windshield. He was unconscious, but I cried out to him anyhow. "George, don't die!" I called. "Please, don't die." I reached inside the vehicle and grasped George's hand.

The paramedics had already pumped his lungs full of air, trying to keep him alive, and his inflated, battered body looked like a grotesque caricature of himself.

I fretted to one of the rescue workers, "Oh, my God, he's so swollen!"

"No, no, no," he said, as he continued to work, trying to extricate George from the vehicle. "We did that because we think his lungs are damaged."

The Williamson County Rescue Squad worked feverishly in their attempts get George out of the crushed vehicle, to no avail. They used everything they had at their disposal—hydraulic saws, the "jaws of life" cutters, air chisels, large wrenches, and strong chains—cutting and prying the wreckage apart so they could get George out. They were racing against time, fearing the demolished vehicle might burst into flames at any moment. It took more than two hours, but they finally were able to saw through enough metal that they could reach in and safely pull George out of the crushed SUV. I stood watching, sobbing, and praying the whole time. "Oh, God, please don't take him yet," I wailed aloud. "I need him; I love him; we've been through so much together." A police officer and a rescue worker stood next to me, one on each side, supporting my arms, holding me up to keep me from collapsing.

Once they had freed George from the wreckage, the firemen and paramedics gently lifted him onto a stretcher and gingerly wheeled him through the weeds toward a medical helicopter that had already landed in a pasture just off Highway 96. George was still unconscious. I stayed right with him, and with the help of a police officer, followed the gurney to the helicopter. "Can I go with you?" I asked as a paramedic climbed into the helicopter right next to George.

"No," he answered, as he began to close the door. "Nobody can get in the helicopter. You will have to drive to the hospital." He shut and latched the door, and a police officer pulled me away.

In a matter of minutes, the chopper was in the air, flying toward Vanderbilt University Medical Center in midtown Nashville.

I later learned that paramedics continued to work on George throughout the flight, monitoring his vital signs. At two points during the short trip from Franklin to Nashville, George flatlined. He died twice on the way to the hospital, and then roused again.

They landed on the hospital heliport, and several orderlies ran to the helicopter to lift George out, whisking him straight to the Emergency Room.

Verb returned home, and another one of our employees, Woody Woodruff, who had rushed to the scene of the accident, offered to drive me to Vanderbilt. Ordinarily a thirty-minute drive or less, it seemed to take forever to get there. Once we arrived, someone ushered me into a private waiting room, as the doctors attended to George.

After a while, a doctor came out of the ER and sat down next to me. "Mrs. Jones, I need to talk with you," he said. The expression on his face looked somber. He said to me, "There isn't much we can do for him. He's very intoxicated." The doctor said that X-rays revealed that George had a punctured lung, a ruptured liver, and his legs were badly mangled, among other injuries. Although he did not have any serious external lacerations, the doctor offered little hope. "He's probably not going to make it," he said. "Your husband is severely injured internally—on the inside of his body."

I said, "Why are you sitting here talking to me when you could be in there trying to save his life?"

My boldness must have taken the doctor aback. He stood up and said, "Well, I'll try, but I don't think it's going to happen." He walked to the door and said, "We'll do the best we can, Mrs. Jones."

Almost immediately, family members and friends showed up at the hospital. My daughter Adina found me in the ER waiting room. Numerous country music friends such as Waylon Jennings, Randy Travis, Faith Hill, and others soon surrounded me and supported me, as did George's band members, the Jones Boys. Connie Smith, a Country Music Hall of Fame member and wife of bluegrass artist Marty Stuart, called and prayed for George, and for me.

When the news media caught wind of the accident, they showed up too, all clamoring for a scoop. It didn't take them long to find one. While George was still unconscious in the hospital, members of the media scoured the wreckage and immediately implied that alcohol had contributed to George losing control of the SUV. Rumors swirled and the police later confirmed that an open container of vodka was found under the front seat.

As soon as news about the wreck became public, multitudes of George's fans poured into the hospital lobby too, many of them praying for George, some simply curious. All seemed deeply concerned for him.

Meanwhile, the doctors transferred George to the intensive care unit after inserting a tracheotomy in his throat. At that point, the doctors were more concerned about saving George's life and weren't worried about how the trach might affect his singing voice. I was allowed in George's unit, along with one other person at a time. He was hooked up to all sorts of machines, monitoring his condition. Amazingly, he had no broken bones, but he looked awful and the doctors continued to question whether he would make it through the night.

I stayed near George's bedside all night long. Mid-morning the next day, Dina was in the ICU along with me when George regained consciousness for a few moments. He couldn't talk because of the trach in his throat, but he looked into my eyes and weakly squeezed my hand.

I knew then that George was going to make it.

The hospital kept George in the ICU for more than a week, then another week and a half in a private room while he recovered. I stayed there the whole time. While he was in ICU, the hospital did not want me to stay in his room all night, but I didn't want to leave. There was a little broom closet of a room that I stayed in. It was freezing cold in there, but I stayed in that tiny room, because I wanted to be close to George.

Alan Jackson came to visit one night, and when he discovered that I was sleeping in the closet, he suggested, "Nancy, why don't you bring George's bus up here and stay in there?"

I said, "That's a good idea, Alan. I didn't even think about that."

I had our driver bring George's tour bus to the hospital parking lot and my son-in-law, Kirk Hohimer, and I lived in it while George was hospitalized. I'd go back and forth to check on George from there. The nurses said, "Please rest and don't worry, Mrs. Jones. We'll call you if he wakes up."

I said, "Okay, I appreciate that." But I still went back to the hospital every day. The doctors permitted me to visit with George in the ICU for only a few minutes at a time.

One morning, they called, so I went in to visit with George. As I was walking down the hallway, before I got anywhere near his room,

I could hear him singing at the top of his voice. "Me and Jesus got our own thing goin.'"

Yeah, I guess so, I thought. It was like, *Golly! He's back!*

As I passed the nurses' station, one of the nurses said, "He's been awake for about thirty minutes, and he hasn't shut up."

When I walked in his room, George perked right up. He said, "Now, there's my sweet wife. I love you, darling."

I hugged him and said, "What are you doing?"

"I'm singing gospel music," George said. "I want you to do something for me."

"What's that?"

"I want you to get in touch with Vestal Goodman," said George. Vestal was a founding member of the popular Southern Gospel music group the Happy Goodman Family. Her recordings had sold millions of copies, and she was a member of the Gospel Music Hall of Fame. More importantly to George, Vestal had a vivacious spirit to accompany her strong voice. With her deeply rooted Pentecostal background, similar to George's, the woman knew how to pray!

I said, "I don't know how to get in touch with her, but I'll try."

"Call Ralph Emery," George suggested. "He knows how to contact Vestal." Ralph had been a popular WSM Radio personality, a host of the Grand Ole Opry nationwide radio show, and had also hosted one of the most watched television shows in country music history, *Nashville Now*. He knew everybody in the Nashville music business and was a good friend of ours. He once gave George a beautiful leather-bound book as a present. The book was titled *All that I Know About Being on Time,* by George Jones. When George opened the book, he found nothing but empty pages!

I called Ralph and, of course, he knew Vestal and was glad to help.

I called Vestal and told her that George had been asking for her.

She was on tour at the time, so she said, "When are you going home from the hospital?"

I told her when the doctors had estimated that George might be released. Vestal said, "I'll be there."

Amazingly, George's condition did not require any major surgery, just rest and recuperation, so when it was clear that George was going to be okay, the doctor said, "I'm going on vacation." Fans and media had dogged the doctor for days since George had been admitted, so he jokingly said, "I'm going far away, so far that I don't even want to hear anything about George Jones."

When he returned a week or so later, he told me that he had gone to an island. "There was nothing there and I didn't want anything there," the doctor said. "I just wanted to go to the beach and back. But I checked in and went to my room and what do you suppose I found? Right there in the room, on a nightstand near the bed, was a book about the life of George Jones." He said, "I can't get away from that man."

I laughed and said, "See, that's what you get for being so mean."

The doctor chuckled as well.

After the wreck, George's doctors wanted to make sure that he was mentally competent, that the force of hitting the dashboard had not damaged his brain, impaired his mind, or caused him to develop dementia. They tested him by asking basic questions such as, "What is the president's name?" and "What is your phone number?" George passed with flying colors until they asked, "And what is Nancy's phone number?"

George had a love-hate relationship with my phone number. Ever since cell phones first became common, George had carried a basic flip phone. No fancy "smart phone" for him, just a simple flip phone with push-button numbers. To make dialing easier for him, George's daughter Susan programmed several of his frequently dialed numbers into the phone. My number was zero, one. But George's fingers frequently landed on zero, zero, which for some reason, connected him to the 911 emergency operator.

"911, what is your emergency?" the operator would ask George.

"I'm not talking to you," George said. "I'm tryin' to call my wife."

Sometimes George might be sitting in a chair in his den, wanting a cup of coffee, and he'd call me on his cell phone—or at least, *attempt* to call me—in the kitchen!

George would hit my number on his phone, and once again, he'd hear, "911, what is your emergency?"

"Honey!" he'd yell loud enough that I could hear him in the kitchen. "Come here and talk to this woman. I didn't call her, but she keeps answering!"

I hurried to George's den and picked up the phone. "Hello?"

The operator said, "Whoever this is keeps calling 911."

"Oh, my," I said. "I don't understand how he's doing it, but we're sorry."

A few minutes later, George did it again. The operator was not happy with him, and George could tell it. "Ma'am," he said, "this is George Jones, the country music singer, and I'm doing what they told me to do. I got one of those flip phones and I'm hitting zero then one, but I keep calling you. I'm sure sorry about that."

"Well, you're dialing 911, Mr. Jones," the operator said.

"Alright, let me see if I can't get that changed," he promised her. He had Susan reprogram his phone so my new speed dial number was zero, *two*. That kept him from dialing 911.

But when they tested his mental competency in the hospital following the wreck, they asked him, "What is your wife's phone number?"

"Oh, that's simple," George answered. "Her number is zero, two."

The doctors nearly decided to admit him for a few weeks longer until I explained to them.

When George was discharged from the hospital, Scott Ulmer, our bus driver, offered to drive us back home to Nestledown in George's bus. On the way, we had to drive past the bridge George had hit. A large portion of the concrete railing was still missing, taped off and guarded by road construction barrels. It was an eerie feeling as we passed that concrete bridge where the accident had taken place, but we were thankful to God and to the many first responders who had helped save George's life.

Passing by the bridge, George said, "I don't understand this, but I need to tell you something. I think I died before I got to the hospital."

"You did?" I asked. I didn't mention that the paramedics had said something similar, that he had actually died twice on the way to the hospital.

"Yeah," George said real seriously. "I saw this huge eagle with the prettiest wings you've ever seen. The eagle came down, picked me up, put me on its back, and flew me above the clouds."

"Really?" I said somewhat skeptically, knowing that George had been drinking that day.

"Honey, you wouldn't believe the colors on that eagle. Beautiful! And it was huge!"

I nodded, trying to imagine what George might have experienced.

"It would have had to been huge to get your big butt on there, George!" Scott spoke up, breaking the moment with some humor.

"Scott, I'm tellin' the truth," George said. "I was on that eagle and flying."

He didn't try to explain any further, but I continued to ponder what George had said. It would be nearly twenty-two years later when I experienced a bit of what George saw.

19
A New George

True to her word, one of the first people to visit George at home was Vestal Goodman—and not merely once. The woman came every day! I took her back to George's room, and the two of them started singing old gospel songs. I didn't even know that George knew some of those songs! But he did, and Vestal drew them out of him. Vestal visited so often that I gave her the entrance code to our front gate so she could come in without calling. Some days when she came, I'd be so tired and wrung out from caring for George, I'd fall asleep on the living room couch.

I said, "I had to come in here to get some rest."

"Lie down, baby," Vestal said with her radiant smile. "I've got this. You just rest."

Vestal would go back to George's room and the two of them would start singing gospel music. I'd hear 'em both back there, just singing up a storm.

When they were done, she'd come back through the living room and I'd still be on the couch, covered by a blanket. She'd say, "Don't you get up, baby. You stay right there. I'll be back tomorrow. And tomorrow I'm bringing homemade banana pudding." And she would! She came every day for nearly a week.

Each day, George looked forward to Vestal's visit, so they could sing gospel music together. But what George didn't know, before Vestal left our home, she paused at the front door, looked back at me, and said, "Guess what I'm doing?" She raised her foot off the ground and then firmly planted it on the floor again.

"I don't know," I said. "What are you doing?"

Vestal smiled and then her face took on a serious, almost stern look. She said, "I just put the devil under my foot, and I just stomped him." She stomped her foot again. "I stomped that devil right outta here."

"Really?" I asked. "Was he in the house?"

"Oh, he wanted to be," Vestal said as she raised her eyes heavenward. "But he ain't. I got rid of him." Vestal's faith was contagious, and I have no doubt that part of George's rapid recovery was due to Vestal's prayers and the music she and George shared. We needed that.

After all, when we got home from the hospital, we were greeted by media swarming all around our property. Even though our house was tucked back off the street, reporters and photographers hounded us at the front gate, calling out questions, harping and barking like a pack of wolves. They snapped photos incessantly, and many photographers wielded powerful binocular lenses through which they could see us even if we were sitting on the front porch. It was impossible to step outside our front door without a high-powered camera lens targeted on us. Most members of the media were kind, but others were downright mean, constantly badgering us about George "falling off the wagon again."

"Hey, George, we thought you stopped drinking years ago!"

"That must have been mighty strong 7UP you were guzzling!"

"Are you still doing cocaine? Or did you give that up as well?"

The comments were snide, vicious, arrogant, and condescending, without a lick of genuine concern for George or compassion for him or me. I was accustomed to dealing with the media, and I'd had to handle a number of messes with George over the years, not to mention the promotion of his final, contentious album with Tammy Wynette. But this was different. This was simply mean, and I was in no mood for it. I just wanted to get away and leave it all behind.

We still owned a home in Lakeland, Florida, so I called Jay, a friend who was an airplane pilot, and said, "I need to get George out of here. Just come. We'll sneak out the back gate and get to the airport so you can take us to Lakeland."

Jay agreed, and we made our escape. He flew us to Lakeland, and although we didn't get totally away from the media frenzy, the chaos around George was less intense in Florida.

George was able to stand up and move around the house a bit, but then, oddly enough, he developed a new malady. He couldn't open his mouth. At first, I thought it was because he'd had the trach in his throat, covering his mouth, and he hadn't talked very much in nearly two weeks. As a result, he seemed to be suffering from lockjaw, a form of tetanus that caused his jaw muscles to tighten so he couldn't open his mouth. His jaw seemed frozen, so I had to pry his mouth open to even get soup in there with a straw. At the time, we didn't realize that the tetanus could interfere with his breathing and even cause death. All I knew was that George was miserable because he was hungry and couldn't eat. Rather than getting stronger, he just kept getting worse. He was weak and listless.

I called the doctor and told him what we were experiencing. He said, "I think you need to come back to Nashville, Nancy."

I said, "No, I don't want to come back because of the media attention."

Only then did he explain the seriousness of George's condition. He said, "Nancy, George is going to die if you don't come back."

George seemed lifeless already, so I reluctantly agreed, and Jay flew us back to Nashville, where the doctors discovered that not only did George have lockjaw, he had developed double pneumonia. Back to the hospital we went.

After George's condition stabilized, the doctor confided to me, "Thank God you came back when you did, because he wouldn't have lasted much longer."

We stayed in the hospital several more days before returning to our home in Nestledown Farms. George was feeble but he soon started making progress. One day I said to him, "George, the doctor says you have to walk."

"Okay. Okay," he agreed somewhat reluctantly, grousing at me as the impatient patient.

We stepped out into the brisk, spring air and slowly walked arm in arm down our long driveway. We walked as far as a bridge entering the subdivision and George did well, but I could tell that he was exhausted.

When we got to the bridge, he sat down on the side of the road. "I'm too tired," he said. "I don't think I can walk all the way back. Go get the golf cart. Please."

I said, "Okay. Just stay here and I'll be right back." I started off in the direction of the house, and as I did, I heard George praying. He said, "God, if you let me get over this, I'll never drink again. I'll never smoke again, and I will be the perfect husband."

I smiled but didn't say anything to George. I'd heard him make lots of bold declarations to me over the years. I had stopped counting how many times he had quit drinking . . . for a day or two, or sometimes a few weeks, or even months. But this was different. He was talking with God, and he was asking for His help.

That's when I believed him.

I returned with the golf cart, picked up George, and headed back to the house. Along the way, he looked at me and said, "I told God I quit."

"I know. I heard you," I replied.

He said, "Honey, you gotta believe me. I'll never touch it again."

I looked over at George, and said, "You know what? I believe you."

And I did!

The next morning, George ran off the guy that had been supplying him with the vodka. "Go find your own place," George told him. The man had been living on our property and he wasn't even an employee of ours. So when George got serious with God, he knew enough that he couldn't allow that fellow who was enabling his habit anywhere near him. The enabler was gone the next day.

That, too, showed me that George was serious about staying clean.

Prior to the accident and our brief trip to Lakeland, I had been so frustrated with George that I was ready to call it quits and get a divorce. But now, divorce was off the table. I was convinced that George's transformation was real.

George remained true to his commitment to the Lord. Maybe it was because it was George's prayer, with him calling out to the Lord personally, not just me praying for him or trying to encourage him to stay sober. But whatever it was, he never again touched alcohol after that. He also never touched a cigarette—and he'd been smoking longer than he'd been drinking; he'd started smoking as a boy of ten. When we'd go out to eat with friends who knew well George's propensity to drink, they'd sometimes ask, "George, is it okay if we order wine?"

"Ain't gonna bother me, son," he'd say. "I don't care."

Our good friends Joe and Theresa Diffie invited us out to a dinner party, but knowing that Joe liked to tip a few drinks, I wasn't sure we should go. "George, there may be folks who are drinking there."

"I don't care," he said. "They'll have the headache the next day, not me."

Sometimes he'd see a young man smoking a cigarette outside and he'd say, "Son, come here. Let me tell you, if you knew what I know, you'd put that cigarette out right now." Or, if we pulled into the mall parking lot and he saw a young woman outside smoking, he'd call her over to the car. "Hey, come here, hon." He'd then encourage her to quit smoking.

George even posted big signs on our property: No Smoking.

So I thought, *Yep. He's serious.*

Yes, he had done that kind of thing before, where he had said, "I'm not gonna drink anymore," and then he had gone back to it again. But this time he didn't. He was through and I'm convinced it was because of his prayer. Something about reaching out to the Lord made a big difference in George. Interestingly, as major US concert promoter Brian Martin pointed out in a full-page advertisement in *Billboard,* "Since 1999, over 200 shows; zero no shows."[1]

From then on, it was no longer me trying to find the hidden vodka bottles to get rid of them. From 1999 to 2013, I got back my husband, a husband I should have had to begin with, a man who trusted God with his strengths and his weaknesses, making him the strongest man I'd ever known. At last, George Jones was a man who wanted to live.

20

Better Choices

Serious consequences sometimes follow foolish actions, and George was no exception to that rule, even though, for years, it seemed he was. He could get into trouble and somehow walk away. But not this time. At some point, after he had sufficiently recovered, George admitted that he had been drinking and driving the day of the accident. We went to court in Williamson County and George pleaded guilty to driving under the influence. The judge ordered George to pay a $550 fine and enter into another rehabilitation program. We also reimbursed the city for the damage done to the bridge and for the cost of the repairs.

Carl P. Mayfield, a popular Nashville radio personality with WSIX, spearheaded a drive to use George's wrecked SUV as a centerpiece for its public service, safe-driving advertisements. They hoisted the vehicle up high on a pole along the highway, the black Lexus dangling in the air where it was clearly visible to all passersby. It was a grotesque but strong message about the effects of drinking and driving.

The media loved it and played it for all it was worth. I was so mad about all the negative publicity, but George just considered it a minor aggravation. He was more concerned about trying to get his health and energy back, and especially his voice.

When he had been hospitalized after hitting the bridge, the

doctors had inserted a tracheotomy down George's throat. Although that was an important part of saving his life, the trach did severe damage to George's vocal cords. Following his recovery, he couldn't reach the high notes as he had previously, including some of the ones he had sung on the new album, *Cold Hard Truth*.

George hadn't been all that excited about recording another major album anyhow. Not that he didn't love singing and performing, but because he was convinced that contemporary "country radio" had left behind artists such as Waylon Jennings, Merle Haggard, George Strait, Randy Travis, and some others. Ironically, all of these artists, along with George, were considered country music superstars, yet country radio rarely played their music. Radio was obsessed with presenting listeners "new country" music, which often sounded more like rock and roll "wannabe music" to George.

But our friend and long time publicist Evelyn Shriver, who had also helped promote Randy Travis's enormous success, was convinced otherwise. When Evelyn became the first female president of a Nashville-based recording company, Asylum, she convinced George that there was still a market for his kind of country and that she could reach that market. "We really want you, George," Evelyn said, "and I guarantee you, we can move some records."

George believed Evelyn, partly because of our friendship and partly because it had been a long time since anyone in the music business had expressed that sort of confidence in George's music. He signed with Asylum and had great fun listening to and selecting songs for the new album. The song "Choices" sounded almost as though George had written it himself about his own life.

Actually, the song had been written by Mike Curtis and Billy Yates, the talented Nashville hairstylist-slash-songwriter who had co-written "I Don't Need Your Rockin' Chair." George had recorded several other songs Billy had written since then. On at least two occasions, Billy played "Choices" for George. Alan Jackson had already passed on the song because he thought it was too much of a downer, but George had known some great success with songs that others thought were too negative—most significantly, "He Stopped Loving Her Today," which even George himself had considered too depressing to ever play on the radio.

As Billy played "Choices" for George, he leaned back and closed his eyes. When he looked up, he said, "No, Billy. That song isn't for me."

Billy was disappointed but undeterred. About a year later, Billy brought the song back to George, and George passed on it again. But when he began considering songs for the *Cold Hard Truth* album, "Choices" seemed right to George. He went into the studio and cut the song with confidence, and the end result dripped with gripping pathos, almost as though George was singing about the many times in his past when he had given in to temptations—especially to alcohol—despite his mama's strong Pentecostal influence during his childhood.

Since the day that I was born
There were voices
That told me right from wrong
If I had listened
No I wouldn't be here today
Living and dying
With the choices I made.

I was tempted
By an early age I found
I liked drinkin'
Oh, and I never turned it down
There were loved ones
But I turned them all away
Now I'm living and dying
With the choices I made.[2]

The song released as the first single from the album on May 8, 1999. The album charted at number five, George's performance of "Choices" won a Grammy Award for Best Male Country Vocal Performance in February 2000, and Billy and Mike were nominated for Grammys as the writers. Not bad for a song that George turned down twice.

But George had recorded *Cold Hard Truth* prior to the accident, when his vocal cords were relatively healthy and had not been impaired by the tracheotomy. When he first went back on stage, he quickly discovered that his injuries had indeed affected his ability to hit some of the high notes. His voice sounded raspy and tired. The audience didn't mind, but it bothered George that he couldn't sing his best.

George doubled down on his efforts to get his voice back in shape. Of course, cuttin' out the drinking and smoking certainly helped. In talking about his renewed commitment to sobriety and how the accident had affected him, George told one writer, "I know a lot of people ain't gonna believe me, but it put the fear of God in me this time. There won't ever be any more drinking . . . in other words, like Hank Williams said, I saw the light. It's a miracle I'm alive."[3]

It took him a while, but before long, George was back singing stronger and better than ever. "Since I quit smoking," he told a friend, "I can hit as high a note as I used to hit when I was only twenty years old."

He was singing so well and his voice was so supple and expressive, he had no trouble at all recording another new album, *The Rock: Stone Cold Country 2001*, released on Asylum Records to strong reviews. Unfortunately, for reasons known only to music industry "gods," Asylum closed its country division shortly after that. Both George and Evelyn were without a label. After leaving MCA Nashville and Asylum Records, George founded Bandit Records—named after our dog—along with Evelyn Shriver, Susan Nadler, and other partners. George later did a gospel recording on the label, *The Gospel Collection*. We signed one artist, Bryan White, but most of the releases from Bandit Records were by George. Bandit remained his label for the rest of his career.

The Country Music Association invited George to sing "Choices" on the 1999 awards show. George was honored at first, but then the producers requested that he sing only a small portion of the song, rather than the entire song. George refused to perform an abridged version of the hit song—it was too special to him—so when the producers declined his request to sing the entire song, George decided not to attend the awards show.

Alan Jackson was so miffed at the CMA's decision that halfway through his performance of his own hit "Pop a Top," during a live broadcast by CBS, Alan cut his own song short, signaled to his band, and they struck up the chorus to George's song "Choices." Alan then walked off the stage and the crowd erupted in a long, loud standing ovation. Many people considered Alan's gutsy performance and the audience's response as one of most notable incidents in the history of the CMA's broadcast. Leave it to George to once again evoke a controversy without even being in the building!

Not long after the CMAs, George was featured in another CBS special in which he sang "Choices." As an expression of his appreciation to Alan for his kind, courageous support during the CMA awards show controversy, before George began the song, he thanked Alan and sang a bit of Alan's song "Pop a Top."

It was Country tradition at its best.

21

Seeing Green; Seeing Red

Some people who didn't know George well thought that he was mean because, in his younger years, he had a reputation for being rowdy and loud. But underneath all that, George was a teddy bear. He had such a heart of compassion.

One night George had played at Harbor Center in Portsmouth, Virginia, and after the show, we were heading up the highway, and our bus driver at the time, Scott Ulmer, was talking on the CB radio as he drove. Shortly after midnight, a Ford Thunderbird in front of us hit the brakes. A tour bus can't stop on a dime, and with Scott on the CB, his reaction time may have been impaired, so we crashed into the back of the Thunderbird. Nobody was injured, but the car was a mess.

George knew that insurance would cover the costs, but that wasn't what mattered to him. He felt so sorry for the couple in the car, he invited them onto the bus and we drove them to Richmond and put them up in a hotel for the night. But not before George signed an autograph for the state trooper investigating the crash. George paid for the victims' room, and Scott made arrangements to get them back home.

On another occasion, we were in Canada on a long tour and our bus was parked at the hotel where we were staying prior to a show. I peered out the window of the bus and saw six kids on the sidewalk gazing in fascination at the large motor coach. When I looked more closely, I noticed that none of the kids had any hair. I told George, "Look at those little kids. I feel so sorry for them."

He said, "I think they got cancer."

I went outside and pulled up a door to one of the storage bays below, and I got six T-shirts, six caps, and six CDs. I took them all on the bus, and George signed every one of them for the kids.

About that time, Bobby Birkhead came on the bus and asked, "What are you doing?"

I said, "I'm giving those little cancer kids caps and T-shirts and CDs all signed by George."

Bobby looked at George and laughed. "They don't have cancer," he said. "They have head lice, so their parents shaved off all their hair."

George laughed too. "I'm sorry they have lice," he said. "But I'm glad they don't have cancer."

Regardless, all six of 'em got T-shirts and caps and autographed pictures and CDs of George Jones.

At all of George's shows, I always sold T-shirts at the merchandise table. I didn't have to do that, and we always had plenty of volunteers who wanted to work the tables, but I loved meeting and talking with the fans, so I spent a good portion of the evening out in the middle of everything, helping folks pick out their George Jones T-shirts, music, or simply talking with them. I was especially helpful to US soldiers. Neither George nor I had any close family members in the military, but we were both intensely patriotic. Any time soldiers came to the merchandise table wearing a US military uniform, I'd wait until they picked what they wanted. Then whenever they tried to pay me, I'd say, "No, no, no. Thank you for your service."

Bobby went on the bus one night and told George, "Whatever we do, don't ever book a show at a military base because we won't have a thing left. Nancy will give away all of our merchandise!"

And I would have.

* * * * * *

George and I had so much fun together and we truly had a great relationship, but part of the reason for that was we weren't afraid to zing one another occasionally. We knew each other well enough to know exactly how to irritate the other person.

George was never materially minded—except about his lawn—and he would have given away almost anything we owned.

On one occasion, we were traveling on the bus and had been to Canada where George had bought me a beautiful pair of cowboy boots. I loved them! I thought, *I'm gonna keep these boots forever. I'll never get rid of them. George bought them especially for me, and he usually doesn't buy something that looks this good.* I kept the boots with me on the bus and wore them for special occasions.

We were at a show one night, and before it was time for George to go on, one of our female background singers stopped by our bus. She was wearing a real cute outfit and George said, "Nancy's got a pair of boots in there that would match your outfit real well. You should wear them."

I was in the bedroom in the back of the bus, and I heard George say, "She don't care. You can have them."

I could hardly believe my ears! The man was giving away my boots! Sure, he had bought them for me, but they were my boots, not his, with which he was being so generous.

Our background singer wore my boots on stage that night.

I was furious! When George came back to the bedroom to get ready for the show, I sat on the far side of the bed and didn't say a word to him. After a while, he noticed that I wasn't getting ready. "Aren't you going to the show?" he asked.

"Nope," I answered curtly. "I'm staying right here on the bus. I don't have any *boots* to wear."

"Ohh," he said. "I have messed up." I just glared at him.

George called our road manager, Bobby Birkhead. "Bobby, I don't know what to do," George told him. "I think I messed up."

He said, "What did you do?"

George said, "I gave away Nancy's pretty boots, the ones I bought her in Canada." George explained that he'd given my boots to our background singer.

"Oh, that's bad," Bobby said in a low whisper. "Do you want me to try to get them back?"

"Can you get 'em in a nice way?" George asked, trying to keep everybody happy.

Bobby approached the singer about the matter, and the next day she came on our bus apologetically carrying the boots. "Nancy, can I talk to you?" she asked.

Still fuming, I answered, "I'm not talking to nobody."

She sheepishly looked down at the floor. "I didn't want the boots," she said sweetly.

"What'd you take 'em for?" I shot back.

She said, "Because George told me that they'd look good with that outfit I was wearing. I'm bringing them back." She lifted the boots chest high and handed them in my direction.

"Oh, no. I don't want 'em now," I said.

She looked at me and spoke quietly. "Nancy, please don't do that to me."

I knew it wasn't her idea to wear my boots, so I let her off the hook. "Okay," I said, nodding my head so she knew that I understood. She placed the boots on the bed and quickly exited the bus.

But I was still mad at George.

I knew that George loved cars and that he had ordered a brand-new Lexus that would most likely be in by the time we returned to Nashville.

I also knew that George Jones hated the color red. I don't mean he disliked it; he *hated* it!

So right in front of George, I called the Lexus dealership and asked for J.R., the manager. When he picked up the phone, I said, "J.R., this is Nancy Jones."

J.R. automatically thought I was calling about George's new car that was on order. "Hi, Nancy!" he said enthusiastically. "I just talked with George a while back about his car."

"That's fine," I said. "You get him one. But I want mine, too."

"What?"

"That's right," I spoke loudly as George eyed me on the phone. "I want a brand-new, red convertible sports coup. *Red*," I emphasized.

"Nancy, are you sure?" J.R. asked. "You know that George doesn't like red? Right?"

I said, "J.R., this car is for me." I saw George flipping channels on the television, pretending not to be listening. So I said, "I want it just as bright red as you can get it."

"Okay," J.R. said. "I'll have it for you when you come home."

Sure enough, when we returned home to Tennessee, both cars were sitting in our driveway—George's black SUV and my *red* sports coup.

I knew that George hated that car, but every day he tried to pretend he liked it. "That really is a pretty car," he'd say, rubbing his chin and walking around the Lexus, but I knew he didn't mean it. He hated it. I had a red sweater one time and George couldn't stand that. "I hate that sweater," he'd say any time I wore it. "It's not the sweater; I just hate red."

George could not leave well enough alone. Once he had purchased a vehicle, he liked to change everything about it, putting chrome on it or different tires, anything, or everything to give it the Jones touch.

One day, he surprised me. "Go look at the tires and rims on your car," George said with a smile. I looked in the garage, and sure enough, George had changed the size of my tires.

"George, you can't do that on a Lexus," I said.

"Why not?" he asked.

"It won't ride right," I said.

Our friend, Herb, had come to visit, so we were going across town to our friend T. G. Sheppard's home, and I had planned to drive my car. George decided not to go, so Herb and I took my car and I let him drive.

Along the way, Herb said, "Nancy, what's wrong with this car? It rides terrible!"

I told Herb about George having the tires and rim sizes changed.

Herb said, "You're gonna have to try to get your tires back."

I called J.R. at the dealership and told him I wanted my original tires and rims. "Oh, I'm sorry, Nancy," he said. "We sold those."

I went in the house and said, "George, you ruined my car."

"Oh, no, no, I didn't."

I said, "Yes, you did. Tell him Herb."

Herb said, "It drives like a logging truck."

George got in my car and took it for a test drive. When he came back, he said with an impish smile, "Well, they sure don't drive the same as they used to, do they?" That rascal sold my car, ostensibly because it didn't drive right. It wasn't till later that I realized that George had done that tire trick on purpose, just to get rid of that red car!

George loved cars; the man would have bought a new one every week if he could have.

And he loved zinging me, sometimes pulling a prank on me, sometimes just doing something with a car to irritate me. For instance, for a while, we had a black Audi. It was a nice car, but George knew it wasn't my favorite.

Nevertheless, a short time after George died, I received a call from the local Audi dealer. "Nancy, George's car is in."

I said, "What car? We just got a new one."

"I know but he ordered this one and gave me instructions to deliver it when he dies."

"What? He actually said that?"

"Yes, ma'am," the dealer said. "And your car is in."

"Do I have to take it?" I asked.

"No," the dealer said. "You don't have to take it. I think George was just trying to mess with you."

That was George, still zinging me, even after he was in heaven. At least he hadn't ordered me a red car.

* * * * * *

I knew that Waylon Jennings was not doing well when he and his wife, Jessi Colter, came out to George's show in Arizona in 2001. Waylon was in a wheelchair. George was shocked to see how much Waylon's physical health had deteriorated, and it broke his heart to see his friend so weak and frail. Nevertheless, George asked, "Do you want to sing a song tonight?"

"Oh, no," Waylon said. "I'll stay right here backstage."

Of course, George introduced Waylon and Jessi to the crowd that evening so they could honor them, and the audience responded with a prolonged, thundering ovation. Jessi sang a song with George and then sang one her hits, one of George's favorites, "I'm Not Lisa."

After the show that night, George walked out with Waylon to his car. George leaned in close to Waylon and the two of them embraced and said goodbye.

When we got on our bus, George looked at me and somberly said, "We'll probably never see Waylon again."

George was right.

The day before Valentine's Day in 2002, we received the sad news that our good friend, Waylon Jennings, had passed away due to diabetes-related illnesses. Waylon and Jessi had been living in Chandler, Arizona, and the last few months of his life were bittersweet. He was inducted into the Country Music Hall of Fame in October 2001, and then two months later, doctors amputated his left foot as a result of the diabetes. Little more than two months after that, Waylon died. He was only sixty-four years old.

When we got the call, I asked George, "Do you want to go to Waylon's funeral?" I knew that George disliked attending funerals, but this was Waylon, one of George's best buddies. Maybe he would want to go.

"I don't believe I do," George said. "I want to remember Waylon the way I remember Waylon . . . as one big, strong man."

"Okay," I said. "We'll just send a big spread of flowers."

George called Jessi and expressed his sincere condolences. Jessi and I stayed in close touch for a long time after Waylon died. Jessi's strong faith in Jesus fortified her for the lonely days and nights ahead.

Losing Waylon at such an early age was shocking, but losing another of George's closest friends, Johnny Cash, within the year forced George to face his own mortality.

Johnny called George the first week in September 2003 and said, "I'd like for you to come out to the house, George. I think I'm about ready to go see the Lord and June." Johnny's wife of thirty-five years, June Carter Cash, had died in May of that year, and her death had hit Johnny hard. Although he was only seventy-one years of age, Johnny was convinced that it was his time to go as well.

"Oh, don't talk like that, son," George said. It made George sad to think of Johnny dying, but Johnny wasn't afraid.

"Well, Little Pal," Johnny replied, "you know when it's time. Why don't you come over and we'll talk." Johnny seemed absolutely at peace.

George and I went to visit Johnny at his home in Hendersonville, about fifteen miles north of downtown Nashville. When we entered the house, Johnny called out to us, his voice weaker than usual but still clear. "I'm in here, Little Pal," we heard him say. We walked deeper into Johnny's home and found that caregivers had moved him out of his and June's master bedroom to a cozy room on the first floor, a sort of study in which they had put a twin-sized bed. His face was drawn and his skin looked awful but his spirit was strong. We greeted each other and talked for a while about mundane matters. Then Johnny got down to it.

"George," he said, "it's time for me to go home."

George nodded. "Well, I've always heard that you'll know when it is time," he said.

"It's time," Johnny said. "I just wanted to see my Little Pal before I go."

"Well, I'm here," George said.

Johnny knew where he was going when he left this world, and he knew also that George had changed since the terrible auto accident in 1999. He had encouraged George and prayed for him so many times over the years. I think he simply wanted to encourage George one more time to stay on the narrow path.

A week later, on September 12, George's birthday, we got the call from Johnny's son, John Carter, that his dad had gone to heaven. George was in his den watching television when we received the news. I went in and quietly said to him, "Johnny's passed." George muted the sound on the television, leaned his head back in the chair, and looked up toward the ceiling, but he didn't say a word. He shed no tears and his face remained calm.

After a while, he spoke. "Today's my birthday, isn't it?" he said.

"Yeah . . ."

"Well, I'll be darned," he said quietly, as it struck him that Johnny had passed on his birthday.

We attended Johnny's funeral at First Baptist Church in Hendersonville, and it was a moving tribute to a great man. Along with the numerous stories told by the Cash family and friends, Kris Kristofferson sang, as did Emmylou Harris and Sheryl Crow. With a twinkle in his eye, Kris added, "Johnny Cash was Abraham Lincoln with a wild side . . . whose work in life has been an inspiration and salvation to so many people around the world."

Franklin Graham, whose father, Billy Graham, was in poor health, preached a moving, biblical salvation message, as Johnny would have wanted.

George remained solemn and stoic throughout.

As George grew older, he continued to keep an intense pace, performing concerts and recording new albums. Every so often, I'd say, "George, why don't we just quit and take it easy?"

"Honey, don't do that to me," he'd say. "I'll know when it's time to come home."

In 2008, we learned some hard lessons about trusting people. We received numerous invitations for George to endorse products, and we always considered them. George's name was on everything from bottled water, to sausage, to dog and cat foods, to events, and even resort communities. One such development was "The Legend," a neighborhood within the Country Crossings resort community in Enterprise, Alabama, about ninety miles from Panama City, Florida, that was promoted by our friend Ronnie Gilley.

We tried to evaluate every opportunity, so we weighed the Country Crossing opportunity carefully, and we really believed that Ronnie Gilley was looking out for our interests.

In 2008, George was listed as an official spokesperson for the development, along with several other country artists, such as Ronnie Dunn and the band Alabama. The developers gave George and me a home in the community and allowed us to stay there for free. They touted the fact that we lived there, although we spent only short periods of time actually living on the premises. The developers built the house, and I decorated it with our furniture—I loved interior decorating—but we didn't really own the home. We owned only our furniture in the house. The developers paid George to do interviews and to represent the property to the public. He occasionally played golf on or near the property, even though George didn't really consider himself a good golfer. Interestingly, he played guitar right-handed and did most everything else right-handed, but when he played golf, he played left-handed. "I can drive the ball a long way," George said, "but I can't putt."

Mostly, when we went to Country Crossing we ate barbecue—George loved that Southern barbecue. The property was lovely and our home was tastefully decorated, so it was refreshing when we could spend time there, even though most of our visits were relatively short-lived.

We still lived in Franklin. On Christmas Eve, the alarm sounded in the Alabama home, and I received a notice on my phone. I called Ronnie Gilley. "The alarm is going off in our house," I told him.

"I'll go check on it."

Ronnie called me back with a report that all was well. But when George and I returned to our home at Country Crossing, we discovered that someone had stolen all of our furniture.

Sadly, not long after that, Ronnie went to prison and the developers sold the property, including the home George and I had enjoyed. Ronnie served several years and then was released, but he must have been too embarrassed to ever see George and me after that. And I never did get our furniture back.

It's always disappointing when people you trust let you down, but George knew that he had let down a few people himself, so maybe that's why he was so forgiving.

In the recording studio, George experienced something similar. His daughter Georgette begged him to record a song with her that she had co-written. Titled "You and Me and Time," the song was a syrupy, lyrical apology for missing all the years together as father and daughter. Granted, almost any father who ever sacrificed time with his family to earn a living could identify with the words of the song, as could many daughters, but George didn't really care for it. Actually, he hated that song. To him, it was simply too smarmy—and that from the man who had made "He Stopped Loving Her Today" one of the most popular country songs of all time. But Georgette nagged him into the studio to record the song.

As we pulled up to the studio, George was complaining but I said, "Oh, just go do it."

George glared at me as he slammed the car door. He was still fuming as he walked toward producer Keith Stegall's studio, when he missed a step, tripped, and fell, breaking his arm. We had to call an ambulance to get George to the doctor's office.

"You see what you did," George said, blaming me for goading him into recording with Georgette.

For some reason, playing guitar proved difficult for George after that fall, and he never again played the guitar seriously on stage. The Jones Boys chided him, “Oh, it’s okay, George. You couldn’t play guitar anyhow!”

But Georgette got her song out on the air and parlayed it into promoting her own interests, which were not always aligned with George’s.

Nearly a decade after her father’s death, Georgette authorized the television series *George and Tammy*, based on a book she had written. The way the filmmakers represented George was appalling, and besides failing to capture his true personality, not to mention the public’s interest, the dramatization was rife with fabrications, mischaracterizations, errors, and downright lies. Maybe “You and Me and Time” will make it better.

22

Christmas at Nestledown

GEORGE WAS NEVER a big fan of Christmas, but his feelings had nothing to do with religion. He had sad memories of Christmas with Tammy Wynette that tainted the holiday for him. On Christmas Eve, Tammy had been crying and carrying on because she hadn't had a hit song in a while. She was all upset and kept him up all night long. George told me, "I was just mad. So the next morning I got up on Christmas Day and I left. I went to Billy's [Sherrill] and we went out on my houseboat on Old Hickory Lake. When I came back, my clothes were in a garbage bag on the front porch on Christmas Day. And she had changed the locks!"

Because of those bad memories, it took a long time for me to get George to like Christmas again, but once he did, he loved it.

Each year we lived at Nestledown, I decorated the whole downstairs of our home. I lined our main staircase with bright-red poinsettias all the way up and across the landing. I hung beautiful lights coming down the long stairway, and I decorated a large Christmas tree there. I put up two more Christmas trees in the living room, one in the kitchen, and one in the dining room. Every time I'd turn on all the decorative lights, George said something such as, "Man, that's beautiful. You did beautiful, honey."

The festive lights brightened his spirits and he'd go around the house singing Christmas songs—especially some of the old, familiar carols he'd learned as a boy in church.

I had always enjoyed decorating the interior of our house for the holidays, and at Nestledown, we had a large fence and gate at the front of our driveway. I decided to decorate that outdoors area with twinkling, colored lights for Christmas. I started with just a few decorations at the front gate. Playing off George's hit song "I Don't Need Your Rockin' Chair," I found a huge rocking chair in Alabama and had it brought to our home in Franklin. That big old oak chair weighed a ton!

We put the rockin' chair out at the front gate with a footstool so Santa Claus could climb up into it and be seated, greeting people from that enormous chair. People started coming from miles around to see the lights and to bring their kids to meet Santa in the rocking chair. Many fans thought that it was George himself playing Santa in that chair. It wasn't; it was usually anyone *but* George.

Each year, our display grew larger and more extravagant, and our decorations grew more extensive, as we added lights and ornaments in the yard and decorated every Bradford Pear tree lining our driveway, similar to what the staff at Opryland Hotel did every year. Before long, we had hundreds of thousands of lights and other large decorations included.

Cruising Nashville-area neighborhoods to view the Christmas displays is always a special aspect of the holiday season, so word soon got out that there was a spectacular array of decorations at the home of George and Nancy Jones. More and more people started driving through our neighborhood looking at the lights.

Wanting to do something good with all the attention, I put out the word, "If you come to see the lights, please bring a gift for the needy." Many of George's fans, as well as people who had never heard of George but loved the Christmas decorations, brought toys and gifts and food and we distributed it to various ministries around Nashville. They, in turn, distributed the gifts to needy families.

I thought, *Hmm, this is pretty good.* So I decorated the whole place, all the way from the front gate up the driveway to the front porch of our house. We bought and hung thousands and thousands of lights. I recruited two strong men to help me, George Lunn and our property caretaker, Mitch Latting. Of course, the Opryland Hotel had had an army of employees to put up the decorations; there were just three of us. We started in September and we wrapped trees all day long for days, hoping to get everything done in time for Thanksgiving, the official opening date we decided to turn on all the lights.

Each year, I purchased more decorations and lights. I enjoyed buying different things such as a huge pre-decorated Christmas tree that we placed out in the middle of the field. I bought a decorative helicopter with all sorts of colored lights displayed. And of course, we had Santa's sleigh and his reindeer flying through the sky.

I made numerous trips to Pigeon Forge, near Gatlinburg, where there was a business that featured unusual Christmas decorations. I bought everything they had that I didn't. Sometimes, the owner would say, "Ms. Jones, we have a great deal in the storage area in the back. We haven't put it out yet."

"I'll take it, man," I'd say, without even seeing the decorations. They were always unique and always delightful additions to our lights and ornaments. Almost anyone who ever saw the Christmas display on our property said it was absolutely gorgeous!

At one point, our friend Conway Twitty let it be known that he planned to close his theme park, Twitty City, located on the north side of Nashville, in Hendersonville. Conway was another Christmas fanatic, and for years, Twitty City boasted one of the most outstanding Christmas displays in the entire South. I bought all of Conway Twitty's lights from Twitty City and added them to our ever-growing display at Nestledown.

George was little help with the decorating, but he was funny. With crowds of people down at our front gate, he'd say, "Honey, I'm going out the back gate. This is ridiculous."

"Okay, fine with me," I told him.

People came from everywhere, from all over Nashville, from various parts of Tennessee, and from out of state—some came from as far away as Canada—just to drive through our neighborhood to enjoy looking at all the lights and decorations. To make it easier for fans and other folks to find us, we even allowed the local newspaper to print our home address and provide directions to our neighborhood.

We had to have state troopers posted at the entrance and exit of our subdivision to direct the traffic from Highway 96.

Of course, any time George and I went out to eat locally during the Christmas season, numerous people came by our table to offer their thanks and words of appreciation. We'd be eating dinner and folks would say, "Oh, George, the Christmas lights at your house are so pretty."

He'd smile that big Possum smile and say, "Oh, thank you so much."

Meanwhile, I'd be glaring at him, thinking, *You dirty dog, George! Taking credit for all the decorations and you never lifted a finger!* It was all in good fun, though. It might be snowing or pouring down freezing rain, and if a light set went out or was disconnected, I'd go out there taking that one off, plugging up another one. I did a lot of that.

When it came to his fans, George's attitude was usually, "Step right up, come on in," but the enormous crowds of Christmas revelers in front of our house wore him out. On one occasion, I convinced George to go down to the front gate to talk with people. Once. That was it. "I'm gonna kill you!" he growled facetiously like a bear. Talking with the thousands of people who showed up every night was not George's favorite thing to do. He always said, "I don't have to talk; my wife will tell you anything you want to know!" He preferred to stay inside the house, especially if there was a football game on television. But I loved going outside for several hours almost every night, talking with folks, helping Santa, receiving the gifts for the Tennessee Baptist Children's Home and other charitable ministries. It made our Christmas so much better than simply going out and buying more stuff that we didn't need for each other.

I stayed out there at the front gate with the people so much during the Christmas season, sometimes George called me from the house. He'd say, "Honey. What are you doing?"

"Well, George, you know what I'm doing."

"Yeah, but when are we going to eat?"

"I can't come up right now," I reminded him.

"Well, I need you to fix a chocolate pie," he said, totally oblivious to the fact that thousands of people were lined up and driving through our neighborhood in their cars to see "George Jones's Christmas lights."

"I'll be there in a minute," I lied. It was several hours before I went back inside. I'm a people person and I enjoyed talking with everyone. I'm glad "George's Christmas decorations" were a blessing to them.

One year, we even decorated the entire front entrance of our neighborhood, so as cars pulled off the highway, they were instantly enveloped by an array of colored lights. It was beautiful.

At our own expense—not the government's or even some organization's—and with the sweat of our own brows, we put up the huge display every year for twelve years. The lights came on at five o'clock in the afternoon and stayed on till midnight every day from Thanksgiving until New Year's Day. Sometimes, we'd still be eating Thanksgiving dinner, and as the afternoon skies darkened, the car horns outside began blowing. People were already out there waiting for the lights to come on. Our electric bill averaged around $1,800 per month because of the extra use, and of course we absorbed those costs as well.

The entire extravaganza didn't cost the taxpayers a dime, and we only did it to bring some joy to folks and to help some children in need. One time we learned that a whole bus was coming, filled with kids that the leaders referred to as "the underground kids." I hurriedly recruited "Santa's helpers" and we decorated the big old barn and had a special barbecue just for the children and their sponsors. I had presents wrapped for each one of the children, and they tore into them, their eyes sparkling and their voices squealing with joy.

I had George's band, the Jones Boys, come out to the barn and play some Christmas music, and some of those kids sang along with them. They got on our stage in the barn and sang up a storm. They were having a blast and I loved it. I said to George, "You know what? This is what God wanted."

"Yeah, yer right, Hon," he said.

It was wonderful to witness their enthusiasm and exuberance. It was a chore to get that done, but most of those kids had next to nothing, and some had no family with whom they could celebrate Christmas, so we enjoyed having them celebrate with us.

The public festivities at Nestledown came to a grinding halt when a guy that had recently moved into our neighborhood griped and complained about all the commotion and the traffic. His house was near the entrance of the subdivision where our property was located, so every car full of cheerful families coming in to see the lights had to pass by his house. Apparently, that irritated him. Especially when he had trouble getting out of his driveway. I called him Mr. Scrooge.

He decided to canvas the neighborhood with a petition prohibiting exorbitant displays of Christmas lights—or some such thing. His efforts were obviously aimed in our direction.

I confronted him one day and said, "You don't have to do all of that. My electricity bill is so high during the Christmas season because of our display. I'll just stop it."

That was the last time we put on the extravagant Christmas celebration, although we always decorated the interior of our home beautifully and had a greatly reduced version of Christmas lights outdoors.

Sad, isn't it? That one grumpy person could steal the joy from so many. On the other hand, just a few of us had brightened the Christmas season for thousands of people for more than twelve years, so I guess the tradeoffs were worth it.

And to see the bright eyes and the expressions of joy on the faces of those children . . . ahh, Jesus and Jones did good.

23

The Power of the Possum

George's reputation, being known as No Show Jones, trailed behind him throughout his career, even after he had established a consistent new track record in which promoters could count on him. He'd smile about the "no shows," but as George looked back, he sometimes felt pangs of remorse for letting down his fans. He knew he'd never live down his controversial past, and he never worried about the performance fees he missed or the millions of dollars of lawsuits that were filed against him. But he did feel badly that hard-working families had taken their time and money to attend one of his shows where he may have been too drunk to perform or simply had not shown up.

His fans' loyalty, however, was astounding. They forgave him again and again. Sure, they'd boo and make a fuss when they learned George was not in the building at a show venue, but they always forgave him and most came back to see him when we booked a make-up show, or the next time George came to town. George never took the love of his fans for granted, and as he aged, he appreciated them even more.

We were together almost constantly during 2013. George had been struggling with health issues, and he seemed to know that this time his body was not going to recover. He called our business managers and lawyers and said, "Now don't you let anyone take advantage of Nancy." I appreciated George watching out for me. He knew he was dying, and he didn't want anyone to hurt me.

George had taught me a lot—about the music business, about cars, about people that I could trust and those who were not trustworthy. Oddly enough, George had taught me to have patience (I'm still working on that one!). I could be brusque because I was always in a hurry to get something done. I've always been rather hyper with a hot temper. George taught me to be calm and to take one day at a time. Moreover, when somebody did George or me wrong, I was quick to write them off. I didn't want to have anything further to do with them. But George would say, "Now, honey, be patient with them. No matter what people do to you, kill 'em with kindness. Give them another chance." George knew that he had been forgiven much, so he was quick to forgive.

As his life on earth faded, George was ready to go. He emphasized that to me, saying, "If God wants to take me, I'm going to heaven and I'm ready."

It made me sad to hear him talk that way, but it also made me glad to know that George was looking forward to heaven.

* * * * * *

We celebrated George's eightieth birthday with a party attended by numerous music notables at Rippy's, a downtown Nashville restaurant known for its barbeque. A cross section of musicians celebrated George that night—everyone from Travis Tritt to Bryan White, from songwriter Billy Yates to gospel artist Guy Penrod. Someone even decorated a cute Possum cake and presented it to George and me.

George had carried that nickname through much of his career, after a radio deejay dubbed him "the Possum," because he said that when he looked at George's face from the side, his nose looked like that of a possum. I'm not sure that George ever agreed with him—at first, he hated the label, but he later embraced the nickname nonetheless. When Ralph Emery, the popular radio and television show host, picked up on the name and started calling George "Possum," the world of country music followed suit. "Well, how about that?" George said. "I've got me a nickname." I thought the nickname Possum was the cutest thing ever. I guess other people did too, because friends and fans called him by the name for the rest of his life.

George was overwhelmed by all the love and attention. "It's wonderful to know that you've got friends left that still love you," he said, "and I love them too."

Later that night, we went to the Grand Ole Opry's Birthday Bash for George, featuring some of George's friends, including Alan Jackson, Joe Diffie, Jamey Johnson, and Lee Ann Womack. The show closed out with a rousing rendition of "I Don't Need Your Rockin' Chair," with George singing along with Alan, Jamey, and Montgomery Gentry.

"I'm just going to try to live the last few years and work a little bit and enjoy myself," he told everyone. But then in case anyone may have gotten the impression that George was done performing, he quickly added, "I'd like to do some duets again, like some of the funny things that Ernest Tubb and Red Foley did a long time ago."

Over the years, George recorded with a wide variety of duet partners, including James Taylor, B. B. King, Elvis Costello, Willie Nelson, Randy Travis, Emmylou Harris, Linda Ronstadt, and even The Rolling Stones' Keith Richards. He recorded an entire album with pop star Gene Pitney in 1965. Oh, yes; there was also that woman named Tammy, with whom George had a number one country hit ("We're Gonna Hold On") while they were married, and two more ("Golden Ring" and "Near You") after they were divorced.

Nobody believed that George was going to slow down—nobody but me. I knew he didn't have much choice.

George turned eighty-one years of age on September 12, 2012. He was hospitalized numerous times in 2012 and early 2013 with various respiratory infections, forcing him to cancel shows—this time with good reason—and reschedule. Shortly after George turned eighty-one, one of our grandkids, Breann, asked him to speak to the grade school kids in her Music History class. George consented and told the kids how he had learned to play guitar on his own. He encouraged the kids to maintain their focus. "Your mind needs to stay very clear," he told them. "Because [if not] you'll grow up with the wrong people around you and you'll never get your life straightened up, unless some good miracle comes along." That was George's subtle way of discouraging the students from drinking or doing drugs. It was his first time addressing a class of school kids, and although they couldn't relate to some of his stories, he enjoyed it and we hoped to do more. Unfortunately, he never got the chance. "The best thing that ever happened to me was the good Lord and marrying a good woman," he told the class. "I think they got together and straightened me up."

George maintained an upbeat attitude even in the face of his deteriorating health. We celebrated our thirtieth wedding anniversary on March 4, 2013. We didn't make a big deal about our three decades together; we simply invited our daughters, Sherry and Adina, to go out to eat with us. None of us could have imagined that we were celebrating

George's and my last anniversary together.

George and I both had known he was going downhill. He prepared to die as best he could, even asking to have our pastor visit him one last time. George knew he was dying, so he told me almost every night, "Don't cry. Be strong. Remember all the things I've taught you."

I told him, "George, I'm going to do everything I can to preserve your legacy. You are a music *icon*."

George looked back at me and smiled. "Honey, I can't even spell that word!" he quipped. "I just want you to go and enjoy life. I've ruined so much of your life."

"No, you didn't," I told him. "It's been fun!"

He never lost his sense of humor and still loved zinging me. One night near the end, when George was getting real weak, I crawled up in the bed with him. He said, "Honey, you're gonna have to get out of the bed. You're too fat!"

He returned to Nashville's Vanderbilt University Medical Center again on April 18 with fever and irregular blood pressure. For a while, he seemed to grow stronger and we thought the doctors might discharge him to go home. Then after further tests, the doctor looked at me across George's hospital bed and said, "He can't go home."

"Yeah, I can," George said weakly.

The doctor looked directly at George. "No, George. You can't."

We all wanted to believe that George would rebound and be back to normal after a few weeks of rest. He had bounced back from the valley of the shadow of death so many times before, we almost took his recovery for granted. But not this time.

George's respiratory problems continued. He was having difficulty breathing and wasn't doing well, so at one point, as I watched George's condition in the hospital bed, I asked him, "Do you want me to call in your kids?"

"No," he gasped.

"George, are you sure? Please, let me call all your kids here to your hospital room so you can say goodbye."

He said, "If you do that, I'm going to kick you out of the hospital!"

He may not have had much strength left, but he was adamant about that point. He did not want to see the three of his adult children who he felt had used him and betrayed him.

I knew he was stubborn, but I didn't want him to have any regrets at this point. "George, are you sure?"

"If you ask me one more time, *you* can go to the house," he said bluntly.

"That's mean," I said.

"I mean it!" George responded. I didn't ask again.

George seemed to sense that he would be leaving us soon, that he was going to die. I kept telling him, "Oh, no, you're not. Stop that." But George knew.

George used to get so mad because Georgette, Jeffrey, and Brian were so mean to Susan. They never acknowledged her. They hadn't seen Susan in decades.

One day, George said, "Bring me a tablet and a pen and an envelope."

"What for?" I asked.

He said, "I'm going to write a letter to Susan. And I'm gonna write a letter to Jennifer, too." Jennifer was Susan's daughter who was pregnant at the time and about to give birth to twins of her own. George said, "But I don't want them to see the letters or know about them. And you give them to 'em when I die."

"I will," I promised through my tears. And I did.

I never asked George what was in those letters. They were

LEFT: Getting ready for an award show was great fun!

ABOVE: Attending an award show with George was always an adventure!

We attended Red Foxx's show in Vegas, and he cleaned up his act just for me!

George enjoyed playing in the country music softball games during Fan Fair and CMA Fest.

We were an affectionate couple!

When George was sober, he was the best man I ever knew.

The entry to our home at Nestledown Farms.
George bid against me on the horse
and other life-sized characters.

We enjoyed having more than one hundred acres
at Nestledown Farms.

ABOVE: Christmas was special at Nestledown.

LEFT: Being silly at Christmastime.

Tanya Tucker and George were buddies.

Tanya was afraid I'd be mad when
she drove George home drunk.
She was right! But I still loved her.

George's crumpled vehicle after slamming into a bridge.

Vestal Goodman and George sang gospel music every day for a week after his accident. Her prayers helped his healing.

After George miraculously survived the horrendous car crash, the county named the highway for him.

Our dog Mandy got thrown in jail with Adina and me while the police "interrogated" George.

To George and me, Bandit was almost human.

George and I loved our dog Bandit so much, we named our record company after him.

George had a great sense of humor, and
he made me laugh more than any comedian!

LEFT: At the close of George's tribute concert, Alan Jackson brought me on stage as the crowd sang, "He Stopped Lovin' Her Today."

BELOW: After George's funeral, Lisa Marie Presley came to visit. She was like another daughter to me.

The Oak Ridge Boys have helped me maintain George's legacy.

Jamey Johnson set the tone for the "Still Playin' Possum" shows.

LEFT: Even after the museum opened, we worked night and day to make it a success. RIGHT: Fans were often surprised to find me cleaning the museum, but it had my name on it, so I wanted it to be excellent.

Kirk West stayed by my side as my medical advocate during my three-month hospitalization. For the next year and a half, he helped me back to full recovery.

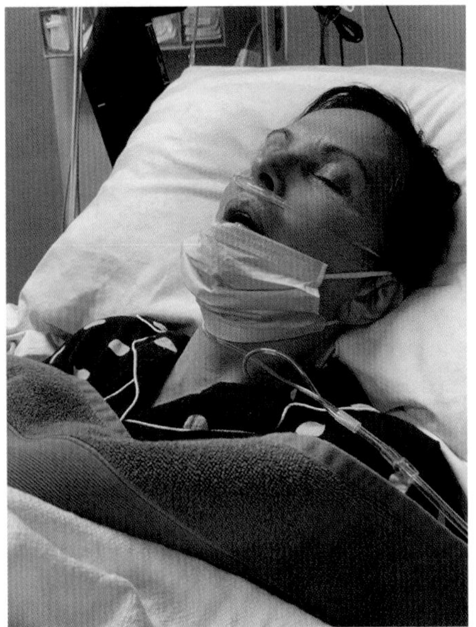

LEFT: COVID-19 nearly killed me, but God kept me alive.
RIGHT: I went from 134 pounds to less than one hundred.

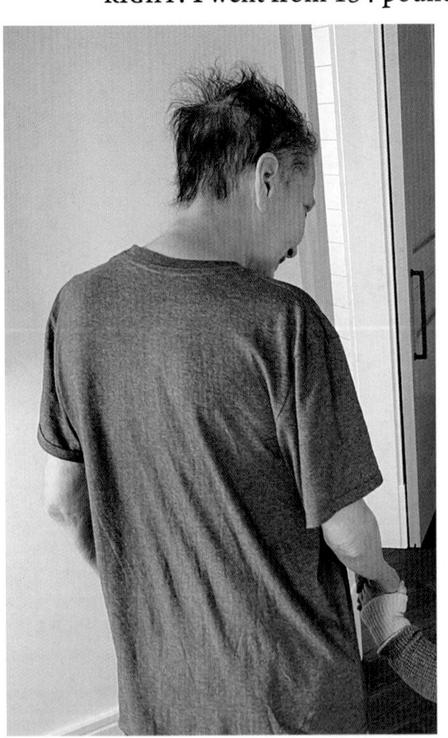

LEFT: Much of my hair fell out during the three months I was hospitalized.
RIGHT: Home at last and praising the Lord!

George and I always had so much fun!

I promised George that I would keep his legacy alive, and I always will.

between George and his daughter and his granddaughter.

It wasn't until nearly 2023 that Susan shared with me the contents of the letter from George. He had written to her, "I love you, Susan."

* * * * * *

Kirt Webster, whose friendship with George and me spanned more than twenty years, including eight years as our primary publicist, stopped by the hospital before going on a business trip across the country. Kirt seemed worried about George's condition. "George, should I stay?" he asked pointedly.

"Naah," George answered. "Go ahead."

Kirt did, but he later wished that he hadn't.

On April 24, George slipped into a semi-comatose condition and never fully regained consciousness. The nurses administered strong medications to keep him from experiencing unnecessary pain. The downside to the medications was that George was no longer communicative. His eyes remained closed, he didn't say a word, and his condition continued to debilitate. He'd been at Vanderbilt University Medical Center for several days suffering from complications in his lungs. The respiratory problems had a big medical name but his personal physician, Dr. Milstone, described it to me as "arthritis of the lungs," making it difficult for George to breathe.

On Sunday morning, I stood at the foot of George's bed along with his doctor. George hadn't spoken hardly at all for days and seemed unable to speak. But then all of a sudden, his eyes popped wide open! I started to step toward him, but the doctor sort of held me back.

Then as clear as I'd ever heard him, George looked up and spoke in his deep, resonant voice, "Well, hello there. I've been looking for you. My name is George Jones."

I believe he was formally introducing himself to God. A few moments later, George was gone.

Of course, God knew George long before George knew God. Before George was even born, God had his days planned out, although George would have been the first to admit that he had messed up plenty of times. Nevertheless, his faith was real, and in the early morning hours of April 26, 2013, George Jones went to heaven.

A week or so earlier, I had been crying and George had called me on it. "Honey, what are you crying for? I've had eighty-one good years, some that I messed up, sure, but now I'm going to heaven."

I knew he was right, and that I would see George again one day—in heaven.

24

Honoring George

I SENT WORD TO KIRT almost as quickly as I did family members because I knew that, as George's longtime publicist, Kirt would want to be involved in helping to get the news out as well as putting together George's funeral. And I needed his help to guide me.

He immediately sent text messages to Garth Brooks, Brad Paisley, Little Jimmy Dickens, and a few others, informing them of George's passing before the news got out to the public. Garth Brooks and Brad Paisley put out the initial press releases informing the country music community of George's passing. By noon that day, Kirt issued a formal press release to the rest of the world.

Brad Paisley sent out a message on Twitter, letting fans know, "My friend, the greatest singer of all time, has passed. To those who knew him, our lives were full. To those of you who don't, discover him now."[4]

I noticed that Brad did not say "the greatest country singer," or "the greatest singer of country music." No, whether Brad had intended to phrase it that way or not, he stated it perfectly: "the greatest singer of all time has passed."

Merle Haggard brought it back home: "The world has lost the greatest country singer of all time."

"Heaven better get ready for George Jones," Alan Jackson said online after receiving the news of George's passing. "He will always be the greatest singer of real country music. There will never be another."

The entire nation seemed to want to say goodbye to George. I always knew that George was highly esteemed, but not even I anticipated the enormous outpouring of love we received from his friends and fans all around the world. In a lighter moment at Nestledown, I joked, "Phones are ringing that I didn't even know we had!"

Following George's death, Kirt, who George affectionately referred to as "Big Daddy," worked closely with me to put together a fitting farewell to George. Already top country music personalities were contacting us with messages such as, "I'm available. Just let me know what you want me to do." Kirt and I pondered how we might squeeze in the many artists and speakers who wanted to honor George.

I told Kirt, "We have to have Vince Gill. We have to have Sweet Pea." George loved Vince as a son. Vince responded affirmatively almost immediately, as did Brad Paisley, Kid Rock, and so many others. Every person that we asked to participate responded, "Yes, what do you need me to do?"

From the outset, I wanted George's fans to be able to attend his homegoing celebration. I felt that George would want it that way. Rather than a stuffy, private funeral, he'd want his friends and fans to gather, pay their respects, and remember the good times.

At the same time, we needed some sort of private visitation where the family and close friends could have a more personal opportunity to say goodbye to George. We decided to hold that private visitation the night before a big public event at the Opry House. George's sons, Jeffrey and Brian, came to honor their father, as did George's daughter, Georgette. We waved and acknowledged each other from across the crowded funeral home, and Brian walked over and hugged me. Not surprisingly, fans soon discovered the location of the private visitation and gathered outside the funeral home in droves. When someone told me that a number of fans were holding vigil outside the funeral home, I said, "Well, invite them in."

In minutes, a long line of fans began streaming through the funeral home, respectfully sharing their stories with country music celebrities and with me. As exhausting as it was greeting and talking to so many people during our family time of grieving, I couldn't help thinking, *George would have wanted it this way.*

We held the public funeral service at the Grand Ole Opry House on May 2, 2013. There was never any real question about where the funeral service should be held. The Grand Ole Opry House was home for George. He had performed there hundreds of times over his career.

Somebody told me that fans began lining up outside the Opry House the day before the service. A line of people waiting to pay their respects stretched all the way out into the parking lot and for hundreds of yards down the sidewalk. When the doors opened, more than four thousand friends and fans from far and wide crowded into the world-famous venue.

A sadness hung over the Opry House, yet there was also a spirit of triumph. George had fought the fight and had finished the race. Many people in the room were Christians who believed that death was not the end. "We grieve but we don't grieve as those who have no hope," the Apostle Paul had taught. So although we were all sad that George was gone, most of us believed that we would see him again in heaven. Because of that, people felt comfortable in laughing or telling funny stories about George. It wasn't a wake; it was sad but still a wonderful celebration of George's life.

Artists presenting humorous or deeply emotional personal stories about George and tribute performances included Randy Travis,

Brad Paisley, Ronnie Milsap, Vince Gill, Patty Loveless, Wynonna Judd, and Alan Jackson.

Former First Lady Laura Bush spoke, as did Tennessee Governor Bill Haslam, former governor of Arkansas Mike Huckabee, CBS reporter and on-air personality Bob Schieffer, Kenny Chesney, and Barbara Mandrell.

Garth Brooks, Trisha Yearwood, Loretta Lynn, Jamey Johnson, and other notable music artists surrounded me on the front row. Our friends and Opry stars John Conlee and Jeanne Pruett sat nearby. The stage was decorated with several large photographs of George, a large rocking chair, and gorgeous displays of flowers, including a special butterfly-shaped arrangement from Dolly Parton.

The service began at 10:00 a.m. as WSM on-air personality Eddie Stubbs welcomed the crowd to the Opry House and then introduced Tanya Tucker, who opened the program by reading the poem "I'm Free," before leading into one of George's favorite hymns, "The Old Rugged Cross," sung by The Imperials.

Our dear friend and former Opry announcer Keith Bilbrey assisted Eddie Stubbs as host for the service. Always kind, Keith had known George through his nightmare years, as well as the years since he had committed his life to Christ, and Keith had prayed for him all the way. He shared his love for George then introduced Governor Bill Haslam, who spoke from his heart about George. The governor concluded by saying, "Tennessee will never stop loving George Jones."

Our pastor, Mike Wilson, helped set the tone by telling the crowd, "It's not a goodbye. It's an 'I'll see you soon.'"

Compliments of George flowed freely that day. Referring to George as an American icon (it was all I could do to keep from smiling), Governor Mike Huckabee said, "If Norman Rockwell had been a singer, he would have sounded just like George Jones."

In one of the more poignant moments in the proceedings, Randy Travis sang a deeply moving rendition of "Amazing Grace," with only his acoustic guitar as accompaniment in the cavernous Opry House. None of us could have imagined at the time that we were hearing the pure, traditional country sound of Randy Travis for one of the last times, as two months later, he suffered a heart infection leading to a debilitating stroke.

The Oak Ridge Boys shared "Farther Along," and Travis Tritt struggled to get through Kris Kristofferson's "Why Me."

Charlie Daniels spoke of George's universal appeal. "He sang for us all," Charlie said. "Happy, unhappy, and everybody in between. George had a song for everybody."

Bob Schieffer spoke of George's youth as well as some of his public struggles with alcohol and drugs. As moderator of CBS's popular program *Face the Nation*, Schieffer had interviewed George in 2009. He told the Opry audience that he got the feeling then that becoming a country music legend was "a surprise to George, and he never quite believed any of it."

He said, "God made just one like him, but aren't we glad He did?" Bob offered a kind compliment: "If 'He Stopped Loving Her Today' saved his career, it would take a good woman to save his life, and it did with Nancy," he said, nodding in my direction. I appreciated Bob's kind words.

Vince Gill—who George always referred to as Sweet Pea—brought us all to tears as he recalled, "George taught us all to sing with a broken heart," and then, joined by Patty Loveless, he attempted to sing "Go Rest High on That Mountain." *Attempted* to sing, because Vince broke down in tears and Patty placed her hand on his shoulder to help him through. Garth and Trisha stood up respectfully and Adina leaned over and embraced me. The audience spontaneously rose to its feet as though to help Vince express what we all wanted to say. Tears flowed freely at the Opry House.

Brad Paisley's eyes welled with tears as he said, "I'm lucky enough to have met George when he had gotten right, beat the demons, found Nancy, and found God." He spoke to younger country music fans and encouraged them to search out George's music and "find out what this ruckus is about. It's worth it." Brad then sang "Me and Jesus," the song I heard George belting out at the top of his lungs in the hospital after his pivotal auto crash when he slammed into the bridge near our home in 1999. Brad and his wife, Kimberly Williams-Paisley, were so kind, caring, and comforting to me.

Kenny Chesney recalled hearing George's voice for the first time while he was in his grandmother's kitchen. One of the first of George's songs that Kenny heard was "Who's Gonna Chop My Baby's Kindlin'?"

Kenny's voice quivered with emotion as he said of George, "He was a larger-than-life figure I thought I would never meet, much less become friends with." Kenny said that he loved George like a father, and "I wanted to come here today to thank George for being George, and for showing me how to be human."

Then before leaving the stage, Kenny turned abruptly back toward me where I was seated on the front row and said, "If you need help chopping kindling, I will be there." And I knew that if I needed Kenny, he would be there for me.

Many speakers extolled the wonders of George's voice and his ability to communicate a song. "When our heavenly Father created George, He gifted him with a magnificent, supremely unparalleled voice," Barbara Mandrell said. She recalled meeting George when she was a thirteen-year-old steel guitar prodigy and he asked her to sit in during his set. "George left his lasting imprint on my heart," Barbara said, "all our hearts." She then pointed us to a greater truth. "He sang for you and me. Now he's singing in glory for the One who created him and gave him that voice."

Former First Lady Laura Bush told of growing up in Texas and listening to George's music. She admitted, "My friends and I must have put a thousand quarters in the jukebox to listen to 'The Race Is On.'" Always sophisticated and classy, in her quiet manner Mrs. Bush evoked some tension-easing laughter when she mentioned that her husband, former President George W. Bush, often listened to George's song "White Lightning" while working out on the treadmill.

George's friend Wynonna Judd sang the classic "How Great Thou Art," a song she had sung at Tammy Wynette's funeral in 1998.

Pastor Mike Wilson offered a benediction, and then Alan Jackson took the stage to perform one of the greatest, yet one of the saddest, renditions of "He Stopped Loving Her Today." All over the Opry House, the audience spontaneously rose to its feet, as though reverently listening to the national anthem. I suppose, in some ways, we were.

When Alan broke off the last note, he removed his white cowboy hat and held it over his heart, as he said through tearful eyes, "We love you, George."

I think Alan spoke for all of us that day.

The service honoring George had lasted more than two hours and forty minutes, yet few people left the Opry House before the final note was sung. Most people didn't want to leave even after that.

As George's casket was wheeled up the center aisle, followed by our family members, George's golden voice filled the Opry House one more time, with "When the Last Curtain Falls." The audience stood in silent respect as George Jones passed by for the final time.

25

Married to the King

I SPENT THE NEXT few months trying to get my bearings. As much as I had known that George was dying, once he was gone, I missed him terribly. I missed the sound of his voice echoing through the large rooms at Nestledown. Instead, our home was filled with the sound of telephones ringing, as people expressed their condolences. Our once vibrant home now seemed like a museum with George Jones memorabilia all over it. Friends stayed in touch and many visited often, but at night, when George and I had often snuggled in bed watching movies, the loneliness grabbed me by the heart and wouldn't let go.

I welcomed friends, old and new, to visit any time. Just to hear their voices in our home brightened my spirits.

One friend who surprised me by visiting was Lisa Marie Presley, the daughter of Elvis and Priscilla Presley. George and Elvis had met in 1955, when George had already scored a big hit with "Why Baby Why" and Elvis was shaking things up with his raucous rendition of rockabilly music. They were moving in different musical directions, but they performed together in Shreveport on the Louisiana Hayride, a venue known as the Deep South's version of the Grand Ole Opry. Indeed, many Opry stars and future country music stars cut their musical teeth on the stage of the Louisiana Hayride.

To George, Elvis seemed friendly but shy, even though he was surrounded by people. Elvis was just a pimply-faced kid, but when he went onstage at the Hayride and did all his shaking, with the girls in the audience screaming and hollering, that made George jealous.

George said, "Hmm, if you can make 'em holler, I'll show you what I'm going to do." He took the stage and performed the upbeat song "Long Tall Sally," and before long, George was shaking all over the stage. So the girls were screaming for George too.

At the intermission, Elvis tried to bring up the subject politely. "Um, George, I do rock and roll; you do country."

George looked back at him and deadpanned, "Well, then what are you doing on this stage, son?"

Elvis went back onstage and shook all over again. That bugged George. "He just don't listen," George said to Elvis's soon-to-be manager, Colonel Tom Parker.

Colonel Parker said, "Now, George, the boy's just starting out. Can't you ease up a bit?"

"Mm-hmm," George nodded. "You need to go find him a rock and roll stage. He's on my country stage."

George wasn't trying to be mean. He just couldn't understand why anyone would book Elvis on a country show such as the Hayride, but the audience loved Elvis and before long, it seemed the whole world did too.

Years later, I bumped into Lisa Marie backstage at the Opry in Nashville. She was not known as the hugging kind, an outgoing woman who was easy to get to know, but for some reason, we hit it off immediately. She held onto my hand, squeezing me as though she were a little girl holding her mama's hand. I liked her but I also felt sorry for her.

I could tell that she was deeply troubled. I thought, *That's one sad girl there.* We exchanged phone numbers that night, but I didn't really keep in touch until I heard from her after George died.

Long before that, when Lisa Marie was pursuing her own music career, she was scheduled to do a show at the Cannery in Nashville. Tony Brown, head of MCA Nashville, invited me to attend and I gladly accepted. I sat at a front table with Priscilla Presley, and I think we talked to each other more than we listened to the music that evening. She was just so sweet and humble, the kind of person who makes everyone around her feel better.

After Lisa Marie's show, Priscilla asked me, "Do you wanna go back and get some pictures?"

"I sure do," I answered.

"Well, come on," Priscilla said. She grabbed me by the hand and guided me backstage, where we took photos together with Lisa Maria. Priscilla and I stayed in touch through the years.

After George's funeral, Lisa Marie wanted to come to visit, and I was delighted to have her. Lisa Marie and her mom had drifted apart a bit after Lisa Marie had married Michael Jackson in 1994, without informing Priscilla before it came out in the news. The marriage lasted little more than two years. Maybe because of the previous tension in their mother-daughter relationship, Lisa Marie regarded me as a substitute mom for a while. I treated her just as I would one of my own daughters. It wasn't a competition. I was glad to be there for her. I felt that I was helping her, and she was helping me. Priscilla often sent me text messages with the theme, "Thank you for being a mom to my daughter."

Lisa Marie was at the house one day a short time after George's funeral when Jon Bon Jovi called. Lisa Marie answered the phone and then looked at me. She said, "Bon Jovi's on the phone. Do you want to talk to him?"

"Who's Bon Jovi?" I asked. Lisa Marie chuckled, rolled her eyes, and handed me the phone.

It never occurred to me that the rock star was calling to offer his condolences about George's passing. "Hello, this is Nancy Jones," I said into the phone and Jon Bon Jovi introduced himself. I could not recall whether we had ever met previously, but he spoke so kindly and respectfully about George.

He said, "George Jones was the greatest singer ever. It doesn't matter the genre. He had the best voice of any singer in the world."

"Thank you, Jon," I said. "That is very kind of you."

"I'm so sorry," he said. "You know, I just love George Jones, and man, what a voice he had."

I said, "Well, I appreciate it." We talked for a while longer, and when I hung up, Lisa Marie said, "I can't believe you didn't know who Bon Jovi was!"

I said, "George knew lots of music folks, but I didn't know some of them."

She thought that was hilarious.

"But I know him now," I told her with a smile.

On Friday, June 7, 2013, little more than six weeks after George went to heaven, I participated in the CMA Fest in Nashville at a special "Remembering George Jones" panel discussion. Scheduled on the dais along with me were Randy Travis, John Rich, Jamey Johnson, and Bobby Birkhead, George's longtime drummer and road manager.

I was nervous about appearing in public so soon after George's passing and even more anxious about speaking in a public forum. I never wanted to be out front when it came to talking onstage.

While eating at a restaurant between Franklin and downtown Nashville, I received a call from Priscilla Presley. She knew that Lisa

Marie and I had struck up a closer relationship after George died. I told her that I was on my way downtown to speak at the CMA Fest event. I said, "I don't know how to do all this. I've never liked a microphone. I've never talked to this many people."

Priscilla understood. "You and I have something in common," she said. "You were married to the King of Country Music. I was married to the King of Rock and Roll. So let me tell you what you do," Priscilla offered. "You hold your head up high."

"Ahh, okay." I said hesitantly.

"And when you walk out on that stage, don't look at anybody," Priscilla suggested. "Look straight ahead and look over top of the audience. They'll think you are looking at them, but keep your gaze focused above their heads. By looking above them, you won't be so nervous, and you can do it."

I thanked Priscilla for her public speaking tip, and we talked all the way as I was driven into town. She was amazingly encouraging.

At the "Remembering George Jones" event, I took Priscilla's advice, especially at the beginning of the session. I looked out at the large audience, but above their heads. After a while, I grew more comfortable and less nervous. Each person on the panel shared emotional, sometimes funny, sometimes poignant stories of their interactions with George. I tried to keep matters lighthearted, sharing the story about getting in the car with George wearing only my underwear. Other stories were more emotional for me, especially when I shared George's final words in the hospital with the audience. I told them about George being in a semi-comatose condition for several days, when suddenly, he woke up and said, "'Well, hello there. I've been looking for you. I'm George Jones.'"

I told the audience, "I believe he was introducing himself to God. A few moments later, George was gone."

It was an emotional moment for the audience, and for me as well. It was also a personal milestone, as I now knew that I could speak about George in public without emotionally falling apart.

Randy Travis had gone into the studio a few days after George died and had recorded a new song: "Tonight I'm Playin' Possum." He performed the song for the first time that afternoon in front of the large crowd of fans and music industry folks, and later that night on the mainstage at Nissan Stadium. In addition to singing "Amazing Grace" at George's memorial service, "Tonight I'm Playin' Possum" was one of the last full songs he'd ever record and sing in public before having a decimating stroke the following month.

It was a few years later before I heard from Lisa Marie Presley again. She wanted to move to Nashville to further pursue her music career and also to escape the clutches of Scientology. I was glad to help her.

We spent a lot of time together, going out to dinner frequently, going to doctors' appointments, and once again, she seemed to regard me as her "Nashville Mother." With good reason, too, because I wasn't bashful about letting her know when I disapproved of some of her actions. For instance, I introduced her to Kid Rock at an album listening party. Privately, I told Lisa Marie, "Kid is a good guy, and we are friends, but don't go to his home." Kid Rock was known to host some rowdy parties, and I didn't think that would be the best environment for Lisa Marie.

"Oh, now you sound like my mama," she said.

Sure enough, she joined the party crowd, and it didn't turn out well for her.

Lisa Marie trusted me and knew that I'd tell her the truth, even if she didn't want to hear it. She'd often call or text me at two or three o'clock in the morning, depressed and discouraged that she'd gotten into another mess. On more than a few occasions, I told her, "What you need is a good butt whipping! You've got to grow up and quit doing things like that. You need to stop pitying yourself." I threatened to turn her over my knee and spank her!

She received my harsh words well because she knew that I loved her.

Eventually Lisa Marie moved back West, but I wished she would have stayed with us in Nashville. Like millions of people around the world, I would be shocked and devastated in 2023, when Lisa Marie Presley died of a stroke and heart attack at only fifty-four years of age. I felt so sorry for her dear children, her husband, and especially for Priscilla. Although she and Lisa Marie had their differences, that was still her precious daughter and she died far too young.

I can't help but wonder if her story may have turned out differently had she remained in a more positive environment.

26

Playin' Possum! The Final No-Show

I knew I needed to stay busy so when Kirt Webster suggested that we start putting together George's monument unveiling and his memorial concert, I was ready to get back to work.

Long before his death, George and I had planned for his farewell concert on November 22, 2013. He knew that he was slowing down, so he had planned to "officially retire" and come off the road. He had always told me, "Mama, don't ask me to come off the road too soon. That would kill me. I'll know when it's time to come home."

And he did.

Earlier in 2013, Kirt, George, and I got together to go over details for George's farewell concert at Nashville's Bridgestone Arena and the events surrounding it, including numerous interviews with the media. Since George was never one who enjoyed doing interviews, Kirt and I were both surprised when he so readily agreed to nearly everything we suggested. I knew instinctively that George was not going to do all those interviews that Kirt was setting up.

"Go ahead and set 'em up, son," George told Big Daddy.

But I knew better.

At one point, Kirt even asked George why he was being so cooperative and conciliatory, agreeing to everything we requested.

George smiled and said, "'Cause I'm not going to be there."

I think he knew, and in late April, George was proved right. He would not be there for his own farewell concert, which we named, "Playin' Possum! The Final No Show."

We meticulously planned for nearly a week-long celebration, beginning on November 18, 2013, with the unveiling of George's monument at Woodlawn Memorial Park, the cemetery where George was buried.

Prior to the unveiling, I announced the creation of a scholarship at Middle Tennessee State University in honor of George. In making the first large donation to the fund, I wanted to establish the scholarship to help struggling students pursue their musical and creative dreams. The second substantial contribution to the scholarship fund for young musicians came from Garth Brooks and Trisha Yearwood.

I told the media, "George would have liked the fact that MTSU attracts so many first-generation college students, as well as students who face financial challenges. Like George, they are hardworking folks who are determined to make their dreams a reality."

Over the years, I stayed in contact with the university, continuing the scholarship, and visiting in the classroom, discussing George, his life, and his music with the students and faculty. In 2023, Professor Odie Blackmon assigned his students to read and report on George's life story. A female student, Hadley Coil, shared her insights from her paper with me: "George admits that he surrounded himself with people who weren't the best influence, making it easy to fall into an addiction trap. He claims it wasn't religion or rehabilitation that saved him, but the love from Nancy that made him want to be a better version of himself . . . George achieved something miraculous . . . he made me feel like I knew him."[5]

I smiled as I read the young woman's paper. I knew that George's legacy would continue to have an impact on future generations.

George was buried, as he had wished, in the center of the sixty-eight plots we owned at Woodlawn Cemetery in Nashville. Seven months later, we erected a large headstone monument on a granite arch with "JONES" etched in it, and the words "He Stopped Loving Her Today" inscribed in large capital letters below a shelf-like ledge covering the top of it. Below the shelf was a guitar, a photo of George and me etched in granite, and another granite stone bearing the title "The Possum." The pillars on each side had George's biographical information and a place for mine. It was a magnificent structure and we dedicated it with a graveside ceremony on November 18, 2013, the opening of the week of special tributes for George, culminating in a memorial concert at Bridgestone Arena in Nashville. Helping me honor George at the cemetery were his trusted producer Billy Sherrill (who eventually was buried nearby), Joe Diffie, Jeannie Pruett, and other key country music influencers.

Almost immediately, fans showed up, wanting to visit the gravesite and the monument venerating George. I didn't mind, and I appreciated their kindness and their love. In fact, when the cemetery put up a fence around our plots and locked the gate, I threw a fit. And so did the fans. I first heard about the fence when a number of fans expressed their outrage on social media sites. Some folks apparently thought that I had intended to keep them away, and they were quite irate.

They were also quite wrong.

I called the cemetery and asked, "Why is there a fence around our plots with a gate closed and locked? I didn't know a thing about a fence out there."

Jeff, the man in charge of the cemetery said, "Well, we put the fence up."

I said, "Well, you can keep the fence, but you can't close the gates."

He said, "Why not?"

"'Cause the fans wanna see George," I told him. "If anything, you ought to put up a sign that says, 'Step right up; come on in.' That's what George would want. That was his attitude toward his fans throughout his life. So don't close that gate again!" (I later had it chained open.)

George's monument had only been in place a short time when I went out to the gravesite one day, and I noticed ashes all over the ledge of George's headstone.

"What is that?" I asked.

A friend with me said, "It looks as if somebody's remains are thrown out here."

"What? That is awful!" I said. I could hardly believe that someone would do such a thing.

I called the funeral director and he hurried out to the cemetery to investigate. He called me back and said, "Yes, that's what it is. Apparently, one of George's fans wanted to be buried next to the King of Country Music. So the relatives put the cremated ashes on top of George's headstone."

I didn't mean anything disrespectful to the dead, but I was mad. I told the funeral director, "Well, get it off that ledge. I don't want that there. That's awful!"

Had the family notified me, I may have said they could put the ashes behind George's monument. Maybe. After all, that was somebody's mother, father, or grandmother. But as it was, they just threw the ashes out on top of George's memorial.

When I calmed down, I realized that the fans weren't trying to vandalize George's gravesite. They were simply trying to do something special for their loved one by placing the ashes right there along with

George. It would have been nice to get permission prior to dumping the remains on the ledge, but I understood . . . kinda.

Then, just as George had planned, we hosted the George Jones tribute show on November 22, 2013. I was hoping for seventy artists, but in fact, more than one-hundred-ten artists turned out to honor George in a sold-out show. Along with George's sister Helen, I sat on the front row, overflowing with bittersweet emotions, as each artist sang one of George's songs. Charlie Daniels, George Strait, Garth Brooks, Blake Shelton, Miranda Lambert, Kathy Mattea, Craig Morgan, Josh Turner, Eric Church, Martina McBride, and so many more presented stellar performances of George's songs. In a somewhat odd but appropriate twist, heavy-metal band Megadeth teamed up with Jamey Johnson on George's song "Wild Irish Rose." Vince Gill wore a special T-shirt bearing the name Sweet Pea. As at George's funeral, his empty rocking chair sat on the stage front and center throughout the evening.

It was an emotionally charged evening for me, but the show also had moments of hilarity. For instance, before performing "Love Bug," Big & Rich (Big Kenny Alphin and John Rich) took the stage by riding on a pair of John Deere lawn mowers—a humorous reminder of George's much overblown (and often mistakenly described), infamous arrest for driving drunk on a lawn mower when Uncle Dub had hidden the car keys to keep him from getting to the liquor store.

Brad Paisley told the audience, "No one was more generous to me than George Jones." Then with perfect timing, Brad quipped, "I know he's looking down at this and saying, 'Son, where's all the money going for this?'"

As he had done at George's funeral, Alan Jackson closed out the more than four-hour-long show by singing "He Stopped Loving Her Today." But this time, after he finished the song to thunderous applause,

Alan motioned for me to join him on the stage. I walked up onto the stage and stood beside Alan as he led the crowd in singing the chorus to "He Stopped Loving Her Today." I could barely contain my emotions as the sound of more than seventeen thousand fans filled the arena and wrapped around my heart.

The following April, a year after George had gone to heaven, I hosted the first of what I hoped would be annual celebrations of George's legacy. I had promised George that I would never let people forget him, so when we planned the anniversary event, we invited the public to attend.

"This day is going to be bittersweet," I told folks prior to the event. "I know how much people loved George, and the love has continued even a year later. I am so fortunate for the friends and fans that George and I made through the years. I want everyone to come celebrate with us, not because he is no longer with us, but to keep his legacy alive."

More than four hundred fans showed up at the cemetery on a clear, crisp April day to celebrate the anniversary of George's homegoing with me. I planted two dogwood trees close to the monument as an expression of George's ongoing influence.

I stood at the podium in front of George's monument and wanted to be strong for George. I assured the group that had gathered to honor George, "I'm not going to cry." They wouldn't have minded if I did, but I didn't.

After the brief ceremony, I remained at the memorial, greeting and hugging every person who came by, until the last person left the cemetery. "I'll be here somehow every year," I told folks.

Nine years later, in April 2023, we celebrated the tenth anniversary of George going to heaven by gathering at the Von Braun Center in Huntsville, Alabama, for the show "Still Playin' Possum, Music and

Memories of George Jones." Once again, some of the biggest stars in country music, including Brad Paisley, Tanya Tucker, Dierks Bentley, Wynonna Judd, Joe Nichols, Jamey Johnson, and twenty-eight other artists joined us to honor George's legacy. Randy Travis had recuperated from the stroke he had suffered ten years earlier but was still unable to sing. Yet he and his wife, Mary, traveled to Huntsville to honor George, as did chef, author, and television personality Paula Deen, who helped Keith Bilbrey host the show. I think George was smiling at us from up in heaven.

At the show, I thanked George's fans for loving him all these years, and reminded them, "I'm never going to let George's legacy die."

27

A Place for George's Fans

Although I was committed to not letting George's legacy lapse in the minds of the public, living in the large, custom-built home George and I had shared together at Nestledown Farms continued to feel like living in a George Jones museum. Everything about the house reminded me of George—which was wonderful—but it also made me lonely for him. At one point before George got sick, we had considered turning our place at Nestledown into a museum similar to what Priscilla Presley had done with her and Elvis's former home, Graceland, in Memphis, but we had decided against it.

After George's passing, keeping up with the more than one hundred acres of prime Tennessee property was a chore for me. I considered my options and decided to sell our home at Nestledown and to downsize to a more manageable house, perhaps in a gated community where much of the maintenance was done by contractors. I put the house and property on the market, but not before I informed George's daughter Susan that we needed to start looking for a new place for her and her family to live, since George and I had built them a home at Nestledown, and it would be sold along with the property.

I was out one afternoon when I received a notice from the real estate agent that a potential buyer wanted to view the house and property. I had errands to run, so I simply extended my time away from Nestledown. Meanwhile, Kirk West, a local businessman, and Jamie Spears, father of Britney Spears, came by the property to check it out.

Jamie had just flown into Nashville for a meeting. Kirk later recalled, "When I picked up Jamie at the airport, I said, 'Hey, George Jones's house is for sale. I'm thinking of buying it and turning it into a Graceland-style museum. Would you want to go see it with me?"

"Yeah, sure, I'll go with you," Jamie said. "I'd love to see it."

So while I was out running my errands, the two businessmen toured my home and property. I arrived home just as they finished up and were walking through the backyard near the house. I greeted them cordially and stepped over to shake hands with them. "Hello, I'm Nancy Jones," I said, extending my hand.

Jamie Spears introduced himself, and we shook hands. Then Kirk West, the taller of the two men, smiled and said, "I'm a hugger." He gave me a great big bear hug. We talked for a while, and I was actually more focused on talking with Jamie, since I knew he hailed from Louisiana, as did I. We probably knew some of the same hoodlums.

The men stayed a short time longer and then left with no offers on the table. But we kept in touch. Kirk knew next to nothing about country music, much less was he a fan, but he knew marketing, and he knew millions of people were familiar with bits and pieces of George's and my story. In our subsequent conversations, I told Kirk, "A lot has been written about George, but few people know the full story."

Kirk was intrigued. We talked more frequently over the ensuing months and we became good friends. Before long, we considered doing business together. Kirk and I also discussed turning the home George and I had shared at Nestledown Farms into a museum. The concept made sense since so many of George's favorite things were at Nestledown. But the more we talked about it, the more we decided that the George Jones Museum would especially appeal to country music fans visiting Nashville, many of whom congregated in the downtown area for shows and large, special events. CMA Fest, for example, regularly brought in more than 150,000 fans to downtown; the annual New Year's Eve "Music Note Drop" concerts downtown exceeded 200,000 fans; not to mention weekly events at the Ryman Auditorium (the original home of the Grand Ole Opry), Bridgestone Arena, and the Country Music Hall of Fame.

I said, "You know, Franklin is about a half hour's drive out of Nashville, and I'm not sure people will come this far. Why don't we try to find a place downtown?"

Kirk went to work and he found a location in downtown Nashville, right on Second Avenue, near Wildhorse Saloon, the Hard Rock Cafe, and just a short walk from the historic Ryman Auditorium, Tootsies Orchid Lounge, and several popular honky-tonks. We would not have to attract tourists; they were already there seven days a week.

We paid $4.35 million to purchase the building and immediately began working on renovations. By then my home at Nestledown had sold, so our goal was to open the museum on the anniversary of George's going to heaven, in April the following year. We started working in the winter and it was freezing cold in that old five-story brick building with no heat.

It was a nightmare from the beginning as the complex seemed haunted by past nefarious people and degenerate activities. Prior to my purchasing it, the building had recently been padlocked by Nashville police due to "persistent criminal activity." When cleaning out the upper levels, Kirk and I discovered rooms painted completely black, replete with "stripper poles," secret rooms and compartments, and evidence of prostitution and human trafficking—all the more reason to renovate the location and replace the evil with something good, fun, and uplifting.

We hired a general contractor who wanted $15 million to renovate the building and bring it up to local codes so we could have guests on all five floors, including a rooftop overview. Shortly after we closed on the building purchase, I met with the general contractor. His renovation schedule was disappointing. "I can have only one floor ready when you open on the anniversary of George's death next April."

I was so upset I started crying—and it takes a lot for me to cry.

Kirk came over to where the contractor and I were sitting, and I told him the situation.

"Whoa, whoa, whoa!" Kirk said. "We need all floors open. We can't just have one floor open."

The contractor was adamant. "Well, I can't do that."

Without missing a beat, Kirk said, "Okay, then. You're fired. I'll do it myself. I will be the general contractor."

The good news about Kirk serving as general contractor was that we were going to save a lot of money. The bad news? We were going to do much of the grunt work ourselves. Kirk and I worked around the clock, seven days a week. We rarely left the building and often worked so late, we fell asleep from exhaustion and slept on the floor.

Kirk and I laid the carpet on the third floor all by ourselves. We worked till two or three o'clock in the morning on our hands and knees, fitting together the carpet squares. We were determined to get it done so we kept going, and when we looked out the window, it was daylight. We'd been working all night long. But we got it done!

Everyone who stopped by seemed convinced that we'd never complete the renovations in time to open on the anniversary. Everyone except Kirk and me, that is. We poured our hearts and souls into that place, not to mention our elbow grease and knuckles. We scrubbed floors, sanitized, shined, and hauled junk. We tore out and hauled away more than one hundred dumpsters filled with debris cleaned out of the building. It was backbreaking work, but we loved it because we felt we were helping to maintain George's legacy and doing something great for the city of Nashville in providing such an entertaining venue at the same time.

We finished up two hours before we were scheduled to have our Grand Opening on April 26, 2015. We had cut it so close that Kirk had to race home to shower and change clothes for the event and consequently missed the ribbon cutting. But we were open and in business and the George Jones Museum soon filled with customers.

The museum had five levels, including a gift shop, two kitchens, a restaurant, event space and music venues, as well as a rooftop entertainment area with a stunning view overlooking the Cumberland River and the Tennessee Titans' stadium. The large, front windows on the ground floor opened so passersby on Second Avenue could hear and see the live musicians performing inside, and they'd hear, "Step right up, come on in," as George's voice would invite them. The interior design was fascinating with exquisite cabinets displaying some of George's most priceless guitars, clothes, and other memorabilia—even the huge rocking chair we'd had out front at Nestledown during Christmas. We hired the company that had helped create the Johnny Cash Museum in Nashville and other museums around the country to assist us in arranging the displays in an easily accessible and understandable way so that whether customers knew a lot or only a little about George, their interest and imaginations could soar.

Even after the grand opening, I worked at the museum every day, often in the restaurant area. We were so busy, packed wall to wall with people—which was a good thing—we were constantly behind in trying to wash silverware and roll it in the napkins, ready for our servers to place at customers' tables. So I jumped right in there and rolled silverware and napkins for hours almost every day. I did not think I was better than anyone else, or that I was too good to do the more mundane, nasty tasks such as cleaning the restrooms.

One night in early 2016, I was on the rooftop cleaning the bathroom when three young women came in. I was concealed behind one of the stalls, cleaning the commode when one of the women pushed open the stall door. "Oh, excuse me," she said.

"No problem," I said, barely looking up from my scrubbing. "If you don't mind, just go to the next stall."

She and her friends went on down the line of open stalls. I continued cleaning, but I could hear the women jabbering. Much to my surprise, they were talking about *me*! One of them said, "Well, I wonder how Nancy is using all of George's money."

Another woman said, "Oh, yeah; she got rich after George died."

I was already fuming as I continued brushing out the commode when I heard the other woman say, "Well, George never cared nothing about Nancy, anyhow. It was all about Tammy."

The longer I listened, the madder I got and the harder I scrubbed that commode.

I was in no mood. I thought, *I am tired. I am hot. I'm filthy from scrubbing and I have to listen to this nonsense!* The more the women spouted their speculations, the madder I got. So finally I stepped out from the stall where I had been scrubbing and glared at the stalls where the women were still gabbing. "Let me tell you something," I yelled. "I am Nancy Jones, George Jones's widow. I am here cleaning commodes. And when y'all come out of those stalls, we'll see if you're big enough to say those things to my face!"

Two of the women came out, took one look at me in my cleaning clothes, and ran off. They didn't even bother washing their hands. They just ran out of the restroom and down four flights of stairs.

The third one stepped out of a stall, and she was huge—I mean she was a large woman! I thought, *Oh, my! What have I done? I'm in trouble now.*

But I was mad too, so I faced that woman and said, "I don't care how big you are; you're not gonna talk about me like that!"

I was talking a bold line, but inside I was praying, *Oh God, please don't let her hit me, cuz I will be dead. She could kill me.*

The woman didn't swing at me. Instead, she just flipped me off and went on out the door. Whether she believed that I was George's wife, I don't know. But I know she wasn't in the building when I went back downstairs.

I cleaned the commodes at the George Jones Museum every night. I also served as the in-residence plumber. If a toilet backed up, I used a plunger to unplug it. Somebody had to do it.

Yes, we had dozens of employees, but we were so busy and usually had a two-hour wait for an open table at the restaurant, so we opened the third floor, which was the event floor. The place was always so crammed full of people having a good time, it was almost hard to walk through without bumping into someone. I couldn't afford to wait till the servers made it all the way upstairs to customers up there, so I started waiting on tables myself, taking the customers' orders.

Almost inevitably, I'd notice someone nudging the person next to them as I took their orders. "That's Nancy Jones! George Jones's wife!" They couldn't believe that I'd be there, much less taking their dinner orders.

I'd say, "Don't give me a tip. We own the place, so no tips are necessary. Just tell me, what would you like to order? Okay, I'm gonna write down what you want. And when I bring it up here, you pick out your food. Because I don't know who gets what."

The customers loved it. Apparently, they felt they were getting more than they had bargained for because Nancy Jones was waiting on their tables. I didn't mind; in fact, I was glad to do it. I wanted it to be known as a place with good customer service and if it meant Kirk and me helping out, we were willing to do it.

Our restaurant managers didn't appreciate it, but I didn't care. It was my name on the door, so Kirk and I would get the orders and take them up to the third floor.

One manager groused, "I wish y'all wouldn't do that."

I turned and said, "We're *not* going to lose a customer!" So I'd take a tray full of food orders upstairs, find the table, and put it down right in the middle. Everybody reached in to get what they had ordered, and they loved it.

But occasionally someone would want to order mixed drinks.

I said, "Now, I don't know how to do that. Y'all just order some beer!"

And they would! And they seemed happy about it.

I was laughing so much and the customers were laughing too. "This is cool," I'd hear them say. They never expected that George Jones's wife would be their server, and they loved that experience. They got an even bigger kick when they saw me bussing tables and hauling off the leftovers from the tables nearby.

Occasionally, when I got really tired, I could lose my patience with a difficult customer.

One guy was sitting at the bar on the restaurant level, and he ordered a steak filet and ate the entire thing. Then he started complaining about the quality of the food. I walked up to him and ripped his hat off and said, "Get out! Our food is great! You ate the whole steak, and now you want to gripe? Get out!" I threw him out of our restaurant.

The place was packed with people almost every afternoon and evening. Since we stayed open later hours, there was little turnaround time. We worked constantly simply to stay caught up. The fans loved it. They enjoyed the food and drinks but even more important to me, they were fascinated by the myriad pieces of George Jones memorabilia, all set in well-marked and clearly explained displays.

It was an enormous amount of work, but I loved making the museum available to the public. Through the museum, long after George's death, I continued to perpetuate his career, as well as giving fans access to George's music, memorabilia, photos, instruments, and the inner workings of his life. Over his more than sixty-year career, George Jones had churned out more than one hundred albums with songs on the *Billboard* charts during five separate decades of his life! There was much to hear and to see.

Moreover, I wanted to make people more aware of the "good George," George's impish sense of humor, as well as his sincere compassion and astounding generosity to people in need, especially regarding children.

By November 2016, I was exhausted. As much as I enjoyed being with the fans at the museum and restaurant, the workload was taking a toll on my health. By then, we employed ninety-two people, and we treated them as family. We wanted them to do well and make a good living, and we knew if we took care of them, they would take care of us.

They did. The entire time I owned the George Jones Museum, only one employee was ever caught stealing from us. We were a family. We visited them in their homes at Christmas and always tried to give more than anyone expected.

When I sold the property, fixtures, furniture, and equipment in November 2016, the hardest part for me was saying goodbye to our employees. Some reporters said I sold the George Jones name and likeness at the same time. That never happened. I leased a *license* to use the name and likeness, as is often done in the music business and others, but no, I have never sold George's name and likeness . . . and I never will.

With the money I had left when George died, I wanted to do something to reward his first daughter, Susan. She had been living on the farm property at Nestledown, so before I sold that home and moved, Susan moved as well. I paid nearly half a million dollars to purchase a house for her in Spring Hill, about a thirty-minute drive away from Franklin. I bought her furniture and paid for all the decorating done at her home.

There were no strings. I looked at it as a gift from George and me. In all the years I had known Susan, she had never asked for anything from her daddy or me. Unlike some of George's other children, she never came with her hand out, with that ugly sense of entitlement. Nor did she ever sell stories about the inner workings of our family to the tabloids, as George was convinced some of his other offspring had done.

She simply lived her life quietly, never drawing attention to herself, even when she attended one of George's shows. Most of the fans didn't know and would never have guessed that Susan was George's daughter. But George never ignored her.

Although the circumstances surrounding Susan's birth were not ideal, George always regarded her as his daughter. Some of his children from other marriages were not so gracious. They preferred to pretend that Susan did not exist, or if she did, that she had no connection to them. The DNA in their bodies would prove differently.

I asked one of George's offspring, "Why are you so mean to Susan?"

His answer shocked me. "Why not?" he said. "She doesn't count."

"What are you talking about?" I pressed. "Everybody counts."

"Well, Daddy got her mama pregnant before they were even married, so he just felt like he had to marry the woman."

"All the more reason to take care of that baby," I said.

But George's other family members didn't see it that way, so they wrote her off, even though George always regarded Susan as his daughter and rightly so. He loved her all his life, and her children as well—as long as they didn't mess up the grass on his perfectly manicured lawn!

I felt strongly, if George was looking down from heaven and saw that I was helping to bless Susan and his family, he'd say, "Good work, honey."

28

POINTING THE WAY

ALTHOUGH I APPRECIATED Kirk West's business acumen and his willingness to work himself to the bone to get the George Jones Museum open, the quality I appreciated most about him was his spiritual concern for people. Kirk really seemed to care about people meeting God.

Despite attending church services earlier in my life, I didn't often find that sort of genuine passion for the Gospel in other people—even some preachers who tried to hang around George and me—and although I believed in God and the truths of the Bible, I really hadn't experienced a personal salvation until I met Kirk. Early in our friendship, he asked me straightforwardly, "Have you said the salvation prayer?"

"Salvation prayer? What is that?" I asked him.

"You know," Kirk said, "admitting that you have sinned and that you need a Savior. The Bible says, 'Believe on the Lord Jesus Christ and you will be saved—and your household.' So the salvation prayer is essentially asking Jesus to save us."

"Oh," I said. "I don't think I've ever done that."

"Well, you can right now," Kirk said. "But it's not merely saying the words. You have to believe it; you have to feel it and express it from your heart." Kirk led me in praying and asking Jesus to come into my life. It was the best thing I ever did. I felt instantly clean. And forgiven. I've truly never been the same since praying that prayer.

I had been attending a church in Franklin and when Kirk met the pastor, he unloaded on him. Kirk is not a quiet guy, so he confronted the pastor boldly. "How dare you say you are a pastor of a church?" he asked the minister. "Shouldn't the number one focus be getting people saved? Getting their souls ready for heaven? Nancy's been attending your church for some time now and she never knew about the salvation prayer."

The pastor mumbled something about how he didn't want to offend me. I guess he figured it was okay if I went to hell, as long as he didn't offend me by telling me I needed Jesus in my life.

When you finally find something real, you not only feel good yourself, you want to tell someone else. Have you ever had a great meal at a restaurant or found a fantastic deal at a department store? You can't wait to tell somebody. That's similar to how I felt about my newfound faith in Jesus. Something about discovering a genuine relationship with God prompted me to want to share His love with everyone I came in contact with, especially my own family members.

In late 2019 and early 2020, my brother Steve's health debilitated to the point that he knew he was dying. By July, he was ready to give up.

I hadn't talked to Steve in a long time. He thought everybody owed him something because he had osteogenesis imperfecta and was confined to a wheelchair or crutches. I felt sorry for him but I also had strong ideas about anyone in our family giving the impression that we deserved any more consideration than someone else.

Kirk and I were talking about some business matters when Steve called me on a Friday and said, "Nancy, I'm dying."

"What? What do you mean you're dying?"

He said, "Yes. The doctor says I'll be dead by morning."

Because I hadn't talked with him in such a long time, his words hit me hard.

"Yeah," he said, "I just want you to know that . . . that I'm dying."

I knew my brother had been in poor health for a long time, so I didn't suggest any more doctors or newfangled treatments. Something inside me let me know that there was only one thing that really mattered. I said, "Steve, are you saved?"

"Am I what?" he asked.

I said, "Do you know the Lord? Do you know the salvation prayer?"

"What is that?" he asked.

My brother and I had rarely talked about spiritual matters, and I was emotionally flustered, so I said, "Listen, I've got somebody here who can help you with this. You repeat exactly what he says and you're gonna go to heaven."

"Okay," Steve said. "Put him on the phone."

I passed the phone to Kirk and he explained to Steve the biblical plan of salvation, that if a person confesses with his mouth Jesus Christ as Lord and believes in his heart that God raised him from the dead, that person will be saved (Romans 10:9). Kirk talked Steve through the salvation prayer and Steve prayed and asked Jesus to come into his life.

Steve died two days later, on Sunday. But we got wind that the day after praying with Kirk, Steve was calling everybody. He thought Kirk was a pastor, so he told his friends, "I talked to a pastor and I said this prayer, and Jesus saved me!" He was telling everybody he knew that Jesus is for real.

My heart overflowed with joy. My brother was that close to dying and being lost for eternity, but now I knew I would see him again someday in heaven. I wondered, though, how his life and especially his attitudes might have been different had he met Jesus years earlier. He may have been a different person. Steve didn't need more money or more medicine. Jesus is what he needed all his life, and although it was late in his life, I was thrilled that Steve had found Him.

My older brother, Bobby, had a similar experience at eighty-one years of age. For most of his life, Bobby was a hellion. He was just wild. After our mama passed away, I tried to watch out for Bobby, even as an adult, but he did not always appreciate my "meddling," especially when it came to the women he dated.

In 2022 he called me from Louisiana and I tried to give him some advice. Bobby did not receive it and flew off the handle, yelling and screaming profanity at me and calling me all sorts of derogatory names.

I said, "What is wrong with you, Bobby? I've never known you to act like this."

Kirk was standing nearby and he could hear Bobby cussing at me. He grabbed the phone and said, "Bobby, I'm coming down there, and you are going to have to deal with me!"

Whether it was Kirk's defense of me or some other reason, Bobby packed up his belongings and moved to a new location.

A few weeks later, Kirk and I went to visit Bobby. He had just wrecked another car, his third. He had only owned the car for three weeks before flipping it as he drove, causing the vehicle to be a total loss.

I said, "Kirk needs to talk to you."

"Okay," Bobby said.

Kirk told him, "Bobby, you have to surrender your driver's license. You're gonna kill somebody."

Bobby nodded. "Well, I can't really see good anymore," he said wistfully.

We had his little granddaughter with us, so I pointed at her and asked, "What would happen if you killed that beautiful child right there because of your reckless driving?"

He said, "I'd never forgive myself."

I said, "Well, then, go with Kirk." They went to the department of motor vehicles and Bobby surrendered his driver's license. Then we took him to the Veterans Administration to help straighten out some of his healthcare issues. We found him an assisted living residence where he could live and he loved it.

Like Steve, Bobby prayed a salvation prayer, asking Jesus to come into his life. Amazingly, his whole attitude has changed. Today, he is a totally different guy. He is as sweet as he can be, just like I used to know him years ago when we were kids. God did that for Bobby. And for Steve. And for me.

29

Sneak Attacks

My doctor prescribed pain medications for me years ago due to neuropathy in my feet. I had endured intense pain for decades and found that certain medications offered some relief. But they were also habit-forming. Although the pain meds helped for a while, the law of diminishing returns eventually set in, and it took more and more pain medication to accomplish less and less relief. That is a classic prescription for addiction. Nevertheless, my doctors kept prescribing more of the addictive drugs and my body responded. Before long, I was hooked.

I talked with my doctor about a possible surgical procedure to deal with the neuropathy, and it seemed feasible, although somewhat out of the ordinary. After careful consideration, I decided not to go through with the surgery, but I still wanted to be free from the pain meds.

I told my doctor that I planned to do my detox on my own, cold turkey.

My doctor said, "Oh, no! Don't do that. Let me prescribe some other medications and we'll bring your levels down incrementally with each dose."

I said, "No, I don't want the drugs anymore."

He said, "You can't do that, Nancy."

I told him, "I'm just going to pray and ask God for His help.

And I did. I asked God to deliver me from the addiction to the prescription drugs—and He did!

I stopped taking the medications, and I'm sure I was no fun to be around for a while. I felt miserable but by mid-May 2021, I was completely off all prescription pain medications. Good thing that I was, as I was about to discover.

* * * * * *

On May 11, 2021, Kirk and I went out shopping and I purchased a new blue-jeans-style jacket for his daughter's birthday. Afterwards, we went to Franklin Chop House, a local restaurant near my home. Kirk pulled the car in the parking lot, and because there were no spots available up close, he said, "I'll let you out here, and you can go in and get us a table while I go park the car."

"Okay, that's fine," I said, as I opened the door and hopped out of the passenger side. Kirk had no sooner pulled away when a lady who was pulling her car out of a parking spot gunned her engine and backed her car right toward me. I let out an ear-piercing scream but apparently the woman couldn't hear me, as she kept coming. The bumper of her car slammed into me, knocking me off my feet, facedown on the ground. My head hit the pavement with an awful thud. It sounded as though someone had just dropped a watermelon on the pavement.

I could feel warm blood oozing under my head on the asphalt.

From where Kirk parked, he heard me yelling, but he hadn't seen me fall. He ran toward the restaurant and found me on the ground, and a woman who looked to be about sixty years of age standing outside her car screaming, "I hit her! I didn't see her. I have insurance." She tried to hand Kirk her insurance card. "I have insurance."

"I don't care about your insurance," Kirk said. "We need an ambulance!" The woman called 911 while Kirk ran back and reached into the car and grabbed the cute blue-jean jacket that I had just purchased that day for his daughter. He wrapped it under my head and used it as a compress to help stop the bleeding. The blood surged into the fabric, soaking it and ruining the new jacket.

An ambulance arrived and the paramedics took me to Vanderbilt University Medical Center, since it was known in the area as a premier facility for head injuries.

Once I arrived in the emergency room, the doctors ran tests for about four hours and, amazingly, couldn't find anything wrong with me. Even more astounding, when they went to stich up the spot from which I had been bleeding so profusely, they could not find any wounds to stitch! The source of all the blood had been healed.

"I don't know what happened," one of the young doctors said.

"I do," I answered with a smile.

It was incredible. Miraculous. It was God.

My lawyer later told me, "Nancy, you know you can sue the insurance company of the woman who hit you," but I said, "Oh, no, no. I'm not suing her. I get to the hospital and I've got a jacket full of blood and the doctors can't find any place that blood came from? Uh-uh, I ain't suing nobody."

"Nancy, are you sure?" the attorney asked.

"Absolutely, I'm sure," I said. "That bill has already been paid!"

30

Lying At Death's Door—Again

As I write these words, the world is several years removed from the cataclysmic upheaval caused by the COVID-19 pandemic. It is easy for some folks to forget how tumultuous those times were—especially for those of us who had near-death experiences with the illness.

In the early part of 2021, Jessica Robertson and her adorable family moved in the home across the street from mine. Jessica is an attorney, and she and her husband, Brent, own a real estate company that specializes in handling high-end, luxury properties. She told Kirk and me when they moved in that they would only be living in the neighborhood for a short while, as they planned to update and then sell their home. Nevertheless, we all quickly became great friends and often shared dinner together as well as good conversations.

Not surprisingly, when news about Covid first became public, Jessica went to work researching information about the virus and how she could best protect her family and friends. The more she learned, the more suspicious she became, not only regarding the source of the virus, but the vaccines the US pharmaceutical industry planned to produce to fight it. "There is an ulterior motive behind this," Jessica told us. "It seems that there are some nefarious agendas in play."

Also an avid researcher, Kirk concurred with Jessica's observations about the COVID-19 virus and the medical treatments offered. Jessica put together a list of simple, practical suggestions to avoid the virus, and what to do or not to do if a person needed medical care during that time.

As we discussed their findings, I became increasingly convinced that if I got sick with the virus, I did not want to be admitted to the hospital. I adamantly told Kirk and others, "Don't take me to the hospital and don't put me on a ventilator if I get sick." Those sentiments were confirmed further by the death of our good friend Joe Diffie, the first high-profile country music artist to die because of COVID-19. The doctors had put Joe on a ventilator in their efforts to help him breathe, but Joe didn't come off the machine alive.

As more information became available about the potential vaccines, Kirk and I decided that, in view of our previous health issues, receiving an experimental vaccine was not in our best interests. We were not interested in being poisoned or having our lungs blown out. As I understood matters, most safe, credible vaccines took as long as fifteen years to create, rather than fifteen months as those being touted to fight Covid. I decided to avoid the vaccines.

By the time I moved across town, Jessica and her family had moved back to their home in Florida. We kept in touch and when Kirk sent a message to the Robertsons that we were sick, Jessica picked up on the urgent need. She researched further and found a doctor in Nashville from whom I could receive fluids by means of intravenous treatments on an outpatient basis.

Ironically, the one medication that was pooh-poohed by many in the medical community was Ivermectin, the very medicine that helped Kirk get back on his feet almost overnight when he was diagnosed with COVID-19.

* * * * * *

After reviving from having no pulse for nearly ten minutes in the doctor's office, I was nearly incoherent when I landed in the hospital with COVID-19 in September 2021, but although my eyes could not stay open, I was conscious. The doctors and nurses made no effort to hide their dire predictions. They were convinced I was going to die.

The hospital admitted me on a Wednesday, and I spent those first two nights alone in the ICU. Even the doctors spaced out their visits because of the Covid protocols. That Friday, two days later, was the first time since the pandemic had begun that the hospital permitted visitors in the ICU.

Kirk entered the room adjacent to the ICU, along with the family members of other patients. The hospital required visitors to sign waivers before seeing their loved ones, declaring basically that the visitors were risking their lives by being there. Once inside, Kirk donned the hazmat suit including a gown, gloves, mask, and face shield. Suited up head to toe, Kirk was permitted to visit with me from noon until two o'clock on Friday. I was glad to see him, but I felt so awful, I wasn't a good patient.

"We need to talk," I told him, as soon as he entered the room. "I'm dying. I'm not going to make it."

"Whoa, whoa, whoa," Kirk replied. "We're not going to talk like that. We're having faith and we're speaking only positive things. We're going to pray and believe, and God is going to get you out of here."

Kirk's faith was bolstered by that of his daughter, Lauren, and her husband, David Peden, who pastor We Are Church Nashville, a congregation in East Nashville. Lauren knew that Kirk was extremely upset by what had happened to me, not to mention that he was just getting over double pneumonia and Covid himself. To encourage Kirk and to pray for me, Lauren and David brought about thirty-five people from their congregation to the hospital.

Due to the COVID-19 restrictions, the hospital would not let them enter the building, so Lauren and David and their fellow believers stood outside the hospital, singing worship songs and praying for me. "You can keep us out of the hospital," Lauren said, "but you can't keep us from praying."

Lauren was solid as a rock. Throughout the ordeal, she declared, "Nancy is going to live and not die. I don't care what the doctors say or what you see. She isn't going *anywhere*." Lauren never waivered in her faith that God would heal me.

The following Wednesday and Friday, Kirk returned for the maximum allowed, two-hour visits. Then the next Monday, he was permitted to stay from eight in the morning till eight at night. When he wasn't actually inside the hospital room with me, he monitored me from home by means of FaceTime on his telephone. That was his visiting schedule for the next week. By that time, I had received a negative test result regarding COVID-19, but my body continued to debilitate. Something was very wrong, and the doctors seemed unable to ascertain what was causing me to degenerate rather than recover. I was weak and extremely sick, losing body weight rapidly. Within four weeks, my weight dropped from 135 pounds to 92 pounds. I was frail, emaciated, and could barely move.

Initially, the orderlies placed my food tray on the other side of the bed, and I couldn't get to it. It was almost as though they didn't want me to eat. When I asked for water, the nurses said, "No, no, no," with no further explanation. Later, when Kirk began visiting me in the room, he brought soup and nutritional shakes for me to drink. Then he realized that those drinks were high in carbohydrates, and since I am diabetic, the shakes could cause my sugar level to spike, slowing my healing. Before Kirk's next visit, he went to a health store and purchased everything he could find that was nutritious with a plant base and low in carbs. But by then, I didn't want anything to eat or drink. My system seemed too far gone.

"You've got to eat, Nancy," Kirk implored. "If you want to live, you must eat. If you want to get well, you have to eat."

"I can't eat," I responded.

Kirk spoon-fed me just to get some nourishment in me, but I still didn't eat much. Ironically, the doctors never fit me with a feeding tube. I had a port in case I needed blood, but nothing for food.

Kirk befriended my lung doctor, who had formerly studied with Dr. Milstone; the lung doctor highly respected our physician's opinions. "Can I just stay here at the hospital in Nancy's room?" Kirk requested. Amazingly, the doctor granted permission for Kirk to stay in my room twenty-four hours a day, as long as he did not leave the hospital. That was fine with Kirk. He ate his meals there, slept in a chair next to my bed (Kirk is six feet, six inches tall, so that chair could not have been comfortable), and stayed in my room, monitoring my condition day and night. He rarely left my side for more than a few minutes.

The doctors recognized that although I was still horribly sick, I seemed to rally simply by having Kirk nearby, knowing that he was watching over every medical procedure the doctors were doing. That was important because when I first had arrived at the hospital, the doctors were adamant that I needed to be vaccinated immediately. "You *will* get the vaccine," a doctor in the ER practically screamed at me. "Do you understand what I'm saying?"

"No!" I cried with what little breath I could muster. "I do not want that shot."

"Well, then, you're going to die," one doctor told me bluntly.

"I don't want the shot," I gasped. "And I'm not going on a ventilator."

It seemed the doctors were more than willing to let me die if I would not receive the Covid vaccine. I didn't understand their motives (and still don't) but it seemed to me that rather than saying, "We helped save Nancy Jones's life," they were more interested in claiming that I died because I didn't receive the vaccine. It was crazy!

Now that Kirk was in the room, I didn't have to concern myself so much with the medical procedures. I knew he was all over them, often annoying the doctors and nurses by his perseverance, but keeping a watchful eye on everything they did to me. He was also quick to sound the alarm for the nurses when anything about my condition changed. That confidence lifted my spirits. A few the doctors expressed quiet appreciation for Kirk's presence and his assistance in keeping an eye on me.

My lung doctor, Stacey Vallejo, told Kirk, "It seems that when you are here, Nancy gets better." That was true. "We've found the cure for her," the doctor quipped, "and it is *you*."

In many ways, Kirk was not only the cure, he was also the physician and nurse on call. He observed everything about my progress—or lack of it—and informed the people supposedly taking care of me. "I'm worried that Nancy is not eating," he texted one of the doctors.

"She's not?" the doctor replied.

"No, she is not," Kirk responded.

"That's a good point," the doctor said. "I'll look into that."

* * * * * *

Although I had survived the immediate Covid threat, I had lost all muscle tone and felt as though my arms and legs had turned to rubber. I could not even sit up in the hospital bed without flopping over. I felt like the cartoon character Gumby. Kirk would slide me up on the pillows, and, *zoop!* Because I had no muscle tone, I simply slumped back down onto the mattress.

Nor could I get out of bed to go to the bathroom. I couldn't control my bladder or my bowels, and since the nurses and orderlies did not frequently come into the room due to Covid protocols, I often lay in my own refuse until I could get someone's attention. The orderlies dressed me in diapers, but I filled them rapidly and repeatedly, long before they found time to change me. It was disgusting and humiliating, but I was helpless to do much about it.

After a while, rather than allowing me to wait in excrement or urine until a nurse or orderly could clean me up, Kirk stepped in to change the diapers. "I'm so sorry," I said to Kirk. I was also so embarrassed. But Kirk was determined to take care of me, even if it meant doing what the orderlies didn't. We went through so many diapers that he ordered extras online and had them shipped to his daughter, who delivered them to the hospital. Like taking care of a helpless baby, Kirk cleaned me up, changed my bedding, and put fresh, new diapers on me, day after day, night after night. One of my doctors commented, "I've never seen a love like that."

All day long, and all night long, every two hours, Kirk rolled me over onto my side to help prevent the onset of pneumonia. First on one side, then after a while, he'd roll me onto my opposite side. "You cannot lay on your back, Nancy," he told me.

I got so mad at him, because I was so miserable, but he would not allow me to stay for long on my back. He also tried to get me to lie on my stomach and I hated it, so I'd fight with him about it as much as I was able. "I don't want to lay on my stomach," I whined. "I get claustrophobic lying on my stomach."

He remained insistent. "Please lie on your stomach, Nancy," he'd plead. "Please, please, please. If you lay on your back, you'll never make it out of here."

I knew he was right, but I didn't care. I felt so awful, dying could only be a relief.

Kirk and I were able to communicate freely, but I did not talk much during those first few weeks in the hospital. Every word coming out of my mouth required massive effort simply to get my lungs to force the words out.

Each day, two big guys came in for what they called "physical therapy." Actually, there wasn't much therapy to it. They simply strapped a belt around me, pulled me out of bed, and plopped me into a chair, and then they'd leave me for an hour or two, sitting in my poop-and pee-filled diaper. They made no attempt to walk me.

After a while, I said, "Kirk, I can't sit here any longer."

He'd find some orderlies to help put me back to bed. "You just can't stay in the bed all the time," one of the nurses chided me.

Making matters even more surreal, everyone who came into the room was dressed in a hazmat suit of some sort. It seemed as though we were all actors in a bad science fiction movie. But this was no movie. This was life and death, and I was definitely not on the "life" side of the ledger.

It was nearly impossible to sleep since I had two oxygen machines pumping full time to give me fifty-five liters of oxygen. The machines sounded like a whirling helicopter propeller on each side of me, *dub-dub-a-dub-dub,* the loud noise adding to the difficulty in communicating.

"Please, Kirk, turn it down," I begged.

"Nancy, we can't turn it down. Your body needs the oxygen," he tried to explain to me.

Early on during my time in the hospital, my nose began to bleed. A male nurse tried his best to stop the bleeding, but it continued for several hours. Within a few weeks in the hospital, my body began bleeding from various other locations. Combined with the diarrhea, I was a mess. Kirk changed my diapers twenty times a day. My body was releasing something constantly, it seemed.

The doctors discovered that I had a bleeding ulcer and took steps to rectify the bleeding. They immediately discontinued all blood thinners that I had been taking and Kirk gave two pints of his own blood to help the doctors revive my system.

Despite being stabilized, with my body so frail and feeble and my weight continuing to plummet, I looked like someone suffering from acute anorexia or, with all respect to those who have experienced such atrocities, a Holocaust survivor. My breathing was shallow, my face appeared sallow, and my legs were as thin as sticks. My skin was peeling off in sheets. Later, my hair began to fall out due to the trauma my body experienced. My hair has always been strong, thick, and wavy, but now, it was dropping off my head in clumps. I also lost a portion of my hearing.

People in the country music community prayed for me and encouraged me. John Rich, Dierks Bentley, Tanya Tucker, and others called often while I was in ICU, and Kirk was able to let me FaceTime with them. Josh Turner faithfully called and prayed for me, as did Randy and Mary Travis. Marsha Blackburn, one of our US Senators from Tennessee, did as well. Many others expressed a desire to come visit me in the hospital, but of course, it would be risky for them, and Covid restrictions prevailed. Early on, we had to inform my own daughters, Adina and Sherry, not to come to the hospital; it was safer for Kirk to be in the ICU with me.

During all those long hours in the hospital, to keep my mind active, I tried recalling George's show sets and the lyrics to his songs. In the early years, George often opened his shows with the song "Why

Baby Why." During the time I was in the hospital with Covid, I remembered all the lyrics to that song and every song on his set list that he planned to do in his show. I knew *every* song and I could remember the lyrics. Oddly, if you were to ask me to recall and recite the lyrics for those songs today, I couldn't do it. But amazingly, while in the hospital, I could.

I spent the next two and a half months in the ICU, taking baby steps and trying to rebuild my body. Nothing seemed to be working. I could barely move my hands and arms. On several occasions, the hospital contacted Kirk and said, "We need that room. When can you move Nancy out?" Apparently, the Covid numbers in Nashville were on the rise, and the hospital was packed with cases. They needed every ICU bed, and they wanted to move me to a standard room.

"We can't do that," Kirk said. "She's still receiving fifty liters of oxygen and can't even walk."

By November, my progress remained minimal, so Kirk called another friend, the CEO at Williamson Medical Center, and said, "We'd like to transfer Nancy."

"Sure, bring her over," our friend said.

With me still in the ICU, the nurse there said, "The doctor won't discharge you from the hospital until you can stand. If you can stand up for ten seconds, they can let you go."

She brought a walker and positioned it near my bed. She and Kirk helped me out of bed, and I grabbed onto that walker with all of my strength. I was wobbly but I stood for ten seconds. "Okay," I said, "I'm outta here!"

Kirk called an ambulance to transfer me to Williamson Medical Center, the hospital closest to my home. I was discharged at eleven o'clock in the morning, and as the nurse wheeled me out of the ICU and down the hallway toward the hospital exit, all the doctors and nurses who had cared for me lined the hallway on both sides as I passed by. They applauded and "We Are the Champions" music played in the background. Kirk looked at the nurse who was pushing my gurney and asked, "Do you do this for everybody?"

The woman looked him square in the eye and said, "People don't leave here."

Going down the hallway, I raised my hands above my head and shouted as best I could, "Praise the Lord Jesus!" I realized more than ever that it was only because of Him that I was still alive.

31

Detecting the Danger Within

The doctors at Williamson Medical Center thought that I might do better at home. They said if my oxygen level could remain satisfactory, I could go home and have a nurse work with me there. As soon as my oxygen stabilized, Kirk said, "Let's get you home!"

An ambulance transported me from the hospital to the house, and I was never so glad to see my own bed.

We thought we were out of the woods and that I was on my way to recovery, but after a week at home, my heart rate remained elevated. I was confined to my bed and still doing the diaper routine. I could barely move, so the hospital arranged for a physical therapist to work with me. She put me in a wheelchair and said, "Okay, I want you to pull yourself out of that chair and stand up."

I tried my best, but I couldn't do it.

Kirk said, "You have to listen to her, Nancy. We want you to get well, so you have to do it."

The therapist returned another day, but I showed no improvement.

Finally, I told Kirk, "Y'all don't understand. I don't feel well. You keep bringing her here, but I feel like I'm dying. My heart is beating so fast I can hear it."

The therapist and Kirk put me back to bed. The doctor theorized that perhaps because I had lost so much weight and muscle tone in my body, almost any kind of exercise could cause my heart rate to go up, since I had not been getting much of a workout for the past few months. That went on for about four days, and my heart rate remained excessively high, somewhere around 140 beats per minute.

Kirk texted another friend of ours, Dr. Alex James Slandzicki, and he came to the house to examine me. We were on familiar terms with the doctor and referred to him as Jamie. I told him, "Something is definitely wrong. I'm dying. I know I am."

"Nancy, you've got to go to the hospital," he said.

I said, "No, I'm not going back to the hospital. I'm not going."

The doctor ordered some blood work done, and a phlebotomist came to the house to extract my blood. The doctor called back and talked with Kirk. He said, "The blood work is okay."

"That's good," Kirk said, "but something's wrong that her heart rate is so high. The last time it happened, she had a bleeding ulcer. So maybe her body is fighting something. I don't really want to take her back to the hospital, but maybe we should?"

The doctor emphatically said, "Kirk, if you don't take her, she's going to die right there in her bed."

Kirk called 911. The paramedics arrived within minutes, and one of them was especially kind. "I can't believe this," he exclaimed when he discovered my identity. "I was part of the crew on the scene at George's wreck in 1999. And now, here I am with you!"

As the attendants prepared to place me on a gurney and in the ambulance for the short trip to Williamson Medical Center in Franklin, I was extremely weak but overflowing with thanks to the Lord. I couldn't breathe well, but I continued to pray aloud as they picked me up and slid me into the ambulance. I said, "Lord, God, Jesus. When I get over this, I'm gonna be praising You and we're going to . . . I'm going to bring so many people to You who are troubled. I don't want trouble with them anymore. I want 'em on their knees. I want 'em praisin' You, Lord God, because without You, we have nothing and people got to start understanding. They've got to come to the Lord Jesus Christ, just like I am. I am overjoyed with what I have, and God, You will see, You will see what I'm going to do. I am not stopping!"

The paramedics smiled. They may have thought that I was delirious. I wasn't. I was thankful to be alive.

At the hospital, the doctors did a CAT scan and ran several tests but did not find anything conclusive. But then an infectious disease doctor came in and looked into my mouth. "Oh, my," he said. "Nancy, your mouth is all white inside. That is not good."

He was concerned that I had either Aspergillus or Candida, both serious infections. He immediately ordered more tests.

The results returned that I was suffering with Candida, a rare and dangerous type of yeast infection. As the doctor examined me, he exclaimed, "It's in the lungs. It's coming up from there!" They did another CAT scan and discovered that 70 percent of my right lung had been eaten away by the Candida and the fungus was already in my mouth and on my tongue.

No wonder I could barely eat. I tried forcing food down, but the irritation was terrible and it hurt. But I was trying to get better, so I struggled to get food into my system.

The doctors discovered that, at some stage of my hospitalization, I had developed pneumonia which was treated with prednisone, and that caused a fungus to grow in my lungs.[6] They estimated that if they had they not discovered the fungus, I would have been a mere day or two away from dying—*again!*

Interestingly, the doctors found the fungus about an hour after I had prayed that heartfelt prayer as the attendants had loaded me into the ambulance. Is there power in praising the Lord? I believe there is. If we can muster our faith to praise Him in the midst of our messes and our problems, He often works miracles. Think about it; I'd been hospitalized for nearly three full months and nobody had discovered the virus, but within an hour of sincerely praising Him from my heart, the doctors had found the problem.

The doctors treated the infection with a slow-acting drug that I would be required to take for more than a year. I remained in Williamson Medical Center for about a week and a half and was then transferred to NHC Place, a rehabilitation center in Franklin. The rehab brought in a bed and a small refrigerator, and Kirk was permitted to stay right in the room along with me. Each day, he and the therapists helped me get out of bed and take a few steps with a walker before plopping down on a chair. I was exhausted from the effort. I hated to see the therapists come, but I knew I needed to move rather than simply lie in bed. "Y'all go away!" I'd say to them, but they understood that I was joking.

During this ordeal, numerous dedicated healthcare workers did their best to care for me during circumstances unlike anything anyone in our world had ever previously experienced, but Carolena, a nurse at NHC, was phenomenal. She would get on her knees in my room at NHC and pray for me. She'd say, "God's good. And you're gonna walk again. You're getting outta here, girl."

"You're going to be fine," she told me. She'd smile and say, "You got too much of the good Lord in you not to make it. Just keep believing." Carolena was an exceptional caretaker and a wonderful encourager to me. We need more people like that in the medical professions, especially in those areas where people are fighting for their lives as I was.

Although I felt a bit stronger, my body was still quite weak. I probably needed to be more careful than I realized. In December, while still in rehab at NHC, I was eating an apple while Kirk had stepped into a restroom to brush his teeth. I experienced difficulty swallowing and part of the apple got stuck in my throat. I started choking violently.

By the time Kirk returned to the room, I was lying flat on the bed, clutching my throat, and making awful noises, and my eyes were rolling back in my head.

Kirk took one look and realized that I was choking. He grabbed me and pulled me upright on the bed. He smacked my back with the palm of his hand, popping the chunk of apple loose and out of my mouth.

For a long moment, we simply looked at each other, not knowing whether to laugh or cry. We had come through so much, the worst that COVID-19 could hit us with, including nearly three months in intensive care, and now I'd almost died from eating an apple. Had Kirk not returned to the room when he had, somebody else might be telling you this story.

We realized that even though we trusted in the Lord, the enemy was not going to give up trying to take me out. Apparently, I was some sort of threat to the forces of hell. If so, I couldn't wait to find out!

32
Recovery

THE DOCTORS DISCHARGED me from rehab a few days before Christmas. For some reason, I was reticent about riding home in a car, afraid of feeling claustrophobic, even though the distance between the hospital and my house was only a few miles. Kirk contacted a private ambulance service and they transferred me home.

When the paramedics wheeled me inside the house, I was overwhelmed by the sight that greeted me. Kirk's daughter, Lauren, had decorated the house for Christmas. George would have been proud of her! Knowing my love for everything Christmas, Lauren even had put a Christmas tree in the bedroom. She used an angel motif throughout the house, so everywhere I looked I was reminded of the angels appearing to Mary, Joseph, and the shepherds in Bethlehem, but also the angels looking out for me. It was so pretty and the decorations made coming home even more special. Tears streamed down my face, tears of appreciation and tears of joy.

I knew that I looked awful; my weight had dropped to ninety-two pounds, and my skin was literally falling off. I had to relearn how to walk, and how to do almost everything, even simple things such as brushing my teeth. My bodily functions were not yet working properly when I left the hospital, and they hadn't improved much when I went home. Nor could I roll over in bed without assistance. I had no physical control of anything—my bladder, my bowels, nothing. I lived in diapers for six months. Because I couldn't control my bodily functions, I did not know when the diarrhea was coming on me. Before I could make my way to the bathroom, I'd be a mess.

Then one day I got up and said, "I don't want any more diapers."

"Wow," Kirk said. "Seriously?"

"Yes," I said, "I think I've got it under control." And I did. I was happy about that. I was able to eat a normal diet, because the doctors wanted me to gain weight. I went from 92 pounds to 131.5, slightly less than my normal body weight of 134 pounds.

In January, I slowly walked from the bedroom to the kitchen for the first time—and that was hard—but it was a grand achievement. A physical therapist came to the house three times a week to work with me. Following one late Tuesday afternoon session, he called Kirk early Wednesday morning to inform us that he had tested positive for Covid. "*Nooooo!*" I said. From then on, we were careful about letting anyone in the house.

For several months after returning home, we kept oxygen tanks in various locations throughout my home and a portable oxygen tank for travel, just in case I needed oxygen in a hurry. Little by little, I was able to wean myself away from relying on the oxygen and breathe normally on my own, even though I was missing most of my right lung. But God may yet decide to heal that, too, which would be okay with me!

God brought me back, and I believe He did so for a reason. I'm convinced He wants me to share with others that He is real, that you can know Him, and that He healed my soul as well as my body. And I give all the glory to God.

I also credit Kirk, because he was my warrior and defender throughout the hospitalization and rehabilitation. He fought for my human rights as well as my patient's rights, when some of the medical people had already given up on me. He watched over every procedure to make sure I received what I needed and that I did not receive treatment that would be detrimental or counterproductive for me, regardless of the prevailing attitudes and instructions from the hospital administration or even the Centers for Disease Control.

* * * * * *

As I share this story with you, my lungs are not yet functioning fully. My right lung registers only 40 percent activity, but I've come a long way and I'm doing great. I walk around the neighborhood most every day. Kirk usually follows behind me on a golf cart in case I get too tired to walk back home.

I know that God is good and God loves me. And on the positive side: after Covid, the neuropathy with which I had suffered for more than thirty years was gone!

It was another seven months before my sense of smell returned. Then, five or six months later, I was almost sorry that it was back. Oddly, everything smelled like curry to me! My food, my soap, even my perfume. But at least my sense of smell is back!

Through it all, God has been with me. Throughout my life with George, He had already given me assignments to get busy for Him—even before George was gone. Like many people, I procrastinated, or I didn't think I had much to say, or I didn't think that I could do anything to really help folks. I think God had already been saying to me, "You need to go out and deliver and save people. You need to do something, Nancy."

Then Covid came and the truth really slapped me in the face. I better understood that my life was but a whisper and could be gone in an instant. Whatever I was going to do for God's sake, I'd better get busy about His business.

More than ever, I realized how many people are hurting and are lost without any hope. I knew then, "It's time to go and do something." So in that respect, the Covid experience drew me closer to God. My number one focus coming out of that was to tell people about Jesus. I didn't care about music, money, fame, or anything else. I was totally focused on God.

Maybe I needed to go through all that simply to get to that point. If so, it was worth it.

Looking back, I see now that I could have died a number of times, but God kept me alive for a reason, and part of that reason was to help save the life and soul of George Jones. And maybe another part of the reason I'm still alive is to tell you these stories, to help save your life—physically and spiritually.

33

Walk Through This World With Me

One of George's and my favorite songs, "Walk Through This World With Me," was recorded on one of his early albums by the same title. George performed the song almost every show he ever did, and it has been sung at untold numbers of wedding ceremonies to help couples express their love. George and I liked to think that the lyrics described our own love story—walking hand in hand, sharing our dreams together. So now that I felt a bit stronger, I not only wanted to tell everyone about what God had done for George, but also what He had done in me. I hoped that people would want to walk with me through this new world I had discovered by following Jesus.

We Are Church Nashville, the congregation in East Nashville pastored by Kirk's son-in-law, specializes in ministering to people who have struggled with all sorts of addictions. Maybe it was divinely orchestrated that the first time I would share my story would be to a group of people learning how to overcome various lift-threatening issues.

I really hadn't planned to say anything on that last Sunday in August 2022. I was simply happy to be able to attend church with Kirk and his kids and grandkids. But once I got in the building and the band started leading the people in praising the Lord, I was so overcome with thanks to the Lord, I could barely contain myself. The worship team completed one song and I walked right up onto the platform and interrupted the service! I had told Kirk, previously, "If I feel like it and God hits me right, I'm gonna get on that stage."

Oddly enough, George used to bring me out on stage occasionally and hold a microphone in front of me. "Say hello to the good folks, honey," he'd say with a twinkle in his eyes.

I always protested, "No, George. No, just leave me alone. I don't want to talk in public. You just sing."

He'd laugh and say to the audience, "She don't like microphones."

But that night at church, I think I might have grabbed the microphone right out of David's hands. I started testifying, telling the crowd what God had done for me. I don't really remember asking David for permission. Nor did David have time to introduce me, but suddenly, there I was, right in the middle of the stage. David stood next to me, offering support if I needed it.

I thanked the people who had prayed for me when I had been in the hospital. "God saved me," I told the audience. I shared about being addicted to prescription painkillers, and how the doctors kept adding more, and I took them. "But when I prayed to God to help me get off those, He did." I told them about being in the hospital during Covid and my debilitating condition. "I lost all of my hair; I lost 70 percent of my lung . . . but 30 percent is working so I have so much to be thankful for!"

I could feel the words bubbling out of me. I had no notes and no prepared speech, only an overflowing heart. "I'm so happy that God loved me . . . and He loves each and every one of y'all," I told the crowd. "Do you have problems? Get on your knees and pray! God will forgive you for everything you've done.

"I love Jesus," I said, "and I'm on fire for Him. I wish every one of you could feel what I feel . . . and you can!"

By the time I was done, I was no longer talking; I was practically yelling with enthusiasm, joy, and heartfelt conviction. "I love God!" I believed that what God had done for me, He could do for other people in the room who had been hurt in some way. Looking back, I now realize that I never even got scared while I was talking—not even for a moment. I was passionate about Jesus and I wanted everyone to know and to experience what He could do in their lives.

This was the first time that I spoke publicly about what I had experienced, not just with Covid, but also about being addicted to prescription painkillers and over-the-counter pain medications.

When I walked down the steps off the platform, people spontaneously surrounded me, praising and thanking God. "I'll sure be praying for you," many said. Others asked *me* to pray for them.

An eighteen-year-old black woman with long dreadlocks came up afterward and asked me, "Can you pray for me?" Tears streamed down her face as she spoke.

"What is it, baby?" I asked her. "What's wrong?" I hugged her and held onto her.

"I have a troubled heart," she said.

Don't we all? I prayed for that dear girl, that God would work a miracle in her life, as He had in mine and so many others.

Later, David quipped to Kirk, "I think Nancy has a bit of Pentecostal in her."

That church service was like a springboard launching me into a totally new lifestyle. I already knew that I wanted to spend the remainder of my life helping people find hope, but now, because I knew the miraculous, healing power of God, I felt I had something more to share with others—something they not only needed, but wanted for themselves. The answer wasn't me; the answer is Jesus.

My lead doctor got upset when he learned that I had spoken in a service at Lauren and David's church. He texted me and said, "You don't need to be in public! It is too dangerous for you yet."

I appreciated his concern, but he didn't understand that indeed I did *need* to bear witness to the miracles God had done in my life, both physically and spiritually. When God does something good for you, you have to tell somebody! Who knows? The very things that you and I have endured may be the things that somebody else needs to hear, to be reminded that there is hope, that God loves us, that He still does miracles, and that nothing is impossible for Him.

* * * * * *

Nowadays, people often ask me, "Nancy, what did you learn through your relationship with George Jones, almost dying several times, and living to tell about it?"

That's easy. I learned that there is a God, honey, and He can save anybody that wants to be saved. All you gotta do is believe. My life-after-life experience helped me get right with the good Lord. Admittedly, Covid and Candida helped me to appreciate every day. It's so easy to take life for granted. Because one minute you can be healthy and the next minute you're dying. So I will never again take the life God gives me for granted.

I want to help people, good people, bad people, religious people, and others who think they are saved and they're not. I want to bring them to God and help them discover a genuine relationship with Him, not merely a religious experience, or a "God bless America" type of Christianity, or a country music tipping of the hat toward God, as George and I did for many years. I want people to find the real thing.

I also have a heart for people who have been abused physically or emotionally or both. Unfortunately, as we have discovered, many people live with abuse—young and old, females and males—physically, mentally, verbally, emotionally, even spiritually. When people have been abused, they often start hating God because they feel abandoned. They rail at God, "Where were you? Why didn't you help me?"

I must admit, there were plenty of times in my life when I thought those kinds of things as well. Especially when I was trying so hard to help George get free from his addictions. But I refused to give up, and I continued to trust that God would bring good out of what the enemy intended for evil.

And God did!

If you know someone being abused or you're married to an alcoholic or drug addict and you really love that person, don't give up hope. Pray; give yourself to God. He will bring you through. Don't belittle or put anybody down or walk past somebody and say, "Oh, he's just an old drunk. She's nothing but an addict." You don't know what's going on inside their heads and their hearts. Instead, do everything you can to help bring that person to God.

Don't give up on people so quickly. "He messed up," or, "She messed up, so I'm outta here. I don't want anything to do with that person anymore."

That was me for a long time.

But Jesus and Jones showed me a better way. Don't hate the person; hate the devil and his demons and what he is trying to do to destroy the life that Jesus died for us to have.

God forgave you; He forgave me. You and I can forgive too.

My message remains simple yet profound: "Lose the hate; get rid of the bitterness and resentment within; learn to love unconditionally, and don't give up on people. When all else fails, hold onto faith, and God will see you through."

Now, regardless of what else you may have seen or read or heard, that's the cold, hard truth about George and me. I loved him then, and I still love him today and always will, but most of all, I love what God has taught me through my life with the King of Country Music. What I've learned through my experiences with George Jones, through my own life-or-death struggles, and how I live today with new priorities focused on helping people in need, including people who have experienced the effects of alcoholism or drug addiction or have suffered physical or emotional abuse, continues to provide hope for others.

I want the world to know that although we all carry heavy loads, life is worth living!

NANCY'S SALVATION PRAYER

A NUMBER OF PEOPLE have asked me what I prayed that truly changed my life. I don't think there is any magic formula, so much as a sincere heart before God, asking for Him to save us, but my personal salvation prayer went something like this:

"Heavenly Father,

I come to you from the depths of my heart, realizing I have sinned. I repent of my sins and confess with my mouth that Jesus Christ is the Son of God and died on the cross for me, paying the penalty for my sins. I believe that You raised Him from the dead.

Lord Jesus, come into my heart and live in me now. I receive You by faith as my personal Lord and Savior. I receive Your Holy Spirit as my Comforter to help me obey You, and do Your will. It is in Jesus' name that I believe and receive the things I have prayed this day. I choose to follow Jesus.

Amen."

If you want to do something similar and trust Jesus with your life and your eternal future, please feel free to use my salvation prayer as an example. Your faith in Jesus Christ is the only sure way to get to heaven, and His Spirit will help you daily with your struggles until you see Him face to face. I know that's where George is, and that's where I'm heading. I sure hope to see you there!

Notes

1. Ken Tucker, "George Jones," *Billboard*, October 28, 2006, 38.
2. George Jones, with Tom Carter, *I Lived to Tell it All* (New York: Random House, 1996), 112.
3. Ibid, 112–113.
4. Joe Chambers, interview by Billy Sherrill, *Musicians Backstage*, September 2004.
5. CMA Close Up, August 1995, 5.
6. Gerry Wood, "George and Tammy Together Again," *Country Weekly*, Volume 2. No. 25, June 20, 1995, 18.
7. Teresa George, *Up Close*, Country Spotlight, Country Music Association, August 1995, 5.
8. Advertisement by Brian Martin Productions, *Billboard*, October 28, 2006, 57.
9. Billy Yates (BMI), Mike Curtis (ASCAP), "Choices," MCA/Universal Music Group, 1997. Used by Permission.
10. Bob Cannon, "George Jones, Making the Right Choices," *Country Weekly*, July 27, 1999, 18.
11. Robert Christgau, "George Jones, an All American Genius," *Billboard*, May 11, 2013, 21.
12. Hadley Coil, "George Jones, I Lived To Tell It All" ("The Life and Music of George Jones," end of course thesis, Middle Tennessee State University Professor Odie Blackmon), March 10, 2023. Used by permission.
13. We were told that the fungus was caused by the medications used to fight the pneumonia, but a report on FOX News suggested that the fungus could also be caused by unsanitary conditions in hospitals or long-term care facilities. See: Amy McGorry, "Frightening new fungus 'candida auris': What is it? Who is susceptible?" Fox News, March 22, 2023, https://www.foxnews.com/health/frightening-fungus-candida-auris-what-it-who-susceptible. Accessed 3-23-23.